SRIMAD BHAGAVATHAM: A SYNOPSIS

DR S RAGHUNATHAN

Made with ♥ on the Notion Press Platform
www.notionpress.com

Dedicated to Shri S P Krishnamoorthy & Radhu Akka

Dedicated to my Father and Mother (Pandit A V Sowrirajan Janaki)

Contents

Contents

Contents

Canto 4

Contents

Contents

Contents

Contents

Contents

Contents

Contents

Contents

Canto 11

Contents

Canto 12

Contents

About The Book

THIS BOOK IS NOT FOR YOU unless your inner conscience says to own it!

I, Dr. S. Raghunathan, the son of Sanskrit Pandit A. V. Sowrirajan from Neyveli, doubted my competence, experience, and religious qualifications to write a book addressing philosophical thinking. Despite following Hindu rituals due to family obligations, I was an atheist. Years ago, Krishna Premi gave me a book called Srimad Bhagavatha Moola Parayana, which I disregarded and left untouched on a shelf for five years.

Then, a remarkable event occurred. A tiny, beautiful baby started communicating with me, imparting instructions and miracles that astonished me. This divine infant punished me when I failed to follow her guidance. Initially, I intended to document the blessings that unfolded in my life and others through chanting Srimad Bhagavatham. However, the baby goddess instructed me to write a book summarising Srimad Bhagavatham with 18000 Sanskrit slokhas of 334 chapter titles.

Today, I humbly present my book SRIMAD BHAGAVATHAM: A Synopsis — a testament to the extraordinary experiences and transformations that transpired through my connection with Srimad Bhagavatham.

My Contact Email-Id:dr.s.raghunathan@gmail.com

Acknowledgements

I want to express my heartfelt gratitude to the following individuals and entities who have played a significant role in creating and completing this book, "Srimad Bhagavatham: A Synopsis."

ChatGPT-3.5: I am deeply thankful for the invaluable assistance provided by ChatGPT-3.5, an artificial intelligence model developed by OpenAI. This AI played a pivotal role in generating insightful content, answering queries, and assisting in research, significantly contributing to this work's quality and depth.

S P Krishnamoorthy: I extend my sincere appreciation to S P Krishnamoorthy, whose guidance, wisdom, and unwavering support have been instrumental throughout this journey. Your expertise and encouragement were the pillars upon which this project was built.

Friends and Family: To my friends and family, thank you for your unwavering belief in me and for being my constant source of motivation. Your encouragement and patience during the long hours of writing are deeply appreciated.

Research Collaborators: I am indebted to the scholars, researchers, and experts in the field of Srimad Bhagavatha who shared their knowledge and insights during my research. Your contributions have enriched the content of this book.

Publishing Team: A special thanks to the dedicated team at Notion Press for their professionalism, expertise, and commitment to bringing this work to fruition and special thanks to Ms Yamini Shekar, Ms. Priyanka Bala, and Mr. Shiraj Abdul

Readers: Last but not least, I extend my gratitude to you, dear readers, for your interest in this book. I hope the synopsis of Srimad Bhagavatham presented here will inspire and enlighten you.

This book would not have been possible without the collective efforts of these individuals and entities. While I have listed specific names, there are many others whose contributions, no matter how small, are deeply appreciated.

Thank you all for being a part of this remarkable journey.

Dr.S.Raghunathan

Canto 1

01-01. Creation

3

The first chapter of the Srimad Bhagavatam, known as "Creation," sets the stage for the entire text. It begins with the sage Suta explaining the importance of hearing this scripture, emphasizing its power to cleanse the mind and lead to spiritual realization.

In this chapter, the sages of Naimisharanya ask Suta to describe the teachings of Srimad Bhagavatam. Suta then narrates how the sage Narada Muni, by his divine grace, enlightened King Vyasadeva about the ultimate purpose of life – devotion to Lord Krishna. This teaching is the essence of the Bhagavatam, emphasizing the path of devotion (bhakti) to attain spiritual enlightenment and liberation.

The chapter ends with a call to earnestly seek such knowledge and devotion. It sets the foundation for the profound teachings found throughout the Srimad Bhagavatam.

01-02. Divinity and Divine Service

In this chapter, the sages of Naimisharanya continue to inquire from Suta about the teachings of Srimad Bhagavatam.

Suta explains that Lord Krishna, descended to this material world in His various incarnations to protect the righteous and annihilate the wicked. The chapter elaborates on the divine attributes of Lord Krishna, emphasizing His omnipotence, omniscience, and omnipresence.

The sages are eager to know more about Krishna's pastimes, and Suta promises to narrate them in subsequent chapters. The chapter underscores the importance of understanding the divine nature of Lord Krishna and cultivating devotion to Him as the means to attain liberation and spiritual enlightenment.

This Chapter highlights the divinity of Lord Krishna and the significance of devotional service to Him as central themes in Srimad Bhagavatam.

01-03. Krsna Is the Source of All Incarnations

In this chapter, the sages of Naimisharanya continue to seek knowledge from Suta regarding the incarnations of Lord Krishna.

Suta explains that Lord Krishna is Godhead's original and supreme personality, and all other incarnations emanate from Him. He describes how Lord Krishna's various expansions and incarnations create and maintain the material universe.

The chapter provides an overview of some prominent incarnations of the Lord, such as the Matsya (fish), Kurma (tortoise), Varaha (boar), and Narasimha (half-man, half-lion) incarnations, each of which played a specific role in the preservation and protection of the universe.

Suta emphasizes that understanding the various incarnations of Lord Krishna and their divine purposes can lead to spiritual realization and liberation.

The chapter highlights Lord Krishna as the ultimate source of all incarnations and explains the significance of these divine manifestations in maintaining the universe and guiding humanity toward spiritual enlightenment.

01-04. The Appearance of Sri Narada

This chapter narrates the divine appearance of the sage Narada Muni and his interactions with the great sage Vyasadeva. Sage Narada arrives at the hermitage of Vyasadeva, who feels sad despite having composed many scriptures. Vyasadeva is perplexed about the cause of his dissatisfaction.

Through his transcendental wisdom, Narada Muni perceives Vyasadeva's inner turmoil. He advises that his discontentment is due to not adequately glorifying Lord Krishna, in his works.

Narada explains that while Vyasadeva had compiled various Vedic literature, including the Mahabharata and Puranas, he had not explicitly emphasized the supreme position of Lord Krishna and His pastimes.

Narada enlightens Vyasadeva about the glory of devotional service (bhakti-yoga) and the importance of chanting the holy names of the Lord. He instructs Vyasadeva to write a scripture that exclusively focuses on the divine pastimes and qualities of Lord Krishna.

Vyasadeva, inspired by Narada's teachings, begins to meditate on the transcendental activities of Lord Krishna. As a result, he enters into a state of profound spiritual realization.

Chapter underscores the significance of glorifying Lord Krishna and His divine pastimes, the transformative power of devotional service and the guidance the sage Narada Muni provided to the great sage Vyasadeva. This chapter marks a pivotal moment in the composition of Srimad Bhagavatam as Vyasadeva embarks on writing this scripture, which is dedicated to the supreme glory of Lord Krishna.

01-05 Narada's Instructions

This chapter continues the conversation between Sage Narada and Vyasadeva, focusing on the importance and essence of Srimad Bhagavatam.

Narada Muni emphasizes the unique and extraordinary nature of Srimad Bhagavatam, describing it as the ripened fruit of Vedic literature. He explains that this scripture contains the essence of all spiritual knowledge and can satisfy the soul's deepest spiritual hunger.

Narada advises Vyasadeva to write Srimad Bhagavatam in a way that directly narrates the transcendental pastimes of Lord Krishna. Doing so will captivate the hearts of those who hear it and lead them toward devotion and liberation.

Narada stresses that glorifying the Lord should be the central theme of Srimad Bhagavatam and that it should be presented in a way that is easily accessible to people of all ages and backgrounds. Vyasadeva, now inspired by Narada's instructions, envisions the form of Lord Krishna and gains insight into His transcendental activities. With this divine vision and inspiration, Vyasadeva begins to compose Srimad Bhagavatam.

Chapter 5 of Canto 1 highlights the significance of Srimad Bhagavatam as the ultimate scripture for spiritual enlightenment and underscores the importance of focusing on the divine pastimes and glories of Lord Krishna within this text. It showcases the pivotal role of Sage Narada in guiding Vyasadeva to compose this sacred scripture, which is dedicated to the glorification of Lord Krishna.

01-06 Conversation Between Narada and Vyasa

In this chapter, Sage Narada continues to impart spiritual wisdom and guidance to Vyasa, reinforcing the significance of devotion to Lord Krishna and the importance of composing the Srimad Bhagavatam.

Narada instructs Vyasa that devotion to Lord Krishna is the ultimate goal of human life and the means to attain liberation. He emphasizes that all other forms of religious practices and knowledge are ultimately meant to lead one to this path of devotion. Narada narrates the story of his previous life, in which he was a Gandharva (celestial musician) and later took up the path of devotion. He shares how he attained his current status as a great sage through the grace of the Lord. Narada advises Vyasa to compile the teachings and pastimes of Lord Krishna in Srimad Bhagavatam, making it the prime focus of the scripture. He suggests that by doing so, Vyasa will uplift himself and benefit humanity by providing the means for spiritual salvation. Now deeply inspired and enlightened by Narada's instructions, Vyasa meditates on Lord Krishna. It seeks guidance on how to describe the Lord's divine pastimes and qualities in Srimad Bhagavatam.

This Chapter underscores the importance of devotion to Lord Krishna as the ultimate path to spiritual realization and liberation. It illustrates the transformative power of Narada's guidance on Vyasa and his commitment to composing Srimad Bhagavatam

01-07. The Son of Drona Punished

In this chapter, we encounter the story of the great warrior Ashvatthama, who seeks revenge for his father's death in the Mahabharata war. After the Kurukshetra War, Ashvatthama, the son of Dronacharya (the Kuru dynasty's military teacher), becomes overwhelmed with anger and grief upon learning of his father's death on the battlefield. In his desire for revenge, he commits a heinous act. Ashvatthama sneaks into the Pandava camp at night and kills the five sons of Pandavas and Draupadi in their sleep. This act shocks and devastates the Pandavas, as the children are innocent and uninvolved in the war.

Draupadi, in her intense grief, appeals to her husband and Lord Krishna for justice. Arjuna, Bhima, and other Pandavas set out to apprehend Ashvatthama.

Eventually, Ashvatthama is captured and brought before the grieving Pandavas. They demand justice for his horrific crime.

Arjuna, known for his compassion and courage, is initially inclined to kill Ashvatthama. However, under the advice of Lord Krishna, he decides to spare Ashvatthama's life. Still, he punishes him by cutting off the jewel on his forehead and removing his ability to use advanced weapons. Ashvatthama is then banished from the Pandava camp.

This Chapter portrays the tragic events following the Mahabharata War, particularly the revenge-driven actions of Ashvatthama and the subsequent punishment meted out to him by Arjuna and the Pandavas. The chapter also underscores the epic heroes' moral and ethical principles, as guided by Lord Krishna.

01-08. Prayers by Queen Kunti

This chapter contains the heartfelt prayers offered by Queen Kunti, the mother of the Pandavas, after the great Kurukshetra War ended.

After the Kurukshetra War concludes and the Pandavas emerge victorious, Queen Kunti, who has witnessed the tremendous loss of life and the suffering caused by the war, offers her prayers. In her prayers, Kunti praises Lord Krishna as recognizing His divine nature and omnipotence. She acknowledges that Krishna is beyond human understanding and that even great sages cannot fully comprehend His transcendental qualities.

Queen Kunti expresses her gratitude to Lord Krishna for His guidance and protection throughout the Pandavas' trials and tribulations, including the attempted disrobing of Draupadi and the challenges they faced in exile.

Kunti prays for continued difficulties and hardships because she believes such trials will keep her always dependent on Lord Krishna and His divine mercy. She values the opportunity to remember Krishna in times of distress.

Finally, Kunti requests Lord Krishna to conceal His divine form as she fears His presence may distract people from their worldly duties.

Chapter 8 of Canto 1 features the beautiful prayers of Queen Kunti, which highlight her deep devotion to Lord Krishna and her understanding of His divine nature. These prayers exemplify how one can maintain a profound spiritual connection with the Lord, even when facing challenges and difficulties.

01-09. The Passing Away of Bhishma

Bhishma Deva, a revered and virtuous warrior, lies on a bed of arrows on the battlefield of Kurukshetra, waiting for the auspicious time to pass away. He has been granted the ability to choose the moment of his death. As Bhishma prepares to leave his mortal body, Lord Krishna and the Pandavas arrive at his side. Bhishma welcomes them and praises Lord Krishna for His role as the charioteer and advisor during the battle. Bhishma offers profound teachings and wisdom to Yudhishthira, the eldest Pandava, on various aspects of dharma (righteousness), including the duties of a king, the qualities of a leader, and the importance of truth and morality. Bhishma also imparts his insights into spiritual knowledge, explaining the significance of devotional service and the importance of surrendering to the Supreme Lord, Lord Krishna.

Bhishma then offers his final prayers and obeisances to Lord Krishna, expressing his desire to merge into the Lord's divine form. At the chosen moment, Bhishma casts off his mortal body and attains liberation. The Pandavas and Lord Krishna pay their respects to Bhishma and perform the proper rituals for his departure. Celestial omens and divine sounds accompany Bhishma's passing. Bhishma's passing portrays the poignant and spiritually significant moment of Bhishma Deva's departure from the world, emphasizing his wisdom and devotion. It also underscores the teachings of dharma and faith imparted by Bhishma in his final moments, providing valuable guidance to both the Pandavas and all readers of the Srimad Bhagavatam.

01-10 Departure of Lord Krishna for Dwaraka

This chapter describes the final moments of Lord Krishna's presence in Hastinapura after the Kurukshetra War and His departure for His kingdom, Dwaraka.

After the Kurukshetra War and the passing away of Bhishma, Lord Krishna decided to return to His city, Dwaraka, along with His Yadu dynasty.

As He prepares to leave, the Pandavas and other residents of Hastinapura, including Kunti and the citizens, are deeply saddened by His departure. They express their love and gratitude to Lord Krishna, who played a pivotal role in their lives. Queen Kunti, in particular, offers heartfelt prayers to Lord Krishna, thanking Him for His presence and blessings in their lives. She acknowledges that Krishna saved them from various calamities and provided them with guidance and protection. Lord Krishna reassures the Pandavas and Kunti that He will always be with them in spirit and that they can remember Him through devotion and prayer. Finally, Lord Krishna departs from Hastinapura, leaving behind His transcendental legacy. As He leaves, His charioteer, Daruka, conveys His message to the residents and assures them that He will always be accessible through devotion.

This Chapter captures the poignant moment of Lord Krishna's departure from Hastinapura after the Kurukshetra War. It highlights the deep bond and devotion between Lord Krishna and the Pandavas, especially Queen Kunti. It underscores the message that the Lord is always accessible to His devotees through heartfelt prayers and love.

01-11. Lord Krishna's Entrance into Dwaraka

This chapter narrates the glorious return of Lord Krishna to His city, Dwaraka, following His departure from Hastinapura.

Lord Krishna arrives at the city of Dwaraka, beautifully described as a prosperous and wealthy kingdom. The residents of Dwaraka, eager to welcome their beloved Lord, celebrate His return with great joy. The citizens of Dwaraka shower Lord Krishna with flowers and offer Him heartfelt prayers, expressing their devotion and gratitude for His safe return.

The queens of Dwaraka, including Rukmini and Satyabhama, eagerly await the Lord's arrival. They receive Him with love and devotion, and their hearts are filled with bliss. Lord Krishna is depicted in His magnificent and charming form, radiating divine beauty and splendour. His presence brings immense happiness to all of Dwaraka.

The chapter also highlights the wondrous events and festivities in Dwaraka as the Lord returns, including the singing and dancing of the citizens and the joyous atmosphere throughout the city.

Lord Krishna's return to Dwaraka symbolizes His eternal connection with His devotees and His role as their protector and beloved deity.

Chapter 11 portrays the grand and joyous reception of Lord Krishna in the city of Dwaraka after He departs from Hastinapura. It illustrates the deep devotion and love of the residents of Dwaraka for their Lord and the blissful atmosphere that permeates the city upon His return.

01–12. Birth of Emperor Parikshit

After the Kurukshetra War and Lord Krishna's departure, the Pandavas ruled Hastinapura as righteous monarchs. Yudhishthira, the eldest Pandava, is their king. At this time, Sage Narada arrives in Hastinapura and meets the Pandavas. He advises them on matters of administration and righteousness.

One day, while the Pandavas are away on a forest retreat, the age of Kali (the age of vice and discord) begins to manifest, and the holy principles of dharma (righteousness) begin to decline. In this deteriorating age, a powerful and venomous snake named Takshaka bites the unborn child in the womb of Uttara, the wife of Abhimanyu and the daughter-in-law of Arjuna. This incident threatens the continuation of the Pandava dynasty.

Upon hearing of this crisis, the sages and citizens of Hastinapura are deeply troubled and turn to Sage Narada for a solution.

Having foreseen this situation, Sage Narada assures them that the child in Uttara's womb is not doomed. He foretells that the child will be a great emperor and that Lord Krishna Himself will protect him.

Subsequently, Lord Krishna intervenes and saves the unborn child, Parikshit, by entering Uttara's womb and countering the effects of the snakebite. This act confirms Parikshit's divine destiny. This chapter sets the stage for the significant role Parikshit plays in the later portions of the Srimad Bhagavatam.

01-13. Dhrtarastra Quits Home

This chapter narrates the events that unfold after Emperor Parikshit's birth and Dhritarashtra's departure from Hastinapura.

Following the birth of Parikshit, Yudhishthira, the eldest Pandava, becomes the king of Hastinapura and rules with righteousness and wisdom.

Dhritarashtra, who had been living in the palace as a retired king, is informed about the birth of Parikshit and the changing political landscape. Dhritarashtra's attachment to his sons, the Kauravas, and his desire for their welfare remain strong.

Vidura, Dhritarashtra's brother, counsels him to retire to the forest for spiritual contemplation and to avoid the conflicts and complications arising from political matters.

Though initially reluctant, Dhritarashtra eventually heeds Vidura's advice and leaves the palace. He prepares for his departure with the help of his wife, Gandhari, and Queen Kunti.

Before leaving, Dhritarashtra seeks the blessings and forgiveness of the Pandavas and expresses his sorrow and guilt for his role in the Kurukshetra War and the suffering it caused.

Dhritarashtra, Gandhari, and Kunti then set out for the forest, accompanied by Vidura, and begin their life of spiritual retreat and meditation.

Chapter 13 portrays the departure of Dhritarashtra from Hastinapura, marking the end of an era and the beginning of his spiritual journey in the forest. It also reflects on attachment, renunciation, and the consequences of past actions.

01-14. The Disappearance of Lord Krishna

This chapter narrates the departure of Lord Krishna from the earthly realm and the reactions of His devotees. The chapter begins by describing how Lord Krishna and His brother Balarama roam the city of Dwaraka, appearing like the moon among the stars. The citizens are immensely joyful in His divine presence.

Meanwhile, Lord Krishna withdraws His inner consciousness from His physical form in a secluded spot. His body, which is eternal and divine, immediately starts to disintegrate. The residents of Dwaraka, including the queens and Yadava warriors, sense something amiss and rush to the spot where Lord Krishna's body is. They are heartbroken and overcome with grief upon seeing His physical form fading away. Great sages and ascetics, who had been meditating on Lord Krishna, arrived at Dwaraka to pay their respects to the Lord and witness His departure.

Lord Krishna's beloved queens, who are deeply devoted to Him, experience a unique and intense separation, heightening their love and devotion. Finally, the Lord's divine charioteer, Daruka, describes Lord Krishna's departure to Arjuna, who is grief-stricken by losing his dear friend and Lord.

Lord Balarama, the Lord's elder brother, also decides to leave His earthly form, and the residents of Dwaraka witness His departure.

Chapter 14 describes the poignant moment of Lord Krishna's departure from the world, leaving behind His physical form. It emphasizes His devotees' intense love and devotion, particularly the queens, and how they cope with the separation. The chapter underscores the eternal nature of the Lord's divine existence beyond the material realm.

01-15. The Pandavas Retire in a Timely

This chapter narrates the events that unfold as the Pandavas, after the departure of Lord Krishna, decide to retire from their royal duties and embark on a journey of renunciation. Following the disappearance of Lord Krishna and the subsequent disintegration of the Yadava dynasty, the Pandavas are left in a state of sorrow and spiritual introspection.

Yudhishthira, the eldest Pandava and the king of Hastinapura feels empty and consults with his brothers and sages regarding their future course of action. After careful deliberation and guidance from philosopher Narada, the Pandavas decide that it is time to retire from their royal responsibilities and embrace a life of renunciation. They plan to leave behind their kingdom and worldly possessions.

Yudhishthira anoints his grandson, Parikshit, as the king and ensures that the kingdom is in capable hands. He instructs Parikshit to rule with righteousness and justice. The Pandavas and their mother, Kunti, embark on a journey to the Himalayas, seeking a life of spiritual contemplation and liberation.

As the Pandavas and Kunti depart from Hastinapura, they are accompanied by a group of sages and ascetics who admire their decision to renounce the world.

Chapter 15 depicts the pivotal moment when the Pandavas, led by Yudhishthira, consciously choose to retire from their royal roles and pursue a life of renunciation. It highlights their commitment to spiritual growth and the principles of dharma (righteousness) as they embark on a journey to the Himalayas, leaving their kingdom and material possessions behind.

01-16. How Parikshit Received the Age of Kali

Emperor Parikshit ruled over the kingdom of Hastinapura with great wisdom and adherence to dharma (righteousness) after being anointed as the king.

One day, while on a hunting expedition, Parikshit becomes thirsty and enters the hermitage of a group of sages. He finds the scholars absorbed in meditation and asks them for water out of thirst and impatience. Parikshit's interruption deeply offended the philosopher and silenced him by placing a dead snake around his neck. This snake, sent by the personified age of Kali, is highly venomous, and its bite will cause Parikshit's imminent death. When Parikshit's ministers and family learn about the curse, they are deeply distressed and inform him of the impending danger.

Parikshit, despite his predicament, remains calm and composed. He accepts the curse as the will of destiny and decides to spend the remaining days of his life immersed in spiritual contemplation and hearing about the glories of the Lord. Parikshit's decision to spend the last seven days of his life attending the divine narrations of Lord Krishna's pastimes from the sage Shukadeva Goswami is highly praised as an exemplary way to prepare for death.

Chapter 16 portrays the incident where the sages curse Emperor Parikshit due to a momentary lapse in judgment. His response to the curse, spending his remaining days in devotion and hearing about Lord Krishna, reflects his wisdom and spiritual commitment. This incident sets the stage for the subsequent chapters of Srimad Bhagavatam, where Parikshit's quest for spiritual enlightenment continues.

01-17. Punishment and Reward of Kali

This chapter discusses the influence of the age of Kali and how dharma (righteousness) was affected during this era. King Parikshit, in his quest for spiritual enlightenment during the last seven days of his life, asks the sage Shukadeva Goswami about the characteristics and influence of the age of Kali.

Shukadeva Goswami describes how the age of Kali, which follows the period of Dvapara, is characterized by a decline in righteousness, truth, and morality. People become more inclined toward sinful activities, and the principles of dharma deteriorate.

Shukadeva Goswami narrates an incident that illustrates the impact of Kali on society. He tells the story of a lowly and sinful personality named Kali, who enters a cow's body to escape Maharaja Parikshit's wrath. Parikshit Maharaja punishes him by striking his head with a golden staff upon discovering the presence of Kali within the cow. However, he spares Kali's life, demonstrating the importance of compassion even in such circumstances.

The cow represents Mother Earth, and Parikshit's actions symbolize the protection of dharma and righteousness. The chapter highlights the necessity of maintaining moral values even in the age of Kali.

Chapter 17 addresses the influence of the age of Kali, characterized by a decline in righteousness and an increase in sinful behaviour. It also underscores the importance of upholding dharma, as demonstrated by Maharaja Parikshit's actions in protecting Mother Earth and punishing Kali while showing compassion.

01-18. Maharaja Parikshit Cursed

This chapter narrates the incident where Emperor Parikshit is cursed by a young Brahmana boy named Shringi in the final days of his life. Emperor Parikshit, during his days of spiritual contemplation and hearing the Bhagavatam from Sage Shukadeva Goswami, continues to rule over Hastinapura with wisdom and righteousness.

One day, while Parikshit is touring his kingdom, he becomes thirsty and enters the ashram (hermitage) of a sage named Shamika. The sage is deeply absorbed in meditation and does not offer the customary respects to the king. Feeling disrespected and slighted by the sage's behaviour, Parikshit places a dead snake on the sage's neck, using the tip of his bow to express his displeasure. The son of the sage, a young Brahmana boy named Shringi, arrives at the ashram and witnesses his father's humiliation. Outraged by the king's actions, he curses Parikshit, declaring that the king will die of snakebite within seven days as retribution for his insult.

Word of the curse spreads quickly, and the citizens of Hastinapura are distraught. They inform Parikshit about the curse, and the king, who is already prepared to leave his body in seven days, accepts the curse as the will of destiny. Parikshit decides to prepare for his imminent departure by renouncing his royal attire, performing austerity, and seeking spiritual guidance from sage Shukadeva Goswami.

01-19. The Appearance of Sukadeva

Following the curse of the Brahmana boy Shringi, this chapter narrates that Emperor Parikshit prepares for his impending death by renouncing his royal attire and performing austerities. As the seven days of his life approach their end, great sages and rishis assemble at the banks of the River Ganges to witness Parikshit's departure and offer spiritual guidance. On the seventh day, when Parikshit is sitting by the river in deep meditation, he is approached by a personified representation of the age of Kali, who appears in the form of a lowly Sudra (an outcaste). Kali chastises Parikshit for using his bow to place a dead snake on the sage Shamika's neck and suggests that Parikshit's actions are unbecoming of a king.

Parikshit responds by explaining the context of his actions and the reasons behind them. He defends his activities to express his duty to protect dharma (righteousness). At this moment, a young and radiant sage, Sukadeva Goswami, suddenly appears on the scene. He is the son of Vyasadeva and is known for his transcendental knowledge and detachment from the material world. The assembled sages revere Sukadeva Goswami despite being born naked and unaffected by material attachments. His divine qualities and wisdom are immediately recognized. The thinkers, including Parikshit, desire to hear the Srimad Bhagavatam from Sukadeva Goswami. Sukadeva agrees to narrate the Bhagavatam to Parikshit, which forms the basis for the subsequent chapters of the scripture.

Canto 2

02-01 The First Step in God's Realization

25

In this chapter, Suta Goswami begins narrating the Srimad Bhagavatam to a gathering of sages in the forest of Naimisharanya. He explains that the ultimate goal of life is to realize Lord Krishna and attain liberation from the cycle of birth and death.

Suta Goswami emphasizes the importance of hearing and chanting the glories of the Lord as the most potent means of achieving spiritual enlightenment. He describes the various incarnations of Lord Krishna and the significance of His pastimes, highlighting how these stories have the power to purify the mind and lead one to self-realization.

The chapter also introduces the concept of "varnashrama-dharma," the social and spiritual duties system in Hindu society, and how it can be executed appropriately to attain spiritual progress.

Chapter 1 of Canto 2 introduces the Srimad Bhagavatam and sets the stage for the profound spiritual teachings in subsequent chapters. It emphasizes the importance of devotion, the significance of Lord Krishna, and the path to ultimate liberation through the study and contemplation of divine stories and teachings.

02-02 The Lord in the Heart

In this chapter, Suta Goswami continues his narration of the assembled sages at Naimisharanya. He explains that the Supreme Lord, the ultimate cause of all causes, resides within the heart of every living being as the Supersoul or Paramatma.

Suta Goswami elaborates on the nature of the soul and the Supersoul, emphasizing that the soul is eternal and distinct from the material body. At the same time, the Supersoul is the divine presence that witnesses the activities of the individual soul and provides guidance. He describes how the Supersoul is all beings' ultimate source of knowledge, remembrance, and forgetfulness.

The chapter also discusses the process of yoga, particularly the practice of dhyana (meditation), to connect with the Supersoul within one's heart. Through disciplined meditation and inner reflection, one can gradually realize one's spiritual identity.

Chapter 2 of Canto 2 delves into the philosophical concepts of the soul and the Supersoul, highlighting their relationship and the importance of self-realization through meditation and spiritual practice. It underscores the idea that one can attain spiritual enlightenment and liberation by understanding and connecting with the Lord within the heart.

02-03 Pure Devotional Service

This chapter focuses on transforming one's consciousness through pure devotional service to the Supreme Lord, Krishna.

Suta Goswami explains that unalloyed devotional service to Lord Krishna is the most potent and effective means to attain liberation and spiritual realization. He emphasizes that bhakti (devotion) is not dependent on one's social status, birth, or knowledge but is accessible to all, regardless of background. Suta Goswami describes how engaging in devotional practices, such as hearing and chanting the glories, naturally purifies the heart and frees one from material attachments. A person's consciousness undergoes a profound transformation by sincerely and selflessly serving the Supreme Lord with love and devotion. This change in heart leads to a complete detachment from material desires and a deep, loving relationship with Krishna.

The chapter also includes stories and examples of great devotees, such as Dhruva and Prahlada, who attained the Lord's mercy through unwavering devotion and completely transformed their hearts through loving service.

Chapter 3 of Canto 2 underscores the supreme significance of pure devotional service to Lord Krishna as the path to spiritual transformation and liberation. It illustrates how devotion can purify one's heart and lead to a deep, loving connection with the Supreme Personality of Godhead.

02-04 The Process of Creation

This chapter provides an elaborate description of the creation of the material universe and the different elements that constitute it, according to Vedic cosmology.

Suta Goswami explains that the universe is created and maintained by the divine will of the Supreme Lord, Krishna. He describes how the primary elements of creation, including the mahat-tattva (the cosmic intelligence), false ego, the modes of material nature (sattva, rajas, and tamas), and the subtle and gross elements, all originate from the Lord's energy.

Suta Goswami elaborates on how cosmic creation occurs in cycles, with periods of manifestation (design), maintenance, and destruction. These cycles, known as yugas, repeat endlessly and are presided over by different celestial personalities, including Lord Brahma, the creator. The chapter also touches upon the concept of time and how it influences the material universe's duration and transformations.

Chapter 4 of Canto 2 provides a detailed account of the creation process according to Vedic cosmology. It emphasizes the role of the Supreme Lord, Krishna, in creating and maintaining the material universe and describes the intricate elements and forces that cyclically shape the cosmos. This chapter offers insights into the metaphysical aspects of the universe's existence as understood in Hindu cosmology.

02-05 Answer to Questions by Parikshit

In this chapter, Parikshit Maharaja, the primary character in the Bhagavatam, continues seeking answers to profound spiritual questions. In this chapter, Parikshit Maharaja inquires from Sukadeva Goswami about various aspects of religious duties and the spiritual path. He asks questions about the best means of attaining liberation, the importance of religious rituals, the significance of different yogic practices, and the nature of the Supreme Personality of Godhead.

Sukadeva Goswami, the sage narrating the Bhagavatam to Parikshit Maharaja, provides detailed and comprehensive answers to these questions. He emphasizes the importance of bhakti yoga, the path of devotion to the Supreme Lord, as the most effective means of attaining liberation. Sukadeva explains that faith in Lord Krishna is superior to other forms of yoga and that one should focus on hearing and chanting the Lord's glory with a pure heart.

The chapter also discusses the essence of dharma (righteousness) and the principles that guide a virtuous and spiritually fulfilling life. Overall, Chapter 5 of Canto 2 continues the dialogue between Parikshit Maharaja and Sukadeva Goswami, focusing on addressing Parikshit's inquiries about the spiritual path, the nature of God, and the means to attain liberation. It highlights the significance of devotion to Lord Krishna and the importance of leading a righteous and virtuous life to achieve spiritual goals.

02-06 Purifying the Heart

In this chapter, Sukadeva Goswami continues his teachings to Parikshit Maharaja, emphasizing the importance of purifying the heart and cultivating devotion to Lord Krishna.

Sukadeva Goswami explains that purifying the heart is essential for spiritual progress. He discusses the influence of the modes of material nature (sattva, rajas, and tamas) on an individual's consciousness and actions. He describes how one can transcend these material modes and attain a state of pure goodness (suddha-sattva) through devotional service to the Supreme Lord.

The chapter provides practical guidance on how to purify the heart, including the importance of hearing and chanting the glories of the Lord, engaging in devotional practices, and associating with devoted and spiritually advanced individuals. Sukadeva Goswami emphasizes that sincere and continuous engagement in these activities can gradually free the heart from material contamination and awaken one's love for God.

Furthermore, Sukadeva Goswami recounts the story of King Khatvanga, who attained liberation by dedicating his life to devotional service and engaging in selfless acts of charity and righteousness.

Chapter 6 of Canto 2 underscores the significance of purifying the heart as a crucial step on the spiritual path. It outlines practical methods for achieving this purification, primarily through devotion to Lord Krishna and virtuous actions. The chapter emphasizes that by purifying the heart, one can attain spiritual realization and ultimately reach the divine destination of the Supreme Lord.

02-07 Scheduled Incarnations

In this chapter, Sukadeva Goswami describes various incarnations of the Supreme Lord and their specific purposes in maintaining and preserving the universe. In His multiple manifestations, Sukadeva Goswami explains that the Supreme Lord descends to the material world to protect the righteous, annihilate the wicked, and reestablish religious principles. He details some of the prominent incarnations, including Matsya (the fish), Kurma (the tortoise), Varaha (the boar), Nrisimha (the half-man, half-lion), Vamana (the dwarf), Parashurama (the warrior with an axe), Rama (the prince of Ayodhya), and Krishna (the Supreme Personality of Godhead).

Each of these incarnations has a specific mission and divine purpose. For example, Matsya saved the Vedas during a cosmic flood, while Kurma supported Mount Mandara during the churning of the ocean. Varaha rescued the Earth from the demon Hiranyaksha, and Nrisimha protected His devotee Prahlada by defeating the monster Hiranyakashipu. The chapter also mentions future incarnations, such as Lord Kalki, who will appear at the end of the current age (Kali Yuga) to eradicate the forces of irreligion and establish a new era of righteousness.

Chapter 7 of Canto 2 highlights the concept of incarnations of the Supreme Lord, known as avatars, and their specific roles in maintaining cosmic order and upholding dharma (righteousness). It illustrates how the Supreme Lord descends to the material world to protect His devotees and reestablish spiritual principles whenever there is a decline in morality.

02-08 Questions by King Parikshit

Parikshit Maharaja continues to seek spiritual wisdom from Sukadeva Goswami, focusing on various aspects of life, death, and the afterlife. Parikshit Maharaja asks Sukadeva Goswami to explain the significance of the time of death, the process of dying, and the effects of one's consciousness at the time of death on the soul's destination. He inquires about the different kinds of births determined by one's karma (actions) and consciousness. Sukadeva responds by elaborating on the importance of remembering the Supreme Lord, especially at the time of death. He describes how one's thoughts and consciousness at the moment of death play a crucial role in determining the soul's next destination. One can attain liberation and avoid the cycle of birth and death by thinking of Lord Krishna and meditating on His divine form. The chapter also includes the story of Ajamila, a sinful man who, at the time of death, unknowingly called out to his son Narayana (a name for Lord Vishnu) and was saved by the Lord's mercy. Sukadeva Goswami uses this story to illustrate the potency of the Lord's holy name and the importance of remembering God throughout one's life, especially at the time of death.

Parikshit Maharaja's questions about the significance of the time of death and its impact on the soul's journey are answered. Sukadeva Goswami emphasizes the power of remembering the Supreme Lord and the potency of His holy name in ensuring a spiritually auspicious outcome at the time of one's passing. The story of Ajamila serves as a powerful example of divine intervention and the importance of devotion, even in the face of a sinful life.

02-09 Answers by Citing the Lord's Version

In this chapter, Sukadeva Goswami responds to King Parikshit's inquiries by summarising Lord Krishna's teachings to the great sage Narada Muni.

Sukadeva Goswami explains that Lord Krishna, in His previous incarnation as Lord Kapila, imparted profound spiritual knowledge to His mother, Devahuti. He describes how Devahuti approached her son Kapila with questions about the nature of the self, the material world, and the path to liberation.

Lord Kapila, in His teachings to Devahuti, covered various aspects of spiritual philosophy, including the nature of the soul (atma), the material elements, the three modes of material nature (sattva, rajas, and tamas), the importance of devotional service, and the process of meditation and yoga. He emphasized that true liberation comes from transcending the modes of material nature and reestablishing one's connection with the Supreme Lord through devotion.

Sukadeva Goswami narrates these teachings to Parikshit Maharaja, concisely summarising Lord Kapila's instructions to Devahuti. He highlights the importance of understanding the spiritual knowledge imparted by the Lord, which can lead to liberation and eternal bliss.

Chapter 9 of Canto 2 focuses on Sukadeva Goswami's explanation of Lord Kapila's teachings to Devahuti. These teachings cover essential aspects of spiritual philosophy and emphasize the significance of devotion and spiritual knowledge in attaining liberation from the material world.

02-10 Bhagavatam: Its Content

Sukadeva Goswami begins by praising the Bhagavatam as the most potent scripture for understanding and realizing the Supreme Lord, Krishna. He explains that the Bhagavatam encompasses various forms of knowledge, including knowledge of the creation and destruction of the universe, the activities of the Lord's incarnations, the principles of devotional service (bhakti), and the descriptions of pure devotees and their divine experiences.

Sukadeva Goswami underscores the importance of regularly hearing and reciting the Bhagavatam, purifying the heart and bestowing spiritual wisdom. He emphasizes that the Bhagavatam's primary focus is the glorification of Lord Krishna and that by hearing these divine narrations, one can transcend material existence and attain the highest spiritual realization.

The chapter also briefly mentions the divisions and structure of the Bhagavatam, which consists of twelve cantos with numerous branches, each containing valuable teachings and narrations.

Chapter 10 of Canto 2 provides a meta-commentary on the Srimad Bhagavatam itself, emphasizing its importance as the ultimate scripture for understanding and realizing Lord Krishna. Sukadeva Goswami highlights the Bhagavatam's content, which includes diverse spiritual knowledge, and encourages regular reading and hearing of its verses to attain spiritual purification and wisdom.

Canto 3

03-01 Questions by Vidura

In this chapter, Vidura, a wise and spiritually inclined character in the epic, asks a series of questions to his half-brother, Uddhava, a devoted disciple of Lord Krishna.

The questions raised by Vidura are deep and philosophical, addressing fundamental aspects of life, the self, and the Supreme Being. He seeks to understand the nature of the self, the material world, the soul's relationship with the Supreme, and the process of attaining liberation or spiritual enlightenment.

In response to Vidura's inquiries, Uddhava imparts spiritual wisdom and knowledge based on the teachings of Lord Krishna. The chapter sets the stage for a profound philosophical discourse that will continue in the subsequent chapters of the Bhagavatam.

Chapter 1 of Canto 3 is an important starting point for the philosophical exploration of spiritual concepts and the quest for self-realization and enlightenment in the Bhagavatam.

03-02 Remembrance of Lord Krishna

In this chapter, Uddhava continues to respond to Vidura's inquiries about spiritual wisdom and the path to enlightenment.

The central theme of this chapter is the importance of remembering and meditating upon Lord Krishna to attain spiritual realization and liberation. Uddhava emphasizes the significance of devotion and surrenders to Lord Krishna, the Godhead's Supreme Personality and the ultimate source of all existence.

Uddhava explains various aspects of devotional service, such as the significance of chanting the holy names of the Lord, engaging in loving kindness, and cultivating a deep attachment to Krishna. He also discusses the nature of the material world and how it can be overcome through spiritual knowledge and devotion.

The chapter highlights the power of sincere and unwavering devotion to Lord Krishna as the ultimate path to transcendental realization and liberation from the cycle of birth and death.

Chapter 2 of Canto 3 of the Bhagavatam focuses on remembering and meditating upon Lord Krishna to attain spiritual enlightenment and liberation.

03-03 Remembrance of Lord Krishna

In this chapter, Uddhava continues to impart spiritual wisdom to Vidura. He emphasizes the importance of devotion and meditation on Lord Krishna to attain spiritual realization and liberation.

Uddhava discusses various aspects of faith, such as the significance of chanting the holy names of the Lord, engaging in loving service, and cultivating a deep attachment to Krishna. He explains that by focusing one's mind and heart on Krishna, individuals can transcend the material world and attain a state of pure consciousness.

Uddhava also delves into the nature of the material world and how it is characterized by suffering, impermanence, and illusion. He describes how attachment to worldly possessions and relationships keeps individuals bound to the cycle of birth and death, and he encourages detachment from material desires.

Throughout the chapter, Uddhava draws upon the teachings of Lord Krishna to emphasize the importance of devotion and meditation on the Supreme Personality of Godhead. He provides Vidura with profound spiritual insights and guidance on self-realization and liberation.

Chapter 3 of Canto 3 of the Bhagavatam underscores the significance of remembering and meditating upon Lord Krishna to transcend the material world, achieve spiritual enlightenment, and attain liberation from the cycle of birth and death. It highlights the path of devotion as the key to spiritual realization.

03-04 Vidura Approaches Maitreya

In this chapter, Vidura approaches the sage Maitreya to seek further spiritual guidance and knowledge. This chapter begins a profound dialogue between Vidura and Maitreya, where Vidura poses questions, and Maitreya imparts spiritual wisdom.

Vidura, eager to understand more about the path of self-realization and liberation, expresses his humility and eagerness to learn from Maitreya. He inquires about various aspects of life, the universe, and the Supreme Being.

Maitreya, in response, begins to share deep philosophical and spiritual teachings. He discusses the universe's creation, the Supreme Lord's role in its maintenance, and the processes of cosmic manifestation and dissolution. Maitreya's teachings touch upon topics like the nature of time, the material elements, and the purpose of life.

This chapter sets the stage for a rich and enlightening dialogue between Vidura and Maitreya, where profound spiritual truths are explored and explained. It signifies Vidura's sincere quest for spiritual knowledge and Maitreya's role as a knowledgeable sage and teacher.

Chapter 4 of Canto 3 in the Bhagavatam introduces the dialogue between Vidura and Maitreya, with Vidura seeking spiritual wisdom and Maitreya imparting profound teachings on various aspects of life, the universe, and the Supreme Lord.

03-05 Vidura's Talks with Maitreya

In this chapter, Vidura continues his conversation with the sage Maitreya, delving deeper into philosophical and spiritual topics.

In this dialogue, Vidura expresses his desire to understand the essential principles of life and spirituality, seeking answers to profound questions about the nature of the self, the Supreme Being, and the material world. Maitreya, who is a knowledgeable sage, responds with enlightening teachings.

Maitreya explains the concept of the eternal soul (atman) and its relationship with the Supreme Lord. He elaborates on the creation of the material universe and how the Supreme Personality of Godhead controls it. Maitreya discusses the modes of material nature (goodness, passion, and ignorance) and how they influence living beings.

The chapter also discusses the importance of devotional service and cultivating a loving relationship with the Supreme Lord. Maitreya emphasizes that true self-realization and liberation can be attained through devotion, surrender, and meditation on the divine.

Throughout the chapter, Vidura listens attentively and continues to ask insightful questions, eager to gain a deeper understanding of spiritual truths.

Chapter 5 of Canto 3 in the Bhagavatam portrays the ongoing dialogue between Vidura and Maitreya, focusing on profound philosophical and spiritual teachings. It addresses questions related to the nature of the self, the Supreme Being, and the material world, highlighting the importance of devotion and surrender to attain spiritual realization and liberation.

03-06 Creation of the Universal Form

In this chapter, the sage Maitreya continues to narrate the teachings to Vidura, focusing on creating the universal form of the Supreme Lord.

Maitreya describes how Lord Vishnu assumed His universal form, known as the "Vishvarupa," during creation. This versatile form is vast and all-encompassing, containing countless universes, planets, living beings, and cosmic elements. Maitreya elucidates how this astral form of the Lord manifests and is the source of all creation.

The chapter explores the intricate details of the universal form, including the various demigods, celestial beings, and divine personalities that make up its components. Maitreya explains the cosmic order and the roles of these religious entities in maintaining the universe.

As the narrative unfolds, Vidura gains a deeper understanding of the grandeur and complexity of the universe and the Supreme Lord's omnipotent presence within it. The teachings in this chapter emphasize the metaphysical nature of the Supreme and His all-pervading influence on material creation.

Chapter 6 of Canto 3 in the Bhagavatam delves into the creation of the universal form of the Supreme Lord, highlighting the intricate and all-encompassing nature of this divine manifestation. It underscores the omnipotence and omnipresence of the Supreme Personality of Godhead within the cosmos.

03-07 Further inquiries by Vidura

In this chapter, the dialogue between Vidura and the sage Maitreya continues as Vidura seeks more profound knowledge about spiritual concepts and the nature of the Supreme Being.

Vidura, who is deeply committed to his quest for spiritual wisdom, poses various philosophical questions to Maitreya. He inquires about the creation of living beings, the origin of consciousness, and the process of attaining liberation (moksha).

Maitreya responds by providing detailed explanations of these topics. He discusses the role of time in the creation and dissolution of the material universe, the influence of the three modes of material nature (goodness, passion, and ignorance) on living beings, and the journey of the soul through various forms of life in the cycle of birth and death (samsara).

Maitreya also explains the significance of devotion to the Supreme Lord, emphasizing that surrendering to the Divine and developing a loving relationship with the Lord is the most effective means to attain spiritual realization and liberation.

Throughout the chapter, Vidura listens attentively and engages in thoughtful dialogue with Maitreya, absorbing the profound spiritual knowledge being imparted to him.

Chapter 7 of Canto 3 in the Bhagavatam features a continued conversation between Vidura and Maitreya, focusing on Vidura's inquiries about creation, consciousness, and the path to liberation. The chapter underscores the importance of devotion and surrender to the Supreme Lord as the key to spiritual enlightenment and independence from the cycle of birth and death.

03-08 Manifestation of Brahma

In this chapter, the narration shifts to the cosmic creation and the appearance of Lord Brahma, the secondary creator of the material universe. The Chapter begins by describing how the Supreme Lord Vishnu, in His Garbhodakasayi form (a universal form of the Lord), lies down within the causal ocean, sometimes called the Garbhodaka Ocean. From the pores of His skin, innumerable universes emanate as bubbles. Lord Brahma was born to carry out the creation task within these universes.

Maitreya, the sage narrating the story to Vidura, explains the details of Brahma's appearance and how he initially finds himself alone in the universe. Brahma then engages in deep meditation to understand his purpose and the source of his existence. Eventually, Lord Vishnu, in His form as Lord Krishna, reveals Himself to Brahma and imparts transcendental knowledge and instructions for creation. The chapter underscores the interconnectedness of the Supreme Lord, the creator (Brahma), and the material universe. It highlights the role of Lord Vishnu as the ultimate source of all creation and how the Lord empowers Lord Brahma to carry out his duties.

Chapter 8 of Canto 3 in the Bhagavatam narrates the emergence of Lord Brahma, the secondary creator, from the pores of the skin of Lord Vishnu, who lies within the causal ocean. It emphasizes the divine guidance given to Brahma by Lord Vishnu and how Brahma is entrusted with the task of creation within the material universes.

03-09 Brahma's Prayers for Creative Energy

In this chapter, Lord Brahma, the secondary creator of the material universe, offers prayers to Lord Krishna, seeking the creative energy required to carry out his cosmic responsibilities. Brahma humbly approaches Lord Krishna and acknowledges his limitations and dependence on his mercy. He expresses his deep gratitude for the opportunity to participate in the creation process but also realizes the need for the Lord's empowerment to perform his role effectively. Throughout his prayers, Brahma extols the intangible qualities and attributes of Lord Krishna, describing Him as the ultimate source of all creation, the Supreme Controller, and the reservoir of all divine qualities. He praises Krishna's inconceivable potency, knowledge, and compassion. Brahma also reflects on the material world's nature and the struggles living beings face in the cycle of birth and death. He seeks the Lord's guidance and blessings to create a world conducive to all beings' spiritual growth and ultimate liberation.

In response to Brahma's heartfelt prayers, Lord Krishna bestows His mercy upon Brahma and empowers him to fulfil his role as the creator. The chapter highlights the profound devotion of Brahma and the importance of surrendering to the Supreme Lord for the successful execution of one's cosmic duties. In summary, Chapter 9 of Canto 3 in the Bhagavatam portrays Lord Brahma's humble prayers to Lord Krishna, seeking the creative energy and guidance required to fulfil his cosmic responsibilities. It underscores the significance of devotion, surrender, and dependence on the Supreme Lord in the execution of one's duties, even for celestial beings like Brahma.

03-10 Divisions of the Creation

Sage Maitreya continues his narration to Vidura, elaborating on the creation process and the different categories of beings within the material universe. Maitreya explains how Lord Brahma, empowered by Lord Krishna, creates various forms of life and species within the material cosmos. These creations are classified into four main categories known as varnas or divisions. These divisions are:

Brahmanas: Those entrusted with the responsibilities of spiritual knowledge, teaching, and priestly duties. Kshatriyas: The warrior and administrative class responsible for protecting and governing society. Vaishyas: The merchant and agricultural class responsible for economic activities and trade. Shudras: The labourer and service class that supports the other three divisions.

Maitreya describes how these divisions are created to maintain order and balance within society, with each category contributing to the overall well-being of the universe. He emphasizes that the primary purpose of life is to engage in one's prescribed duties (dharma) with devotion to the Supreme Lord, ultimately leading to spiritual realization and liberation. It discusses the varnashrama dharma concept, which outlines individuals' duties and responsibilities based on their varna and ashrama (stage of life). Maitreya underscores the importance of performing one's duties selflessly and in devotion to the Supreme.

Chapter 10 of Canto 3 in the Bhagavatam provides insights into the divisions of creation within the material universe, emphasizing the significance of performing one's prescribed duties in a spirit of devotion to the Supreme Lord.

03-11 Lord Krishna's Entrance into Dwarka

This chapter marks a significant turning point in the narrative as it focuses on the return of Lord Krishna to His city of Dwarka after His victory over the demon Bhaumasura.

In this chapter, Lord Krishna and His queen, Satyabhama, defeat and subdue the powerful demon Bhaumasura in a fierce battle. After the victory, Lord Krishna and Satyabhama return to Dwarka, where the city's residents joyfully welcome them. The citizens, overwhelmed with devotion and love for Krishna, celebrate His return enthusiastically.

The chapter describes the opulence and grandeur of Dwarka, adorned with beautiful gardens, palaces, and streets made of gold. Lord Krishna's entrance into the city is described as a magnificent event, with citizens showering Him with flowers, singing His praises, and expressing their deep affection.

Amidst the festivities, Lord Krishna's queens, including Rukmini and Satyabhama, express their love for Him, and Krishna reciprocates with affectionate responses. The chapter also highlights the exchanges between Krishna and His devotees, underscoring the intimate and loving relationship that devotees share with the Supreme Lord.

Chapter 11 of Canto 3 in the Bhagavatam portrays a joyous and celebratory scene in Dwarka as Lord Krishna returns after defeating Bhaumasura. It illustrates the deep love and devotion that Krishna's devotees have for Him and provides a glimpse into the opulent and divine atmosphere of Dwarka, Krishna's city.

03-12 Birth of Emperor Parikshit

This chapter narrates the significant events surrounding the birth of Emperor Parikshit, who later becomes an important figure in the Mahabharata and is known for his devotion to Lord Krishna.

The chapter begins with the curse of the sage Shringi, who becomes angry when King Parikshit, in a moment of arrogance, places a dead snake around the neck of the sage while he is deep in meditation. The sage's father, Samika Rishi, learns of this incident and predicts that King Parikshit will die from a snake bite within seven days due to his son's curse. Upon hearing the curse, King Parikshit renounces his kingdom and seeks spiritual wisdom in his remaining days. He goes to the banks of the Ganges River, where he meets various sages and saints. Among them is the excellent sage Shukadeva Goswami, known for his knowledge of the Bhagavatam.

While King Parikshit is sitting by the Ganges, awaiting his imminent death, he is approached by his ministers, his queen Uttara (who is pregnant), and other citizens. At this moment, Lord Krishna's son, Lord Siva, intervenes to protect Parikshit's unborn child from the imminent snake bite. Siva enters Uttara's womb and protects the child from harm. The chapter concludes with the birth of Parikshit's son, Janamejaya. Janamejaya is born free from the curse and inherits the throne after his father's passing. This chapter serves as the backdrop for the subsequent events in the Bhagavatam. It sets the stage for the narration of spiritual wisdom by Shukadeva Goswami to Emperor Parikshit, which comprises the core of the text. It highlights the consequences of one's actions and the power of divine intervention in the face of adversity.

03-13 The Appearance of Lord Varaha

This chapter narrates the divine appearance of Lord Varaha, an incarnation of Lord Vishnu as a boar, to rescue the Earth (personified as the goddess Bhudevi) from the depths of the cosmic ocean.

The chapter begins with describing a great demon named Hiranyaksha, who submerges the Earth into the cosmic ocean through his immense strength and power. This act disrupts the cosmic balance and causes chaos in the universe.

Seeing the dire situation, Lord Vishnu incarnates to rescue the Earth as Varaha. He descends into the cosmic ocean and engages in a fierce battle with Hiranyaksha. The conflict between Varaha and the demon is described in detail, highlighting the divine prowess of Lord Vishnu.

Ultimately, Lord Varaha defeats Hiranyaksha, rescues the Earth, and lifts her from the ocean with His tusks. The goddess Bhudevi, grateful for the Lord's rescue, offers prayers of devotion and gratitude to Lord Varaha. The chapter includes these heartfelt prayers in which Bhudevi extols the glories of the Lord and expresses her love and reverence.

This chapter is a significant narrative of one of Lord Vishnu's incarnations, emphasizing His divine intervention to protect and restore balance in the universe. It underscores the concept of divine compassion and the importance of devotion and surrender to the Supreme Lord, as seen through Bhudevi's prayers of gratitude.

03-14 Pregnancy of Diti in the Evening

This chapter narrates the story of Diti, one of the daughters of Daksha Prajapati, and her desire to conceive powerful sons through a specific ritual called "Garbhadhana."

Diti is married to the sage Kashyapa, and she approaches him with a request to perform the Garbhadhana ritual during an auspicious time known as "Sandhya" (the evening twilight). Diti desires sons who can be as powerful as her nephews, the demigods Indra and other celestial beings. Kashyapa, a wise and compassionate sage, agrees to Diti's request but warns her about the importance of maintaining purity during the ritual. He instructs her on how to perform the way properly, emphasizing the need for cleanliness and a peaceful state of mind. However, due to her impatience and restlessness during the ritual, Diti makes a mistake by allowing the evening to turn into the nighttime. As a result, her sons are born with a fierce and destructive nature. These sons become known as the "Maruts" or "Storm Gods" and are associated with thunderstorms and natural calamities.

The chapter is a cautionary tale about the importance of performing rituals with discipline, purity, and patience. It also illustrates the consequences of impulsive actions and how they can lead to unexpected outcomes. Chapter 14 of Canto 3 in the Bhagavatam narrates the story of Diti's desire for powerful sons, her request to Kashyapa for the Garbhadhana ritual, and the unintended consequences that arise due to her impatience during the ceremony. The chapter underscores the significance of proper conduct and mindfulness in performing religious traditions.

03-15 Description of the Kingdom of God

In this chapter, the sage Maitreya continues to describe to Vidura the metaphysical nature of the Supreme Lord's abode, Vaikuntha, and the various divine aspects of this spiritual realm.

Maitreya explains that Vaikuntha, the kingdom of God, is beyond the material realm and is eternally free from the influence of the three modes of material nature (goodness, passion, and ignorance). It is the supreme abode of Lord Vishnu (Krishna), where He resides with His eternal associates in a state of eternal bliss and harmony. Vaikuntha is a place of unlimited luxury and beauty, adorned with divine lakes, rivers, gardens, and palaces. The residents of Vaikuntha, including Lord Vishnu's consorts like Lakshmi, serve the Lord with unwavering devotion and love. The chapter provides vivid descriptions of the opulent surroundings and the transcendental qualities of the Lord and His devotees in this spiritual realm.

Maitreya also explains the nature of the Supreme Lord's form, which is spiritual, metaphysical, and all-attractive. The Lord's condition is beyond the limitations of the material body and is eternally youthful and beautiful. This chapter elucidates the concept of Vaikuntha and the spiritual realm, highlighting the eternal nature of the Supreme Lord and His abode, where the material miseries do not exist, and devotees enjoy perpetual bliss and service.

The chapter describes Vaikuntha, the kingdom of God, and emphasizes the metaphysical nature of the Supreme Lord and His divine abode. It serves as an essential element in the broader narrative of the Bhagavatam, emphasizing the spiritual dimension beyond the material world.

03-16 Jaya and Vijaya, Cursed by the Sages

The chapter begins with the sage Sanandana and his companions approaching the gates of Vaikuntha to visit Lord Vishnu. However, Jaya and Vijaya, who are highly loyal to the Lord and protective of His abode, prevent the sages from entering. The scholars are surprised and question the gatekeepers about their actions, emphasizing that all souls are equal in the eyes of the Supreme Lord.

In their determination to protect the sanctity of Vaikuntha, Jaya and Vijaya commit an offence by blocking the sages' entry. The philosophers respond by cursing the gatekeepers for descending to the material world and taking birth three times as demons. They decree that the porters will only be redeemed and return to the spiritual world upon being killed Himself by the Lord.

As a result of the curse, Jaya and Vijaya are born as the demon brothers Hiranyakashipu and Hiranyaksha in their first birth, Ravana and Kumbhakarna in their second birth, and Shishupala and Dantavakra in their third birth. In each of these lifetimes, they engage in adversarial roles against various incarnations of Lord Vishnu before finally attaining liberation at the Lord's hands. This chapter serves as an essential narrative within the Bhagavatam, illustrating the significance of devotion and humility in the spiritual realm. It also highlights the deep love and protectiveness that the Lord's devotees have for Him, even at the cost of making mistakes. Ultimately, the curse on Jaya and Vijaya serves as a means to facilitate the Lord's divine pastimes and to demonstrate His mercy in redeeming His devoted gatekeepers.

03-17 Victory of Hiranyaksha

In this chapter, the narrative continues with Hiranyaksha, endowed with immense strength and power, becoming a formidable adversary in the material world. He challenges the cosmic order and creates havoc by submerging the Earth in the cosmic ocean, much like his birth as Bhaumasura.

Hiranyaksha's actions threaten the universe's balance, causing both celestial beings and earthly inhabitants distress. The gods, led by Lord Brahma, approach Lord Vishnu for assistance in dealing with this calamity. Vishnu agrees to incarnate on Earth to confront Hiranyaksha and restore order. In a fierce battle, Hiranyaksha and Lord Vishnu engage in a cosmic struggle. Hiranyaksha displays his immense power, and the fight between the two is described in vivid detail. Ultimately, Lord Vishnu, in His form as Lord Varaha (the boar incarnation), defeats Hiranyaksha and rescues the submerged Earth by lifting her with His tusks. The chapter concludes with Lord Varaha's victory and the restoration of the Earth to its proper place in the universe. This divine victory highlights the concept of the Supreme Lord's incarnations for the protection and well-being of the cosmic order, emphasizing His compassion and commitment to maintaining balance and order in the material world.

Bhagavatam narrates the intense battle between Hiranyaksha and Lord Vishnu in His Varaha incarnation, emphasizing the importance of divine intervention in preserving cosmic harmony and the role of the Lord's incarnations in protecting the universe from disruptions caused by powerful demons.

03-18 Diti Vows to Kill King Indra

This chapter focuses on the aftermath of the battle between Lord Varaha (Vishnu in His boar incarnation) and the demon Hiranyaksha. After Hiranyaksha's defeat and death at the hands of Lord Varaha, the goddess Diti, who is Hiranyaksha's sister and was deeply affectionate toward him, becomes overwhelmed with grief and anger. She vows to seek revenge against King Indra, the king of the heavenly demigods, whom she considers responsible for her brother's demise.

Diti performs austerities and penances to seek a powerful son who can fulfil her vow. She carefully follows the instructions given by her husband, the sage Kashyapa, to ensure the success of her endeavour. Kashyapa instructs her to observe a specific vow and remain pure.

However, as time passes, Diti becomes impatient and neglects her vow by becoming involved in actions that disrupt her purity. One evening, when she is about to approach her husband for the conception of her desired son, a storm brews in the heavens. The sage Kashyapa arrives and realizes that Diti's impatience has caused a disturbance in the cosmic balance.

Kashyapa explains to Diti that her impurity has resulted in the birth of her sons as the Maruts, the storm gods, who will be known for their aggressive and destructive nature. This chapter is a cautionary tale about patience, purity, and adherence to spiritual instructions. It highlights the consequences of impulsive actions and the disruption they can cause in the cosmic order.

03-19 The Killing of the Demon Hiranyakashipu

55

Hiranyakashipu is a mighty demon who has gained immense strength through austerities and penance. He becomes arrogant and believes himself to be invincible. He challenges the authority of the demigods, particularly Lord Vishnu, and forbids the worship of the Lord.

Hiranyakashipu's son, Prahlada, on the other hand, is an ardent devotee of Lord Vishnu and refuses to obey his father's orders. Despite facing persecution and attempts to dissuade his devotion, Prahlada remains steadfast in his faith. Hiranyakashipu's anger escalates, and he confronts Prahlada with the intent to kill him. At this critical moment, Lord Vishnu appears in a unique and fearsome form known as Lord Narasimha—a half-man, half-lion incarnation. Lord Narasimha emerges from a pillar in Hiranyakashipu's palace to protect Prahlada.

A fierce battle ensues between Lord Narasimha and Hiranyakashipu. Lord Narasimha's form embodies the qualities of both man and beast. He defeats Hiranyakashipu neither inside nor outside but on the threshold, demonstrating that He cannot be defeated by man or beast during day or night. Lord Narasimha ultimately vanquishes Hiranyakashipu, saving Prahlada and re-establishing the cosmic order. This divine pastime illustrates the omnipresence and omnipotence of the Supreme Lord, emphasizing that He appears to protect His devotees and maintain righteousness in the universe.

03-20 Prahlada Pacifies Lord Nrisimhadeva

This chapter continues the story of Lord Narasimha's appearance and the aftermath of His battle with the demon king Hiranyakashipu. After defeating Hiranyakashipu, Lord Narasimha remains in extreme anger and agitation. His form is fearsome, with blazing eyes and a terrifying demeanour. The demigods and celestial beings, who had been unable to alleviate the Lord's anger, turn to Prahlada, a devoted and sincere bhakta (devotee) of the Lord, for assistance.

Prahlada approaches Lord Narasimha with deep humility and offers heartfelt prayers. He glorifies the Lord's transcendental nature, describing Him as both fearsome and merciful, and explains that the Lord's anger and compassion manifest His divine qualities. Prahlada expresses his unwavering faith and love for the Lord, acknowledging that his presence is the ultimate source of protection and salvation. As Prahlada continues to offer his prayers, Lord Narasimha's anger gradually subsides, and He becomes pleased with Prahlada's devotion. The Lord blesses Prahlada and grants him his heartfelt desire—to free his demoniac father, Hiranyakashipu, from the cycle of birth and death.

This chapter emphasizes the power of genuine devotion and the potency of heartfelt prayers in pacifying the Supreme Lord's anger and earning His divine mercy. It highlights Prahlada's unwavering faith and dedication as an exemplary model for all devotees. Ultimately, it showcases the Lord's boundless compassion and willingness to forgive even the most sinful souls when approached with sincerity and love.

03-21 Conversation Between Manu and Kardama

This chapter features a dialogue between Manu, one of the ancient progenitors of humankind, and Kardama Muni, a great sage and husband of Devahuti. In this conversation, Manu expresses his concerns about his descendants' welfare and spiritual progress, particularly in the age of Kali (the present age characterized by degradation and moral decline). He seeks guidance from Kardama Muni on ensuring that his progeny remains virtuous and spiritually inclined.

Kardama Muni responds by imparting spiritual wisdom and instructions on navigating the challenges of the material world. He emphasizes the importance of performing one's prescribed duties (dharma) and engaging in devotional service to the Supreme Lord to attain spiritual enlightenment and liberation. Kardama Muni also shares his life experiences and the significance of practising detachment and renunciation in pursuing spiritual growth. He highlights the value of self-realization and the need to transcend material desires and attachments. Throughout their conversation, Manu listens attentively and seeks clarifications on various spiritual topics, demonstrating his eagerness to understand and implement the sage's teachings.

Chapter 21 of Canto 3 in the Bhagavatam presents a philosophical and practical dialogue that underscores the importance of spiritual knowledge, devotion, and the pursuit of dharma as essential tools for navigating the material world and attaining spiritual realization, particularly in the challenging age of Kali.

03-22 The Marriage of Kardama Muni

Kardama Muni, after imparting spiritual wisdom to Manu and his wife Shatarupa, decides to undertake a life of solitude and meditation to deepen his spiritual practice. However, at the behest of Lord Brahma, Kardama Muni agrees to marry Devahuti, the daughter of Manu, as part of Lord Vishnu's divine plan to extend His dynasty on Earth.

Kardama Muni approaches Manu and seeks the hand of Devahuti in marriage. Manu, recognizing Kardama's spiritual stature, readily agrees to the marriage. The wedding ceremony is conducted with great opulence and divine splendour. It is described in the chapter as a celestial event attended by numerous demigods and religious personalities. After their marriage, Kardama Muni and Devahuti lead a life of both worldly and spiritual responsibilities. Kardama imparts profound spiritual teachings to Devahuti, guiding her on the path of devotion, self-realization, and detachment from material pursuits. Devahuti, in turn, serves her husband with utmost dedication and humility.

The chapter illustrates the divine plan's importance and celestial personalities' role in facilitating the Lord's purposes on Earth. It also highlights the harmonious balance between spiritual pursuits and worldly duties within the context of a Vedic marriage.

Chapter 22 of Canto 3 in the Bhagavatam recounts the divine marriage of Kardama Muni and Devahuti, emphasizing their dedication to spiritual growth and fulfilling their worldly responsibilities as part of the Lord's divine arrangement.

03-23 Devahuti's Lamentation

Despite receiving profound spiritual teachings from Kardama Muni, Devahuti still experiences a sense of dissatisfaction and lamentation due to her attachment to material desires and the worldly comforts she has renounced. She reflects on the ephemeral nature of material life and expresses her longing for liberation from the cycle of birth and death. In response, Kardama Muni imparts further spiritual wisdom to Devahuti, explaining the nature of the material world and the soul's journey through different lifetimes. He emphasizes the importance of detachment, renunciation, and devotion to the Supreme Lord to attain spiritual realization and liberation.

Kardama Muni also introduces Devahuti to bhakti yoga (the path of devotion), guiding her in cultivating a loving relationship with the Supreme Personality of Godhead.

The chapter underscores the profound spiritual transformation that Devahuti undergoes under the guidance of her husband. Her lamentation catalyzes deeper spiritual understanding, and her sincere inquiry leads to the revelation of higher truths about the nature of the self and the ultimate goal of human life, which is to attain spiritual realization and liberation.

Chapter 23 of Canto 3 in the Bhagavatam portrays Devahuti's lamentation and her quest for spiritual knowledge, which leads to further teachings by Kardama Muni on the path of bhakti yoga and the importance of detachment and devotion in achieving spiritual enlightenment and liberation.

03-24 The Renunciation of Kardama Muni

This chapter describes the culmination of Kardama Muni's life as a great sage and his decision to renounce the material world in pursuit of higher spiritual realization. Kardama Muni has imparted profound spiritual teachings to his wife, Devahuti, and she has achieved a high level of spiritual understanding and self-realization through his guidance. Seeing her spiritual progress, Kardama Muni decides it is time for him to embark on a journey of renunciation and meditation.

Before departing, Kardama Muni arranges for his daughter, Kapila Deva, an incarnation of Lord Vishnu, to guide Devahuti in her continued spiritual journey. Kapila Deva will provide Devahuti with further spiritual instructions and insights. Kardama Muni takes a vow of silence and meditates on the Supreme Lord within his heart. He gradually withdraws his senses from external objects and enters a deep state of meditation. His meditation is so intense that he becomes oblivious to the external world. Devahuti, deeply saddened by her husband's departure, continues her spiritual practices and meditation under the guidance of their son, Kapila Deva. Kapila Deva imparts profound knowledge to Devahuti, explaining the nature of the material world, the soul, and the path to liberation through devotion and expertise.

The chapter highlights the theme of renunciation and the pursuit of spiritual enlightenment. It underscores the significance of self-realization and the role of spiritual guides in guiding seekers on their path to liberation. Kardama Muni's renunciation exemplifies a sage's detachment from material life and dedication to pursuing spiritual wisdom.

03-25 The Glories of Devotional Service

Kapila Deva explains that devotional service to the Supreme Personality of the Godhead is the most direct and effective means of attaining spiritual realization and liberation. He describes the characteristics of pure devotion and emphasizes that it is not dependent on rituals, birth, or social status. Anyone can engage in devotional service with sincerity and dedication, regardless of background.

Kapila Deva also delves into bhakti-yoga, the path of loving devotion to the Supreme Lord. He elucidates that pure devotional service involves external rituals, a deep internal connection, and love for the Lord. Such faith leads to a state of samadhi, where the devotee is fully absorbed in the loving service of the Lord. Throughout the chapter, Kapila Deva highlights the metaphysical nature of the Supreme Lord and the soul. He explains that understanding the eternal relationship between the individual soul and the Supreme Soul (God) can attain liberation and freedom from the cycle of birth and death. Kapila Deva's teachings emphasize that true spirituality goes beyond rituals and dogma and centres on developing a loving relationship with the Supreme Lord through devotional service. He guides Devahuti and, by extension, all seekers on the path of pure devotion, showing how to attain ultimate spiritual realization and liberation.

Bhagavatam presents the importance of cultivating a loving relationship with the Supreme Lord as the ultimate goal of spiritual practice and the means to attain liberation.

03-26 Fundamental Principles of Material Nature

Kapila Deva explains that the material world, consisting of the physical universe and all living beings, is governed by the three modes of material nature: goodness (sattva), passion (rajas), and ignorance (tamas). These modes influence the thoughts, actions, and characteristics of all beings. Kapila Deva elaborates on the functions of the three methods, emphasizing that goodness leads to knowledge and purity, passion leads to desire and attachment, and ignorance leads to delusion and confusion. He explains how these modes bind individuals to the cycle of birth and death, causing them to wander within the material world.

Kapila Deva elucidates the role of the individual soul (atma) in the creation process and the importance of transcendental knowledge in achieving liberation from material bondage. Throughout the teachings, Kapila Deva emphasizes the need for self-realization and the cultivation of spiritual wisdom to transcend the influence of the modes of material nature. He encourages Devahuti to practice meditation and contemplation on the Supreme Lord to attain spiritual realization. Bhagavatam comprehensively explains the fundamental principles of material nature and how the three modes of goodness, passion, and ignorance influence the material world and the individual soul. Kapila Deva's teachings underscore the importance of spiritual knowledge and self-realization to break free from the cycle of birth and death and attain liberation.

03-27 Understanding Material Nature

Kapila Deva explains that the material world is governed by the three modes of material nature: goodness (sattva), passion (rajas), and ignorance (tamas). These modes influence the behaviour, desires, and consciousness of living beings. He elaborates on how these modes create a complex web of desires and attachments, leading individuals to wander within the cycle of birth and death.

Kapila Deva emphasizes the importance of transcending the modes of material nature through spiritual knowledge and devotion to the Supreme Lord. He describes how cultivating pure love (bhakti) can free one from the entanglements of worldly life and lead to liberation. The chapter also discusses the concept of the "Supersoul" (Paramatma) and the "individual soul" (jivatma). Kapila Deva explains that the Supersoul, an expansion of the Supreme Lord, resides within the heart of every living being and witnesses all their thoughts and actions. On the other hand, the individual soul is influenced by the modes of material nature and is caught in the cycle of samsara (repeated birth and death).

Kapila Deva advises Devahuti on meditation and contemplation to connect with the Supreme Lord within the heart. He emphasizes the importance of detachment, renunciation, and devotion in achieving self-realization and liberation. Throughout the chapter, Kapila Deva's teachings stress the significance of understanding one's true nature as a spiritual being and the importance of seeking the shelter of the Supreme Lord for liberation from the material world's cycle of suffering and bondage.

03-28 Kapila's Instructions

Kapila Deva explains that pure devotional service to the Supreme Lord is the highest path to attain spiritual perfection. He describes the various elements of bhakti, including hearing and chanting the glories of the Lord, remembering the Lord, serving the Lord's form, and offering prayers and worship with devotion. Kapila Deva emphasizes cultivating a loving relationship with the Supreme Lord through heartfelt love and surrender. He explains that engaging in these devotional practices with sincerity and devotion can gradually purify the heart and transcend the modes of material nature.

Kapila Deva also discusses the significance of association with advanced devotees and the role of a spiritual guide (guru) in one's spiritual journey. He advises Devahuti to seek the association of devotees and to approach a spiritual teacher who can impart transcendental knowledge and guide her on the path of devotion. Throughout the chapter, Kapila Deva's teachings stress the potency of devotional service in purifying the consciousness and awakening one's innate spiritual nature. He encourages Devahuti and all seekers to embrace the path of devotion and cultivate a loving relationship with the Supreme Lord as the surest means to attain liberation and eternal bliss.

Bhagavatam provides profound instructions on the principles and practices of devotional service as taught by Kapila Deva. It underscores the importance of sincere devotion, association with devotees, and guidance from a spiritual teacher in one's journey toward self-realization and liberation.

03-29 Explanation of Devotional Service

Lord Kapila explains that devotional service is superior to all other forms of yoga and is the most direct means of attaining the Supreme Lord. He describes how devotional service encompasses various activities, such as hearing and chanting the glories of the Lord, meditating on His divine form, and engaging in acts of loving kindness to Him.

Kapila Deva emphasizes cultivating a loving relationship with the Supreme Lord through devotion and surrender. He explains that devotion is not a mere formality but a heartfelt offering of love and service to the Lord, transcending ritualistic practices. Kapila Deva describes the attributes of a genuine bhakta (devotee) and explains that devotion is not limited by one's material situation, social status, or external circumstances. It is a matter of the heart and soul. Furthermore, Lord Kapila elucidates the concept of the "living entity" (jiva) and the "Supersoul" (Paramatma) residing within the heart. He explains that the soul is eternal and distinct from the material body, and it can achieve liberation by realizing its true identity as a servant of the Supreme Lord. Throughout the chapter, Kapila Deva's teachings stress the significance of pure devotion, selfless service, and love for the Supreme Lord to transcend the material world and attain spiritual realization and liberation. He encourages Devahuti and all seekers to embrace devotional service as the highest path to achieving the ultimate goal of life.

03-30 Kapila of Adverse Fruitive Activities

Kapila Deva explains that the material world is characterized by pursuing worldly desires and actions to achieve temporary gains. He describes the adverse effects of such fruitive activities, which lead to bondage in the cycle of birth and death (samsara). The chapter delves into karma, emphasizing that the laws of cause and effect govern all actions in the material world. Kapila Deva explains how individuals accumulate karma through activities, determining their future experiences and circumstances.

Lord Kapila further elaborates on how people become entangled in the cycle of karma and transmigration, which leads to suffering and continued material existence. He highlights the futility of pursuing worldly desires and the need for transcendental knowledge to break free from this cycle. Kapila Deva emphasizes the significance of spiritual wisdom (jnana) and devotion (bhakti) in attaining liberation from material bondage. He explains that by cultivating knowledge of the self, realizing one's spiritual identity, and engaging in loving devotion to the Supreme Lord, one can transcend the influence of karma and attain spiritual liberation.

Kapila Deva's teachings stress the importance of shifting one's focus from material pursuits to spiritual realization. He encourages Devahuti and all seekers to engage in devotional service and seek transcendental knowledge to attain liberation and eternal happiness.

03-31 Activities of Kapila

Lord Kapila explains that His teachings guide humans toward spiritual realization and liberation. He reveals that His teachings encompass knowledge of the self (atma), knowledge of the Supreme Lord (Paramatma), and the path of devotion (bhakti). Kapila Deva describes how, as a young boy, He left home and withdrew to a solitary place in the forest to engage in deep meditation and contemplation. Through His meditation, He realized the Supreme Truth and attained a state of transcendental bliss.

Lord Kapila withdrew His external consciousness during His meditation, resembling a dormant child. However, within His inner consciousness, He remained fully aware of the spiritual truth and the eternal relationship between the individual soul and the Supreme Soul. Kapila Deva elaborates on the importance of meditation and contemplation to understand the metaphysical nature of the self and the Supreme Lord. He explains that self-realization leads to liberation from material bondage and the cycle of birth and death.

The chapter emphasizes the significance of surrendering to the Supreme Lord with devotion and cultivating a loving relationship with Him as the ultimate goal of human life. Kapila Deva's teachings emphasize the transformative power of spirituality and the path to transcendental knowledge and liberation.

Bhagavatam provides insights into Lord Kapila's divine activities and the importance of meditation, self-realization, and devotion in attaining spiritual realization and liberation. Kapila Deva's teachings serve as a guide for seekers on the path of spiritual awakening and transcendence.

03-32 Entanglement in Fruitive Activities

Kapila Deva explains that the material world is a place of constant flux and temporary pleasures, where people engage in various actions to fulfil their desires. These actions are driven by attachment and the pursuit of sense gratification, resulting in the accumulation of karma (the law of cause and effect). The chapter highlights how the cycle of karma binds individuals to the material world, causing them to take birth again and again in different species. Kapila Deva elaborates on the intricacies of karma and the consequences of one's actions, emphasizing that even seemingly virtuous deeds can lead to further entanglement if performed with the desire for personal gain or material enjoyment. Kapila Deva advises Devahuti to cultivate detachment from the material world and seek transcendental knowledge and devotion to attain liberation. He explains that one can transcend the influence of materialistic desires and achieve spiritual realisation by understanding the eternal nature of the self (atma) and its relationship with the Supreme Soul (Paramatma).

Throughout the chapter, Kapila Deva's teachings underscore the importance of breaking free from the cycle of karma and material bondage through self-realization and devotion to the Supreme Lord. He encourages Devahuti and all seekers to redirect their focus from worldly pursuits to pursuing spiritual knowledge and love as the path to liberation and eternal happiness. Bhagavatam addresses the entanglement of living beings in materialistic and fruitive activities and the consequences of karma.

03-33 Activities of Kapila

Lord Vishnu continues to impart spiritual wisdom and guidance to His mother, Devahuti, on the path of self-realization and liberation. Kapila Deva explains that one's material existence is characterized by pursuing worldly desires, which lead to various activities and attachments. These attachments create the cycle of birth and death (samsara) and keep the individual bound to the material world.

Kapila Deva describes the importance of transcending material desires and developing spiritual knowledge to attain liberation. He teaches Devahuti about the nature of the self (atma) and the Supreme Soul (Paramatma) and how realising their eternal relationship leads to freedom from material bondage. Kapila Deva encourages Devahuti to engage in devotional service and surrender to the Supreme Lord with love and devotion.

Lord Kapila also elucidates the process of gradual detachment from material existence and the importance of cultivating virtues such as humility and compassion. He explains that one can attain liberation and eternal happiness by letting go of material attachments and developing spiritual qualities. Throughout the chapter, Kapila Deva's teachings stress the transformative power of spirituality and the path to transcendental knowledge and freedom. He is a compassionate guide, providing Devahuti and all seekers with the knowledge and practices needed to achieve spiritual realization and liberation from the material world.

Canto 4

04-01 Genealogical Table Manu

In this chapter, the sage Narada visits King Prachinabarhi and instructs him on the importance of family and progeny. He explains the lineage of the daughters of Manu, who played a crucial role in populating the world after a great deluge.

Sage Narada visits King Prachinabarhi and begins a discourse. Narada emphasizes the importance of having a family and offspring to continue one's lineage and engage in virtuous activities. He describes the origin of the daughters of Svayambhuva Manu, also known as the Prachetas. These daughters include Akuti, Devahuti, and Prasuti.

Akuti married Ruchi, and they gave birth to Yajna and Dakshina. Narada narrates their story and their contributions to society. Devahuti, the daughter of Manu, married Kardama Muni, and they had several children, including Lord Kapila, who became a renowned sage and teacher. Prasuti married Daksha, and they had many daughters, including Sati (who later became the consort of Lord Shiva) and Parvati.

Narada continues to stress the significance of fulfilling one's duties, maintaining family traditions, and following a path of righteousness. This chapter sets the stage for the subsequent teachings and stories within Srimad Bhagavatha and highlights the importance of family and lineage in spiritual and moral life.

04-02 The Daksha-yajna Incident

Daksha organizes a great yajna known as the "Daksha-yajna" to perform a ritual to glorify all the demigods and divine beings, except for Lord Shiva. Daksha had a grudge against Shiva because he did not approve of his daughter Sati's marriage to the ascetic Lord Shiva. Despite her father's objections, Sati decides to attend the yajna to see her relatives and participate in the event. She arrives at the Yajna site, where Daksha disrespects her and criticizes Lord Shiva.

Sati becomes deeply distressed by her father's behaviour and the insults directed at her husband, Lord Shiva. She then gives up her body in protest and self-immolates in the Yajna fire. The news of Sati's self-immolation reaches Lord Shiva, who is deeply saddened and angry upon learning about the mistreatment of his wife and the disrespect shown to him. Lord Shiva creates the terrifying form of Veerabhadra from a strand of his hair to avenge Sati's death. Veerabhadra and his army of powerful beings disrupt Daksha's yajna, causing chaos and destruction.

The demigods and other celestial beings are at the Yajna site and appeal to Lord Shiva to calm his anger and restore order. Lord Shiva agrees, but only after Daksha is brought back to life with a goat's head instead of his original head.

This chapter highlights family conflict, devotion, and the consequences of disrespecting divine personalities. It also underscores the power and ferocity of Lord Shiva when provoked, as well as the deep love and devotion between Lord Shiva and Sati.

04-03 Talks Between Lord Shiva and Sati

The chapter begins with the aftermath of the Daksha-yajna incident. Lord Shiva, accompanied by his followers and associates, leaves the Yajna site after the disruption caused by Veerabhadra. Sati's self-immolation has deeply affected Lord Shiva and overwhelmed him with grief. He decides to leave the material world and deeply meditate to introspect and recover from the emotional turmoil.

Lord Vishnu's eagle carrier, Garuda, carries Sati's lifeless body to her father Daksha's residence. The sight of Sati's body causes great sorrow among her relatives. Sati's father, Daksha, and her sisters are grief-stricken by her death and realize the gravity of their actions. They understand the consequences of mistreating Sati and Lord Shiva. Meanwhile, Lord Shiva enters a state of meditation in the Himalayas, wholly absorbed in the thoughts of Sati. His reflection is so intense that it causes disturbances in the universe.

Sati, an incarnation of the goddess Adi Parashakti, the primordial energy, is born again as the daughter of Himavan, the king of the Himalayas, and his wife Mena. She is named Parvati.

The chapter describes the beauty and virtues of the young Parvati as she grows up in the Himalayas, deeply devoted to Lord Shiva. In Daksha's palace, there are discussions about the need to reconcile with Lord Shiva and seek his forgiveness for their actions. Daksha realizes the significance of Lord Shiva in the cosmic order.

This chapter highlights the themes of devotion, repentance, and the cyclical nature of life and death.

04-04 Sati Quits Her Body

The chapter begins with Sati's deep desire to see Lord Shiva again after her self-immolation in the Daksha-yajna incident. Her love and devotion for Lord Shiva are unwavering. Sati, in a state of intense meditation and contemplation, decides to quit her mortal body as a means to reunite with Lord Shiva. She chooses to renounce her physical form as an act of devotion.

The gods and celestial beings become aware of Sati's determination to give up her life. They are filled with awe and concern about her decision. Through her yogic powers, Sati creates a divine fire within her body. She sits within this fire, and her body is consumed by its flames.

Sati's body is reduced to ashes, so her divine consciousness merges with the cosmic consciousness. Her sacrifice profoundly impacts the universe and is seen as a significant event in the Hindu tradition. Lord Shiva, still in deep meditation in the Himalayas, becomes aware of Sati's sacrifice through his inner vision. He is grief-stricken by Sati's loss but understands her devotion and purity.

The chapter concludes with Lord Shiva lamenting the loss of Sati and expressing his profound sorrow. He carries a portion of her ashes with him, which marks a turning point in his life as he meditates and seeks spiritual solace. This chapter emphasizes themes of devotion, self-sacrifice, and the transcendence of the physical body in the pursuit of spiritual union.

04-05 Frustration of the Sacrifice of Daksha

After the disruption of the Daksha-yajna and the self-immolation of Sati, Lord Shiva's followers, known as the Bhutas and Ganapatyas, are furious with Daksha for his disrespect towards Lord Shiva. Daksha, realizing the gravity of his actions and the consequences of his disrespect towards Lord Shiva, decides to perform another yajna to rectify his past mistakes. This yajna is intended to appease Lord Shiva and seek his forgiveness.

Daksha's yajna is organized with great pomp and grandeur. He invites various demigods, sages, and celestial beings to participate, hoping for their blessings and support. The scholar Narada, who profoundly understands the cosmic order and past events, attends Daksha's yajna and observes the proceedings.

When Daksha begins the yajna, it becomes evident that he has not invited Lord Shiva, which further angers the followers of Shiva. Narada points out the irony of Daksha trying to perform a yajna without including the principal deity of yajnas, Lord Shiva. The assembled sages and celestial beings become critical of Daksha's actions and advise him to seek reconciliation with Lord Shiva instead of continuing with the yajna without him. Despite the warnings and counsel, Daksha remains adamant and proceeds with the yajna without Lord Shiva's presence, causing further discord and tension.

This chapter underscores the consequences of arrogance, ego, and disrespect towards divine personalities and the importance of recognizing and rectifying one's mistakes. It sets the stage for the continuing conflict between Daksha and Lord Shiva and the eventual resolution of their differences.

04-06 Brahma Satisfies Lord Siva

After the failed yajna organized by Daksha and the ongoing conflict between Daksha and Lord Shiva, Lord Brahma becomes concerned about the discord among the demigods and celestial beings. Lord Brahma decides to mediate between Lord Shiva and Daksha to resolve their differences and restore peace in the universe. He acknowledges Lord Shiva's greatness and the importance of his presence in the cosmic order.

Lord Brahma, the creator of the universe, approaches Lord Shiva, who is in deep meditation in the Himalayas and offers him heartfelt prayers and words of reconciliation. He regrets the recent events and requests Lord Shiva's forgiveness.

Lord Shiva, known for his generosity, is pleased with Lord Brahma's sincere apology and willingness to reconcile. He agrees to end his meditation and participate in Daksha's yajna. Lord Shiva also expresses his desire to see Daksha's yajna succeed and to restore harmony among the demigods and celestial beings. He emphasizes the importance of unity among the divine personalities. Lord Shiva and Brahma then join the other demigods and celestial beings at Daksha's yajna, signifying their reconciliation and the end of their conflict.

This chapter highlights the significance of reconciliation, forgiveness, and unity among divine beings. It shows the wisdom and maturity of Lord Brahma and Lord Shiva in resolving their differences for the greater good of the cosmic order and the preservation of harmony in the celestial hierarchy.

04-07 Indra Offends His Spiritual Master

The chapter describes the heavenly abode, where Indra and the demigods reside. This celestial realm is known for its opulence and divine beauty. Indra, the king of the demigods, becomes proud and arrogant due to his position and the indulgence of his kingdom. His ego leads him to neglect his spiritual duties and responsibilities. Brihaspati, the spiritual preceptor of the demigods, notices Indra's neglect and advises him to rectify his behaviour. He emphasizes the importance of humility, devotion, and righteousness.

However, Indra does not heed Brihaspati's advice and increasingly neglects his spiritual practices and duties. During this time, the demon king Bali Maharaja gains power and influence. He begins performing sacrifices and charity with great devotion, which pleases Lord Vishnu. Impressed by Bali's dedication, Lord Vishnu tests him by taking the form of a dwarf Brahmana named Vamana.

Vamana Brahmana approaches Bali Maharaja during one of his grand sacrifices and requests a small piece of land that can be covered by three of his footsteps. Bali Maharaja, known for his generosity, agrees to Vamana's request. However, Vamana, in his divine form, expands to cover the entire universe in three steps, symbolizing the all-encompassing nature of the Divine.

In response to Bali Maharaja's devotion and humility, Lord Vishnu blesses him and grants him a place in the heavenly abode alongside the demigods. Indra, witnessing Bali's newfound success and realizing his arrogance and neglect, approaches Brihaspati for guidance and expresses remorse for his actions.

04-08 Dhruva Maharaja Leaves Home

The chapter begins with the introduction of Dhruva Maharaja, a noble and pious prince. Dhruva is deeply devoted to Lord Vishnu and desires to attain a higher position than his father, King Uttanapada, to earn his stepmother's affection. Dhruva's stepmother, Suruci, whom the king favours, harshly criticizes and insults him for wanting to sit on his father's lap, which he believes will earn him the king's love. King Uttanapada, under the influence of Suruci, cannot provide Dhruva with the affection he seeks.

Heartbroken and determined to earn the love of his father and the respect of the entire universe, Dhruva decides to seek Lord Vishnu and obtain a higher position. He sets out for the forest, renouncing his royal comforts and luxuries. Dhruva encounters the great sage Narada Muni in the woods and expresses his desire to find Lord Vishnu. Narada teaches Dhruva about the path of devotion and instructs him on the mantra "Om Namo Bhagavate Vasudevaya," which will help him attain his goal. Dhruva engages in intense meditation and austerities, standing on one leg with his mind fully absorbed in Lord Vishnu's contemplation. His determined penance shakes the heavens, and the celestial beings become alarmed by his extraordinary devotion.

Lord Vishnu, pleased with Dhruva's unwavering devotion and penance, appears before him in his divine form. Dhruva is initially unable to speak in the presence of the Lord. Still, he eventually expresses his desire for a position more significant than Lord Brahma's and seeks a place that will never be destroyed.

Lord Vishnu blesses Dhruva, assuring him of his request and granting him a place as the polestar (Dhruva Loka) in the celestial sphere, a fixed and eternal position. After attaining his desired boon, Dhruva continues to meditate upon Lord Vishnu and offers prayers of gratitude. Lord Vishnu instructs Dhruva to return to his kingdom and fulfil his responsibilities as a ruler.

04-09 Dhruva Maharaja Returns Home

After attaining the divine blessings of Lord Vishnu and being granted the eternal position of Dhruva Loka (the polestar) in the celestial sphere, Dhruva Maharaja returns to his kingdom. Upon his return, Dhruva Maharaja is warmly received by his father, King Uttanapada, and his stepmother, Suruci, who had previously mistreated him.

Dhruva Maharaja takes up the responsibilities of ruling the kingdom and maintaining the welfare of the citizens. The kingdom flourishes with prosperity and happiness under his just and righteous rule. Despite being the ruler, Dhruva Maharaja remains detached from the material world and is constantly devoted to Lord Vishnu. He lives a life of virtue and righteousness, setting a high standard for his subjects. Dhruva Maharaja imparts spiritual wisdom and guidance to his citizens, teaching them the importance of devotion to the Supreme Lord and the transient nature of material pursuits.

As time passes, Dhruva Maharaja's thoughts turn toward Lord Vishnu, and he decides to renounce his royal responsibilities and retire to the forest for a life of meditation and devotion. Before departing for the forest, Dhruva Maharaja bids farewell to his family and citizens. His return to the forest is celebrated as a glorious and transformative journey, inspiring others to turn to devotion.

This chapter emphasizes balancing one's worldly responsibilities with spiritual pursuits. It serves as a lesson in leading a life of virtue and devotion, even in positions of power and authority.

04-10 Dhruva Maharaja's Fight with the Yakshas

After leaving his kingdom and taking up a life of meditation and devotion in the forest, Dhruva Maharaja continues his spiritual practices with great determination and purity of heart. One day, while Dhruva is engaged in meditation, a group of Yakshas, known for their mischievous and sometimes aggressive nature, approaches him. They try to disrupt his meditation and mock his austerities. Undeterred by the Yakshas' provocations, Dhruva Maharaja remains focused on his devotion to Lord Vishnu and meditates steadfastly.

The Yakshas, impressed by Dhruva's unwavering devotion and fearless attitude, decide to test his strength and wisdom. They transform themselves into fearsome forms, causing the trees and animals in the forest to tremble. A fierce battle ensues between Dhruva and the Yakshas. Despite their formidable powers, Dhruva Maharaja, filled with divine strength and guided by his devotion, defeats the Yakshas one by one. The Yakshas, realizing their defeat and recognizing Dhruva's spiritual prowess, approach him humbly and reveal their true identity. They explain that Lord Vishnu sent them to test Dhruva's determination and devotion.

Having passed the test, Dhruva Maharaja feels deep satisfaction and gratitude to Lord Vishnu for his blessings and guidance. The Yakshas then depart and return to Lord Vishnu, reporting the successful completion of their mission.

04-11 Supersoul Realizes Supersoul

The chapter begins with Devahuti, the mother of Lord Kapila, expressing her eagerness to learn transcendental knowledge from her son. She recognizes Him as her guru (spiritual teacher) and herself as a humble disciple. Lord Kapila praises Devahuti's humility and eagerness for spiritual knowledge. He explains that the knowledge He will impart will help her achieve liberation from the material world. Lord Kapila describes the nature of the self (atma) and the Supreme Self (Paramatma or the Supersoul). He explains that the soul is eternal, unchanging, and distinct from the physical body. At the same time, the Supreme Soul, the Supersoul, resides within the hearts of all living beings and is the ultimate controller of the universe.

Lord Kapila elaborates on the processes of creation, maintenance, and destruction of the material universe. He emphasizes that the material world is temporary and full of suffering. Devahuti asks Lord Kapila about attaining liberation from the cycle of birth and death. Lord Kapila explains that by cultivating knowledge, devotion, and meditation on the Supreme, one can achieve independence and return to the spiritual realm.

Lord Kapila describes the characteristics of a self-realized soul free from material desires and ego. Such a soul is immersed in transcendental love and devotion for the Supreme Lord. He further explains the significance of commitment to the Supreme and the transformative power of bhakti (devotion) in elevating the soul to the highest spiritual realization. Lord Kapila's teachings emphasize the importance of cultivating knowledge, love, and meditation on the Supreme to attain spiritual liberation and realize the eternal nature of the self.

This chapter is a profound exposition of spiritual knowledge and philosophy, focusing on the relationship between the individual soul and the Supreme Soul and the path to liberation through devotion and self-realization. It is a foundational text in the Bhagavata Purana for understanding the nature of the self and the spiritual journey towards the Divine.

04-12 Conversation – Parikshit and Shukadeva

King Parikshit, the grandson of Arjuna and a great devotee of Lord Krishna, has been cursed to die within seven days by a Brahmana boy. Accepting his fate, he renounces his kingdom and spends his remaining days seeking spiritual knowledge and enlightenment. Hearing about King Parikshit's decision and impending death, great sages and saints from various parts of the universe assemble to offer their respects and wisdom. Among the philosophers who arrive is Shukadeva Goswami, a renowned and self-realized sage known for his deep knowledge of the scriptures and devotion to Lord Krishna.

King Parikshit feels blessed upon seeing Shukadeva Goswami and realizes he has a rare opportunity to gain spiritual knowledge from a great sage before his imminent death. King Parikshit inquires about the path of self-realization and the means to attain liberation, expressing his eagerness to hear about Lord Krishna and His pastimes. Shukadeva Goswami, in response to the king's inquiry, begins narrating the Srimad Bhagavatha, a sacred text that contains the transcendental pastimes of Lord Krishna, His devotees, and various philosophical teachings.

This chapter highlights the importance of seeking spiritual knowledge and guidance from realized sages and the eagerness of King Parikshit to hear about the Divine before his imminent departure from the world.

04-13 The Descendants of Dhruva Maharaja

The chapter begins by describing Dhruva Maharaja's glorious reign as a just and righteous king after his return from the forest. Dhruva Maharaja ruled for 36,000 years, during which the earth experienced a period of unprecedented peace, prosperity, and righteousness. Dhruva's rule was marked by a strict adherence to dharma (moral and ethical principles), and he performed many sacrifices and acts of charity to benefit his subjects.

The chapter lists the names of Dhruva Maharaja's sons, who became powerful kings and rulers in different parts of the world. Some of his notable descendants include Arka, Bharmyashva, and Muchukunda. The descendants of Dhruva Maharaja continued to rule with righteousness and devotion to Lord Vishnu, maintaining the high standards set by their illustrious ancestors.

The chapter emphasizes the importance of a virtuous and spiritually guided lineage, where the principles of dharma and devotion are upheld and passed down through generations. While this chapter primarily consists of genealogical information, it highlights the virtuous legacy of Dhruva Maharaja and his descendants, who continued to follow the path of righteousness and devotion to Lord Vishnu. It also reinforces the significance of maintaining the values of dharma and spirituality within a royal lineage.

04-14 The Story of King Vena

King Vena becomes the kingdom's ruler after his father's demise but fails to uphold the principles of dharma and righteousness. His oppressive rule leads to unrest, corruption, and lawlessness in the kingdom. The sages and wise advisors of the domain become deeply concerned about King Vena's actions and their detrimental impact on society. They decide to take action to rectify the situation.

The sages, led by Sage Atri, gather together and perform a sacrifice to invoke the divine personality who can deal with King Vena's tyranny. In response to their gift, a divine being named "Dharmashila" appears from the altar of the yajna (sacrifice). Dharmashila embodies the principles of righteousness and is empowered to correct the wayward king.

Dharmashila confronts King Vena and tries to instruct him in the principles of dharma and morality, but King Vena remains obstinate and disrespectful. In response to King Vena's irreverence and wickedness, Dharamshala punishes him by striking him on the thigh with a blade of grass. This act causes King Vena to fall dead. With the demise of King Vena, the kingdom is left without a ruler. The sages decide to perform a ritual to churn the king's body, from which a new ruler will emerge. During the churning ceremony, a brilliant and virtuous personality named Prithu emerges from King Vena's body. Prithu is hailed as a righteous and capable ruler who will restore order and righteousness in the kingdom.

This chapter introduces King Prithu, who becomes a legendary and virtuous ruler known for his dedication to dharma and the welfare of his subjects.

04-15 King Prithu's Appearance and Coronation

After King Vena's demise, the sages and citizens of the kingdom eagerly anticipate the emergence of a new ruler from the churning of Vena's body, which the philosophers are performing. From the churning, a brilliant and divine figure named Prithu emerges. He is not born from a mother's womb but created by the churning process. Prithu's appearance radiates purity and righteousness. Recognizing Prithu's extraordinary qualities and divine nature, the sages and citizens of the kingdom enthusiastically welcome him as their new ruler and offer him their allegiance.

King Prithu, embodying the qualities of a righteous king, takes on the responsibility of ruling the kingdom. He is committed to establishing dharma (moral and ethical principles) and ensuring the welfare of his subjects. Several significant accomplishments mark Prithu's reign. He performs a great sacrifice called the "Prithvi Yajna" (surrender to the Earth) to nourish and provide abundance to the Earth, which had been rendered barren by the misrule of King Vena. During the sacrifice, Mother Earth appears before Prithu and praises his efforts to restore her fertility and well-being. She offers her blessings and resources to support his rule.

King Prithu's rule is characterized by just governance, the protection of dharma, and the welfare of his subjects. He ensures that the kingdom prospers and the citizens are happy and content.

This chapter highlights the virtuous and divine nature of King Prithu, his commitment to restoring righteousness and prosperity, and his special connection with Mother Earth.

04-16 King Prithu's Appearance and Coronation

King Prithu's extraordinary qualities and divine origins are described in this chapter. Prithu is born from the dead body of King Vena and is hailed as an incarnation of Lord Vishnu. He is a virtuous and influential ruler who brings prosperity to the earth by personally ploughing the land to release its resources.

Prithu's coronation as king is a significant event in this chapter, and it marks the beginning of a golden age of righteousness and abundance. The text emphasizes the importance of a righteous ruler in ensuring the kingdom's and its people's well-being.

This chapter highlights the rise of King Prithu as a just and capable leader who plays a pivotal role in the welfare of his subjects and the Earth itself.

04-17 Mahārāja Prithu Becomes Angry

In this chapter, King Prithu becomes concerned about the Earth's reluctance to yield its resources despite his efforts to plough and cultivate them for the welfare of his subjects. He perceives the Earth as a cow withholding its milk, and he decides to take action to rectify the situation.

Prithu becomes angry at the Earth's uncooperative nature and threatens to punish it. In response, the personified Earth, Bhumi Devi, appears before Prithu and explains her concerns and fears regarding his intense efforts to extract resources. She expresses her willingness to cooperate but requests moderation in her exploitation.

Prithu, being a just and compassionate ruler, listens to Bhumi Devi's plea and agrees to a more balanced approach to resource extraction. This chapter emphasizes the importance of respecting and nurturing the Earth and its resources for the well-being of all living beings.

This chapter portrays King Prithu's interaction with Bhumi Devi and his commitment to finding a harmonious balance in utilizing the Earth's resources while maintaining its fertility and abundance.

04-18 Prithu Maharaja Milks the Earth

In this chapter, King Prithu continues to bring prosperity to his kingdom and ensure the Earth's fertility. He metaphorically "milks" the Earth, symbolizing his responsible and sustainable use of its resources.

Prithu, with a plough in his hand, ceremoniously prepares to extract the Earth's wealth. However, the Earth, personified as Bhumi Devi, willingly cooperates with him now that a balanced approach has been established. As a result, the Earth yields abundant resources for the welfare of Prithu's subjects.

This chapter highlights the idea of responsible stewardship of the Earth's resources and the importance of maintaining a harmonious relationship with nature. King Prithu's actions symbolize the ideal of a righteous ruler who ensures the well-being of the people and the environment.

This chapter depicts King Prithu's successful efforts in extracting resources from the Earth while maintaining ecological balance and harmony, emphasizing the importance of sustainable and responsible governance.

04-19 King Prithu's One Hundred Horse Sacrifices

91

In this chapter, King Prithu performs one hundred horse sacrifices (Ashwamedha Yagnas) as part of his royal duties and spiritual practices.

Prithu's horse sacrifices are elaborate ceremonies meant to demonstrate his prowess as a ruler and his devotion to the Supreme Lord. The rituals involve the release of a sacred horse to roam freely, and Prithu's soldiers protect the horse. Any challenges to the horse's freedom are met with battles and offerings to various demigods.

These sacrifices are conducted with great amenities, and Prithu ensures that all necessary arrangements are made for the successful completion of each one. These sacrifices are seen as devotion and bring prosperity and blessings to Prithu's kingdom.

This chapter narrates the performance of one hundred horse sacrifices by King Prithu, showcasing his devotion to the divine and his commitment to fulfilling his royal duties while ensuring the welfare of his people.

04-20 Lord Vishnu's Appearance

This chapter's extraordinary event occurs during King Prithu's hundred-horse sacrifices. Lord Vishnu, the Supreme God, makes a divine appearance in the sacrificial arena.

As Prithu performs the sacrifices with great devotion, Lord Vishnu appears before him in His four-armed form, adorned with divine attributes. This divine presence fills the entire assembly with awe and reverence. Prithu and the assembled sages offer prayers and worship to Lord Vishnu.

The chapter emphasizes the significance of devotion and the presence of the divine in the lives of the faithful. Lord Vishnu's appearance reaffirms Prithu's righteousness and dedication as a ruler and a devotee.

This chapter narrates the extraordinary event of Lord Vishnu's divine appearance during King Prithu's sacrifices, highlighting the importance of devotion and divine intervention in the lives of the faithful.

04-21 Instructions by Maharaja Prithu

In this chapter, King Prithu imparts valuable instructions and wisdom to his subjects and the assembled sages.

Prithu emphasizes the importance of dharma (righteousness) and living a virtuous life. He advises his citizens on the path of morality, ethics, and the duties of a ruler. Prithu stresses the need for a just and compassionate government that serves the well-being of all its citizens.

Additionally, he discusses the significance of devotional service to the Supreme Lord and how it can lead to spiritual liberation. Prithu's teachings encompass various aspects of life, including pursuing material and spiritual well-being.

This chapter presents the wise teachings of King Prithu, emphasizing the importance of righteousness, ethical governance, and devotion to the Supreme Lord as essential elements of a fulfilled and meaningful life.

04-22 Prithu with the Four Kumaras

In this chapter, King Prithu encounters the Four Kumaras, renowned sages and eternal youths.

When the Four Kumaras arrive at Prithu's palace, the king initially fails to recognize them due to their youthful appearance. Prithu realizes their spiritual greatness despite their youthful looks and respectfully welcomes them. The sages explain that they remain young due to their devotion to Lord Vishnu.

During their conversation, the Four Kumaras impart spiritual knowledge to Prithu, emphasizing the importance of devotion to the Supreme Lord and the futility of material pursuits. They stress the significance of transcending worldly attachments to attain spiritual enlightenment and liberation.

This chapter narrates King Prithu's encounter with the Four Kumaras, who provide him with profound spiritual teachings, highlighting the path of devotion and renunciation for achieving spiritual realization.

04-23 Maharaja Prithu's Going Back Home

In this chapter, the life story of King Prithu reaches its conclusion as he prepares to leave his earthly body and return to the spiritual realm. As Prithu approaches the end of his life, he renounces his royal duties and enters deep meditation, fully absorbed in the thoughts of the Supreme Lord, Vishnu. The assembled sages and citizens witness his divine departure as his body transforms into a radiant, glowing form.

Prithu's transcendental departure signifies his attainment of liberation, and he merges into spiritual existence. The citizens and sages express their deep gratitude and sorrow at his departure, recognizing his exemplary leadership and devotion.

This chapter portrays King Prithu's departure from his mortal body, signifying his attainment of spiritual liberation and the end of his illustrious reign as a righteous and devoted monarch.

04-24 Chanting the Song Sung by Lord Shiva

In this chapter, Lord Shiva recites a beautiful hymn praising the Supreme Lord, Vishnu, and the importance of devotional service.

The chapter begins with Lord Shiva, who is present at the assembly, responding to the inquiries of the sages. In his response, he recites a poetic and devotional composition known as the "Shiva-Pancha Ratna" or "The Five Jewels of Lord Shiva." In this hymn, Lord Shiva glorifies the qualities and divine manifestations of Lord Vishnu.

Lord Shiva emphasizes the significance of surrendering to Vishnu and engaging in devotional service as the highest path to spiritual realization. He also describes various incarnations and pastimes of Lord Vishnu, highlighting His omnipotence and compassion.

This chapter features Lord Shiva's recitation of a holy hymn extolling Lord Vishnu's greatness and the importance of devotion as the supreme path to spiritual liberation.

04-25 The Characteristics of King Puranjana

97

In this symbolic chapter, the story of King Puranjana is narrated to convey spiritual lessons. King Puranjana is portrayed as an ordinary soul entangled in the material world, symbolized by the city of "Puranjana." He marries a beautiful woman called "Puranjani," representing the attachment to the earthly body and senses. The chapter illustrates how Puranjana becomes preoccupied with material desires and pleasures.

As the story unfolds, it becomes clear that King Puranjana is an allegory for the conditioned soul, and his life in the material world represents the entanglement of the soul in worldly pursuits and desires.

This chapter presents the allegorical tale of King Puranjana to teach profound spiritual lessons about the soul's entanglement in the material world and the importance of seeking liberation from such attachments through spiritual knowledge and devotion.

04-26 Kṣemī, the Demon

In this chapter, the narrative shifts back to a more traditional storyline involving a demon named Kṣemī. Kṣemī is a powerful demon who can assume various forms and wreak havoc. He approaches the hermitage of a sage named Karabhājana Muni, intending to cause destruction. However, the sage recognizes the demon's evil intent and engages him in a philosophical discussion about the nature of the soul, the body, and the Supreme Lord.

The demon Kṣemī gains spiritual insight through their conversation and eventually renounces his demonic nature. He then departs to engage in penance and spiritual practices, seeking liberation.

This chapter serves as a reminder of the transformative power of spiritual knowledge and discussion, even for those deeply entangled in ignorance and darkness.

This chapter narrates the encounter between the demon Kṣemī and the sage Karabhājana Muni, highlighting how spiritual discourse can lead to a change of heart and a desire for spiritual growth and liberation.

04-27 Attack by Candavega

In this chapter, the allegorical story of King Puranjana continues. The chapter describes how King Puranjana, representing the conditioned soul, becomes absorbed in sense gratification and material pursuits, symbolized by his city. Meanwhile, a powerful demon named Candavega, representing the force of time, launches an attack on Puranjana's city.

The battle between Candavega and Puranjana's soldiers symbolizes the inevitable passage of time and the destructive nature of material existence. Despite the valiant efforts of Puranjana's forces, they are ultimately defeated by time, and Puranjana's city is reduced to ruins.

This chapter serves as a symbolic reminder of the impermanence of material life and the need for the soul to seek spiritual realization beyond the cycle of birth and death.

This chapter continues the allegorical story of King Puranjana and emphasizes the transient nature of material existence, illustrating the relentless force of time and the importance of spiritual awakening.

04-28 Puranjana Becomes a Woman

In this symbolic chapter, the story of King Puranjana takes a further twist. King Puranjana, who represents the conditioned soul, transforms his next life. He is reborn as a woman and marries a man named Malayadhvaja. In this new life, Puranjana, now a woman, experiences the ups and downs of family life, symbolizing the ever-changing nature of material existence.

The chapter emphasizes the concept of the eternal soul taking on different material bodies and experiencing various roles and relationships in the cycle of birth and death. The symbolic narrative teaches profound spiritual lessons about the soul's journey and the impermanence of material life.

This chapter continues the allegorical tale of King Puranjana, highlighting the soul's transmigration and its experiences in different bodies and roles within the material world.

04-29 Talks – Narada and Pracinabarhi

In this chapter, the sage Narada engages in a philosophical dialogue with King Pracinabarhi. Narada imparts spiritual wisdom to the king and his sons. He discusses the concept of renunciation and the importance of focusing on the eternal, spiritual path rather than the temporary pleasures of the material world. Narada also describes the process of self-realization and attaining liberation from the cycle of birth and death.

The chapter emphasizes the need to detach from worldly attachments and pursue spiritual knowledge to attain a higher consciousness and eternal happiness.

This chapter features the enlightening conversation between Sage Narada and King Pracinabarhi, highlighting the significance of spiritual wisdom, renunciation, and the path to liberation from the material world.

04-30 The Activities of the Pracetas

In this chapter, the focus shifts to the Pracetas, the sons of King Pracinabarhi, and their spiritual journey. The Pracetas embark on a long period of meditation after receiving wisdom from Sage Narada and austerities in the depths of the ocean. They devote themselves to Lord Vishnu, focusing their minds and hearts on the Supreme.

During their meditation, the Supreme Lord, Vishnu, is pleased with their dedication and appears before them. He imparts spiritual knowledge and blessings, encouraging them to continue their devotional practices and fulfil their duties as responsible rulers in the future.

This chapter emphasizes the power of devotion, meditation, and austerities in attaining the divine and balancing spiritual pursuits with worldly responsibilities.

This chapter narrates the spiritual journey of the Pracetas, highlighting their dedication to Lord Vishnu and the divine blessings they receive, underscoring the significance of devotion and balancing spiritual pursuits with worldly duties.

04-31 Narada Instructs the Pracetas

In this chapter, Sage Narada continues to guide and instruct the Pracetas, the sons of King Pracinabarhi, on their spiritual path.

Narada further elaborates on the importance of devotional service and the significance of connecting with the Supreme Lord, Vishnu. He emphasizes the power of meditation, chanting, and hearing the glories of the Lord as essential practices for spiritual growth and realization.

Narada also narrates the story of a king named Puranjana, illustrating the entanglement of the soul in the material world and the consequences of being overly attached to worldly pleasures.

This chapter reinforces the teachings of detachment, devotion, and self-realization to attain spiritual enlightenment and liberation from the cycle of birth and death.

This chapter continues Sage Narada's guidance to the Pracetas, emphasizing the significance of devotional practices and the pursuit of spiritual knowledge to transcend the material world and attain higher consciousness.

Canto 5

05-01 The Activities of Maharaja Priyavrata

This chapter describes the life and accomplishments of Maharaja Priyavrata, one of Lord Brahma's sons. Priyavrata was initially reluctant to rule the kingdom but later accepted the responsibility. He divided the world into continents and oceans, introducing a system of governance. The chapter also mentions his spiritual pursuits and devotion to Lord Vishnu. It highlights Priyavrata's virtuous life and commitment to worldly and spiritual duties.

05-02 The Activities of Maharaja Agnidhra

In the Activities of Maharaja Agnidhra, the narrative shifts to Maharaja Agnidhra, another son of Lord Brahma. This chapter mainly focuses on Agnidhra's meditation and deep fascination with a celestial nymph named Purvacitti. Despite his spiritual inclinations, he becomes infatuated with her beauty and pursues her. The chapter discusses Agnidhra's interactions with Purvacitti and how he eventually attains her companionship after intense penance. This episode is an allegory for the distractions and attachments that can hinder one's spiritual journey, even when initially committed to meditation and devotion.

05-03 Rishabhadeva's Appearance

King Nabhi and Queen Merudevi were devout and performed severe austerities to seek the blessings of Lord Vishnu for a child. In response to their devotion, Lord Vishnu agreed to be born as their son.

The chapter describes how Lord Rishabhadeva, an incarnation of Lord Vishnu, appeared in Queen Merudevi's womb and the divine qualities that marked His birth. It also highlights the great significance of His image and teachings for the spiritual well-being of humanity. This event underscores the importance of divine intervention and devotion in the Bhagavata Purana's narrative context.

05-04 The Characteristics of Rishabhadeva

This chapter describes the divine qualities and teachings of Lord Rishabhadeva, who is considered an incarnation of Lord Vishnu. Lord Rishabhadeva exemplifies the highest level of spirituality and detachment.

The chapter highlights the following aspects of Lord Rishabhadeva's life: His renunciation of the throne: Lord Rishabhadeva, though capable of ruling a kingdom, chose to lead a life of a wandering ascetic to impart spiritual wisdom to humanity.

His teachings: Lord Rishabhadeva delivered profound instructions on the principles of dharma (righteousness) and the path of self-realization. He emphasized the importance of detachment, self-control, and devotion to God.

His compassion: Lord Rishabhadeva exhibited great compassion for all living beings, treating everyone equally and selflessly sharing wisdom.

His transcendental qualities: The chapter describes Lord Rishabhadeva's physical and spiritual attributes, marking Him as Godhead's Supreme Personality.

This chapter underscores the significance of Lord Rishabhadeva's life and teachings as a guiding light for those seeking spiritual enlightenment and the path to liberation.

05-05 Lord Rishabhadeva's Teachings

Lord Rishabhadeva imparts profound spiritual wisdom to His sons and the assembled sages. He emphasizes the importance of self-realization and the path to liberation.

Essential teachings from this chapter include:

Detachment: Lord Rishabhadeva stresses the need for separation from material possessions and desires, as attachment to them leads to suffering and bondage.

Austerity and Self-Control: He advises the practice of asceticism and self-control as essential for spiritual growth. These disciplines help in conquering the mind and senses.

Equality and Compassion: Lord Rishabhadeva teaches that one should see all living beings equally and treat them with compassion. This attitude promotes spiritual advancement.

Surrender to God: He emphasizes surrender to the Supreme Lord as the ultimate goal. One can attain liberation by dedicating one's life to God's service and offering devotional worship.

This chapter serves as a valuable source of spiritual guidance. It underscores the timeless teachings of Lord Rishabhadeva for seekers on the path of self-realization and devotion to the Divine.

05-06 The Activities of Lord Rishabhadeva

This narrative continues to focus on the life and teachings of Lord Rishabhadeva. This chapter explicitly details His actions and spiritual practices during His time as an avadhuta, a liberated soul living outside society's conventions. Key points from this chapter include:

Lord Rishabhadeva's Renunciation: Lord Rishabhadeva chose to live like an ascetic despite being utterly detached from material life. He wandered naked and unperturbed by worldly affairs.

Teaching by Example: By His actions, Lord Rishabhadeva taught the importance of renunciation and detachment. He demonstrated that true happiness and liberation come from detaching oneself from the material world.

Transcendental Behavior: The chapter describes Lord Rishabhadeva's extraordinary behaviour, which included acts that seemed unconventional to ordinary people. However, His actions were beyond material understanding, serving as a powerful spiritual lesson.

This chapter emphasizes the concept of detachment and the need to transcend the material world in one's quest for spiritual realization. It showcases Lord Rishabhadeva as the ultimate example of a liberated soul unaffected by ordinary life's materialistic pursuits.

05-07 The Activities of King Bharata

The focus shifts to the life and experiences of King Bharata, a descendant of Lord Rishabhadeva. This chapter highlights his exemplary devotion and his spiritual transformation during his rule.

King Bharata's Early Life: King Bharata initially ruled his kingdom with excellent efficiency and dedication. However, he maintained an inner detachment from worldly affairs and was deeply absorbed in meditation and devotion.

Attachment to a Deer: While living in the forest as a hermit, King Bharata became attached to a young deer, distracting him from his spiritual practices. He cared for the deer and thought of it constantly.

Renaming as Jadabharata: King Bharata was born a deer due to his attachment after his death. In his next human birth, he was known as Jadabharata. He concealed his intellectual abilities and appeared to be a dull-witted, ignorant person to avoid worldly entanglements.

Inner Realization: Throughout his life as Jadabharata, he maintained his devotion to the Supreme Lord and achieved self-realization. He ultimately attained liberation through his unwavering faith.

This chapter serves as a profound lesson on the importance of detachment and devotion, illustrating how even an emperor like King Bharata chose a life of spirituality and ultimately attained liberation through his steadfast dedication to the Divine.

05-08 A Description Bharata Maharaja

This chapter provides further insight into the character and spiritual journey of King Bharata (formerly known as Jadabharata). It elaborates on his wisdom, devotion, and detachment from worldly affairs.

King Bharata's Ascetic Life: The chapter describes how King Bharata lived as a renunciant, not attached to any material possessions or relationships. He was solely focused on his spiritual pursuits.

Bharata Maharaja possessed a profound knowledge of the self and the Supreme. He maintained stability in all situations, treating happiness and distress with indifference.

Detachment and Disguise: Even though he possessed deep wisdom, King Bharata appeared foolish and ignorant to avoid entanglement in worldly matters. He performed his duties forcefully and never let his actual spiritual knowledge be known.

Renunciation and Meditation: Bharata Maharaja engaged in meditation and devotional practices, seeking the highest realization and liberation from the cycle of birth and death.

This chapter underscores King Bharata's remarkable spiritual journey and commitment to a life of detachment and devotion, demonstrating the path to transcendence and self-realization.

05-09 The Supreme Character of Jada Bharata

This chapter elaborates on his interactions with his fellow travellers and the lessons he imparts through his actions and words.

Jadabharata's Silence: Despite his profound wisdom and spiritual realization, Jadabharata maintained an appearance of ignorance and mainly remained silent. He chose not to engage in idle conversations with ordinary people.

Interactions with a Rogue: Jadabharata's path crosses with a rogue king who attempts to make him his servant. Jadabharata complies but remains unattached to the situation, exemplifying his self-realization.

Spiritual Instructions: When questioned by the rogue king, Jadabharata delivers a series of enlightening teachings on the nature of the self, the material world, and the importance of devotion to the Supreme Lord.

Demonstration of Detachment: Jadabharata's unwavering detachment is evident as he remains calm and indifferent to the harsh treatment he receives from the rogue king.

This chapter highlights Jadabharata's remarkable character, commitment to spiritual realization, and ability to impart profound wisdom through his actions and minimal words. It serves as a lesson in detachment and devotion to the Supreme, even in challenging circumstances.

05-10 Discussion – Rahugana and Jadabharata

This chapter explores a philosophical dialogue between King Rahugana and Jada Bharata. This conversation delves into profound spiritual truths and the nature of the self.

King Rahugana's Humility: King Rahugana, who was initially proud and impatient, humbly approaches Jadabharata after being chastised for mistreating him. He seeks wisdom and guidance.

Teaching on the Material Body: Jadabharata explains the temporary nature of the physical body and how it is merely a vessel for the eternal soul. He emphasizes realizing one's true identity beyond the material covering.

Detachment and Devotion: Jadabharata advises King Rahugana to cultivate detachment from bodily identification and focus on devotional service to the Supreme Lord to attain liberation.

Analogy of the Chariot: Jadabharata uses the analogy of a chariot to explain the relationship between the body (the chariot), the soul (the passenger), and the mind and senses (the horses). He stresses the need for the soul to control the mind and senses.

This chapter is a profound philosophical discourse illustrating the importance of humility, self-realization, and devotion in pursuing spiritual enlightenment. It showcases the timeless teachings found in the Bhagavata Purana.

05-11 Jada Bharata Instructs Maharaja Rahugana

The narrative continues with the philosophical dialogue between Jadabharata and King Rahugana. This chapter further explores spiritual wisdom and the nature of the self.

King Rahugana's Questions: King Rahugana continues to seek guidance from Jadabharata, expressing his genuine curiosity about spiritual matters and the true path to liberation.

The Analogy of the Snake and the Rope: Jadabharata explains the concept of misidentification using the analogy of mistaking a rope for a snake. In the same way, people mistakenly identify with their material bodies, causing suffering.

Importance of Guru: Jadabharata emphasizes the necessity of a spiritual guru (spiritual teacher) to guide one on self-realization. He describes how such a guru can help remove the ignorance that binds individuals.

Detachment and Self-Realization: Jadabharata reinforces the significance of detaching from material desires and cultivating devotion to the Supreme. He emphasizes that one can transcend material bondage by understanding the soul's eternal nature.

This chapter continues the profound philosophical dialogue between Jadabharata and King Rahugana, providing valuable insights into the nature of the self, the role of a spiritual guru, and the path to spiritual enlightenment.

05-12 Conversation – Rahugana and Jadabharata

The philosophical dialogue between King Rahugana and Jadabharata continues. This chapter delves deeper into the nature of the self, the futility of material pursuits, and the importance of devotion.

The Impermanence of the Body: Jadabharata explains how the material body is temporary and subject to birth, death, and decay. He emphasizes that identifying with the body leads to suffering and bondage.

Transcending Material Desires: Jadabharata advises King Rahugana to renounce material desires and attachments, as they are the root cause of entanglement in the cycle of birth and death.

Devotion to the Supreme: Jadabharata underscores the significance of devotional service to the Supreme Lord as the most effective means of attaining liberation. He describes various forms of devotion, such as hearing and chanting the glories of the Lord.

The Role of a Spiritual Teacher: Jadabharata highlights the importance of a qualified spiritual teacher (guru) in guiding one on the spiritual path and imparting knowledge of the self and the Supreme.

This chapter provides further insights into the teachings of Jadabharata, emphasizing the need to transcend material identification, cultivate devotion to the Divine, and seek guidance from a spiritual guru on the journey to self-realization and liberation.

05-13 Further Talks - Rahugana and Jadabharata

The philosophical discourse between King Rahugana and Jadabharata continues. This chapter delves deeper into spiritual wisdom and self-realization.

Transcending Material Designations: Jadabharata advises King Rahugana to go beyond material designations like "king" or "beggar" and recognize the soul's eternal nature, distinct from the external bodily identity.

The Illusion of the Material World: Jadabharata explains how the material world is like a dream or an illusion, and one must awaken to spiritual consciousness to escape this illusion.

Detachment and Devotion: The chapter reiterates the importance of separation from material attachments and emphasizes the significance of devotional service to the Supreme Lord as the path to liberation.

The Role of Spiritual Knowledge: Jadabharata stresses the value of spiritual knowledge in dispelling ignorance and the need for sincere inquiry into the nature of reality.

This chapter continues the profound philosophical dialogue between Jadabharata and King Rahugana, offering deep insights into the nature of the self, the illusory nature of the material world, and the path to spiritual enlightenment through detachment and devotion.

05-14 Prahlada Maharaja

The focus shifts to the life and teachings of Prahlada Maharaja. Prahlada was the son of the demon king Hiranyakashipu but possessed unwavering devotion to Lord Vishnu.

Hiranyakashipu's Displeasure: Despite his father's antagonism towards Lord Vishnu, Prahlada remained steadfast in his devotion to the Supreme Lord. This unwavering faith displeased Hiranyakashipu, who attempted to dissuade Prahlada through various means.

Prahlada's Teachings: Prahlada Maharaja imparts profound spiritual wisdom, emphasizing that devotion to the Supreme is the ultimate purpose of human life. He highlights the futility of material pursuits and the transient nature of worldly pleasures.

Miraculous Protection: Despite several attempts by Hiranyakashipu to harm Prahlada, the Lord miraculously protects him each time, illustrating the power of divine devotion.

Prahlada's Humility: Prahlada Maharaja exemplifies humility and compassion even in the face of adversity, earning the respect of the demigods and sages.

This chapter is a significant episode in the Bhagavata Purana, showcasing Prahlada Maharaja's unwavering devotion to Lord Vishnu, his resilience in the face of adversity, and his teachings on the importance of commitment and spiritual realization.

05-15 Instructions for Civilized Human Beings

The sage Narada imparts valuable guidance to King Yudhishthira on various aspects of human life and duty.

Human Duties: Sage Narada emphasizes the importance of following one's prescribed duties (dharma) based on their varna (occupation) and ashrama (stage of life). By doing so, individuals contribute to society and attain spiritual progress.

Transcendence through Bhakti: Narada explains that the ultimate goal of life is to transcend material existence and attain the Supreme through devotional service (bhakti). He encourages devotion to Lord Krishna as the highest form of worship.

The Importance of Temples: The sage discusses the significance of temples and places of worship in facilitating devotion and spiritual growth.

Detachment and Self-Realization: Narada emphasizes the need for separation from material possessions and desires and encourages self-realization through meditation and spiritual practices.

Influence of Association: The chapter underscores the impact of association with devotees and the importance of choosing a company wisely to stay on the path of spiritual growth.

This chapter serves as a comprehensive guide on leading a righteous and spiritually fulfilling life, emphasizing devotion to the Supreme as the ultimate purpose of human existence. It also highlights the significance of harmonising one's social and familial responsibilities with spiritual pursuits.

05-16 Puranjana Material Pleasures

This chapter narrates the tale of King Puranjana and his pursuit of material enjoyment, ultimately leading to spiritual realization.

King Puranjana's Material Pursuits: King Puranjana becomes obsessed with material pleasures and indulges in various sensory experiences, symbolizing the typical worldly pursuits of individuals.

Symbolism of City and Body: The chapter draws parallels between King Puranjana's city, where he lives, and the physical body. The city represents the material body, and its various residents symbolize the senses and their objects.

The Arrival of Time: Time, personified as a powerful personality, eventually arrives to take King Puranjana away. KALA represents the inevitable nature of time leading to death and the soul's departure from the physical body.

Spiritual Realization: King Puranjana, in his last moments, reflects on his life of materialism and realizes the futility of his pursuits. He turns his thoughts toward self-realization and the Supreme Lord.

This chapter serves as an allegory, illustrating the transient nature of material life and the importance of turning towards spiritual realization and devotion to the Supreme as the ultimate goal of human existence.

05-17 The Descent of the River Ganges

This chapter recounts the divine story of how the holy river Ganges descended to Earth.

Bhagiratha's Penance: King Bhagiratha, a descendant of the great sage Sagara, embarks on intense penance to bring the Ganges down to Earth to purify the ashes of his ancestors. His ancestors had been cursed, and their souls could only attain liberation by bathing in the sacred waters of the Ganges.

Lord Shiva's Role: Bhagiratha's penance impresses Lord Brahma, who then appeals to Lord Shiva to help. Lord Shiva agrees and allows the Ganges to flow through his matted hair, reducing the river's force and preventing her from causing devastation on Earth.

Ganges' Descent: With Lord Shiva's consent, the Ganges descends from the heavenly realms to Earth, following the path created by Bhagiratha's penance. Her purifying waters become a lifeline for countless souls seeking spiritual redemption.

Significance of the Ganges: The chapter highlights the immense spiritual importance of the Ganges River in Hindu culture and how her waters are believed to cleanse one's sins and purify the soul.

This chapter portrays the extraordinary efforts of King Bhagiratha and the divine intervention of Lord Shiva in bringing the sacred river Ganges to Earth, emphasizing the profound spiritual importance of this holy river in Hindu tradition.

05-18 The Prayers by Jambudvipa

This chapter presents prayers and glorifications of the Supreme Lord by the residents of Jambudvipa, one of the continents in the cosmic geography described in the text.

Praises of the Lord: The residents of Jambudvipa express their devotion and gratitude by offering heartfelt prayers acknowledging the Supreme Lord as the ultimate source of creation, maintenance, and destruction of the universe.

Descriptions of the Lord's Characteristics: The prayers highlight the Lord's qualities, such as omnipotence, omniscience, and compassion. They describe how He takes various forms to protect and guide His devotees.

Desire for Devotion: The residents of Jambudvipa express their willingness to develop unwavering devotion to the Lord and seek His blessings to overcome the material illusions that keep them entangled in the cycle of birth and death.

Importance of Spiritual Knowledge: The chapter underscores the significance of spiritual knowledge and devotion to attain liberation and ultimate union with the Supreme.

This chapter serves as a devotional expression of reverence and surrender to the Supreme Lord. It emphasizes the importance of spiritual knowledge and devotion in the quest for spiritual enlightenment and liberation.

05-19 A Description of the Island of Jambudvipa

This text provides a detailed description of Jambudvipa, one of the seven main islands in the cosmic geography of the Bhagavata Purana.

Geographical Layout: The chapter outlines the geographical features of Jambudvipa, including its mountains, rivers, and forests. It describes the universe's arrangement of the seven continents and seven oceans.

Mountains and Rivers: The text mentions significant mountains like Sumeru and Himavat and rivers like the Ganges, Sindhu, and Yamuna, considered sacred in Hindu tradition.

The Importance of Jambudvipa: Jambudvipa is the most prominent and essential of all the continents due to its unique spiritual significance. It is the land where most religious activities occur, especially those related to the Supreme Lord.

Spiritual Significance: The chapter underscores that although Jambudvipa's physical features are important, its primary significance lies in its place for spiritual advancement and devotion to the Supreme Lord.

This chapter serves as a cosmological and geographical description, providing a framework for understanding the Bhagavata Purana's narrative and highlighting the spiritual importance of Jambudvipa within the context of the text.

05-20 The Structure of the Universe

This text offers a detailed and intricate description of the cosmology of the universe, including its various dimensions and realms.

The Universe's Layers: The chapter describes the universe as consisting of numerous planetary systems, with each method having multiple layers or realms. These realms include heavenly planets, earthly planets, and lower, hellish regions.

Description of the Earthly Realm: The text elaborates on the earthly realm, describing the continents, oceans, and mountains. It explains how Jambudvipa is the central continent and the primary location for human habitation.

Dimensions of Time: The chapter discusses the concept of time in the universe, including the divisions of time, such as yugas (ages) and kalpas (cosmic cycles). It highlights the cyclical nature of time and the regular periods of creation, maintenance, and destruction.

Celestial Geography: The chapter provides insights into the geography of the angelic realms, describing the features and residents of heavenly planets, demigods, and divine beings.

Purpose of the Description: It is emphasized that understanding the cosmic structure is essential for comprehending the nature of the material world and the significance of human existence within it. It also underscores worldly life's transient and temporary nature compared to the eternal spiritual reality.

This chapter elaborates on the Bhagavata Purana's cosmological framework, helping readers understand the universe's structure and relationship to the spiritual journey described in the text.

05-21 The Movements of the Sun

This chapter provides a detailed account of the sun's movement within the universe according to Vedic cosmology.

The Sun's Orbit: The chapter explains that the sun orbits Mount Meru, the central axis of the universe, along with its entourage of planets. This description offers an alternative cosmological perspective to the modern heliocentric model.

Sunrise and Sunset: It elaborates on how the sun rises in the eastern hemisphere and sets in the western hemisphere, affecting day and night on different planetary systems.

Different Lokas (Realms): The text mentions various planetary systems and realms, each having unique characteristics and durations of day and night based on the sun's movement.

Significance of Time: The chapter underscores the importance of understanding the movement of celestial bodies as it relates to time measurement in Vedic cosmology. It highlights the cyclical nature of time and its role in material creation.

Spiritual Perspective: While the chapter provides detailed astronomical information, it also reminds readers of the Bhagavata Purana's primary focus on spirituality and the path to transcendence.

This chapter offers insights into the Vedic understanding of the sun's movement within the universe and its role in measuring time in various realms. It provides a unique cosmological perspective in the context of the Bhagavata Purana's broader spiritual teachings.

05-22 The Movements of the Planets

This chapter provides a detailed account of the movements of the planets within the universe according to Vedic cosmology.

Planetary Orbits: The chapter explains the orbits and movements of the planets within the universe. It describes their trajectories around Mount Meru, the central axis of the universe, and how they affect different planetary systems.

Names of Planets: The text lists the names of various visible and invisible planets in Vedic cosmology. These include the sun, moon, Mercury, Venus, Mars, Jupiter, and Saturn.

Time Measurement: The chapter highlights the significance of understanding planetary movements for accurate time measurement in Vedic astronomy. It explains how the positions of celestial bodies are used to determine auspicious times for various activities.

Cyclical Nature of Time: It reiterates the cyclical nature of time and the periodicity of the material universe's creation, maintenance, and destruction.

Spiritual Perspective: While the chapter provides intricate astronomical details, it emphasizes the ultimate goal of spiritual realization and liberation as the central theme of the Bhagavata Purana.

This chapter offers a comprehensive overview of the movements of the planets within the Vedic cosmology, demonstrating the precision with which ancient Indian astronomers and sages understood the universe. It also serves as a reminder of the spiritual context in which these cosmological discussions are presented in the Bhagavata Purana.

05-23 The Shishumar Stotra

This chapter features a profound hymn known as the Shishumar Stotra, which Lord Rishabhadeva recites. This hymn describes the cosmic form of the Supreme Lord as the divine Shishumar, a celestial being with a unique and majestic appearance.

The Cosmic Form: Lord Rishabhadeva describes the cosmic form of the Shishumar, a celestial being that encompasses the entire universe. This form consists of various planets, stars, and galaxies arranged in a specific order.

Vedic Cosmology: The hymn provides insights into Vedic cosmology, depicting the arrangement of the universe as understood in ancient Indian scriptures.

Mystical Symbolism: The Shishumar Stotra is rich in esoteric symbolism, highlighting the interconnectedness of all celestial bodies and their role in the grand cosmic design.

Devotion to the Supreme: Lord Rishabhadeva recites this hymn to emphasize the significance of commitment to the Supreme Lord, who is the ultimate controller and source of all creation.

Spiritual Teachings: While the chapter delves into the cosmic and mystical aspects of the universe, it ultimately serves as a means to convey spiritual teachings about the importance of recognizing the divine presence in all aspects of creation and the path to liberation through devotion.

This chapter is a unique and metaphysical hymn that provides a glimpse into the deep spiritual understanding of the cosmos within the Bhagavata Purana, emphasizing the central theme of devotion to the Supreme as the ultimate purpose of life.

05-24 The Subterranean Heavenly Planets

This chapter provides insights into the existence of celestial realms beneath the Earth's surface, describing subterranean heavenly planets and beings.

Subterranean Worlds: The chapter introduces the concept of subterranean heavenly planets located beneath the Earth's surface. These realms are inhabited by celestial beings who possess unique qualities and abilities.

Description of the Inhabitants: It describes the residents of these subterranean heavenly planets, such as the Nagas (serpent beings), Gandharvas (celestial musicians), Siddhas (perfected beings), and Charanas (singers of the Gandharvas).

Lifestyles and Activities: The text explains the lifestyle and activities of these celestial beings, including their enjoyment of divine music, dances, and beautiful surroundings.

Spiritual Knowledge: The chapter highlights that despite their opulent surroundings, the residents of these realms are highly advanced in spiritual knowledge and virtue.

Vedic Cosmology: It provides further insight into Vedic cosmology by suggesting the existence of vast, multi-dimensional universes and realms beyond what is perceivable on the Earth's surface.

This chapter elaborates on the diversity and complexity of the Vedic universe, introducing readers to the concept of subterranean heavenly realms and their inhabitants. It emphasizes the coexistence of material and spiritual dimensions in Vedic cosmology and the importance of spiritual knowledge and virtue even in celestial realms.

05-25 The Glories of Lord Ananta

This chapter glorifies Lord Ananta, also known as Lord Balarama, who is the elder brother of Lord Krishna and an incarnation of Lord Vishnu.

Lord Balarama's Appearance: The chapter describes the divine appearance of Lord Balarama in the womb of Devaki as a response to the prayers of Vasudeva and Devaki, whom the wicked King Kamsa imprisoned.

Balarama's Exploits: It narrates various pastimes and heroic deeds of Lord Balarama, such as His slaying of demons like Dhenukasura and Pralambasura and His role in the killing of Kamsa.

Balarama's Virtues: The chapter extols the virtuous qualities of Lord Balarama, including His unparalleled strength, beauty, knowledge, and devotion to Lord Krishna.

Balarama's Role in Creation: Lord Balarama is described as the source of Lord Krishna and the instrument through which the entire cosmic creation is manifested. He expands Himself as the unlimited serpent Ananta upon whom the universe rests.

Spiritual Significance: The chapter underscores the spiritual significance of Lord Balarama and His relationship with Lord Krishna, highlighting their roles in the divine pastimes (Lila) for the upliftment of devotees.

This chapter serves to emphasize the greatness and divine nature of Lord Balarama, highlighting His pivotal role in the spiritual narrative of the Bhagavata Purana and His eternal connection with Lord Krishna. It reinforces the teachings of devotion and surrenders to the Supreme Lord.

05-26 A Description of the Hellish Planets

This chapter provides a detailed account of the various hellish realms in the afterlife, where souls suffer due to their sinful actions.

Hellish Realms: The text describes the different difficult planets and the types of punishments inflicted upon sinful souls. These realms are depicted as places of extreme torment and suffering.

Karma and Consequences: It explains that the sufferings on these hellish planets are the direct consequences of one's sinful activities and negative karma accumulated during earthly life.

Descriptions of Hellish Punishments: The chapter elaborates on the specific punishments in each hell, including extreme heat, cold, biting insects, and various types of tortures designed to purify the soul of its sinful tendencies.

Temporary Nature: While these hellish punishments are severe, it is emphasized that they are quick and serve as a means for souls to atone for their sins before being reborn in the material world.

Opportunity for Redemption: The chapter suggests that even in hell, souls may have moments of realization and introspection, offering them the chance to seek redemption and spiritual growth.

This chapter is a cautionary tale illustrating the consequences of sinful actions and the importance of living a righteous and virtuous life. It emphasizes the concepts of karma and the need for moral and spiritual development to avoid the suffering associated with hellish realms in the afterlife.

Canto 6

06-01 The History of the Life of Ajamila

In this chapter, the story revolves around Ajamila, who starts as a pious Brahmin but later falls into a life of sinful activities. Ajamila gets entangled in a life of debauchery, including an association with a prostitute. He eventually becomes the father of several children with the prostitute and names one of them Narayana, one of the names of Lord Vishnu.

As Ajamila's life nears its end, he becomes distressed and calls out the name "Narayana" in fear of approaching death. At this moment, the Vishnudutas, messengers of Lord Vishnu, appear to protect Ajamila and save him from the clutches of the Yamadutas, who are the messengers of Yamaraja, the god of death. The Vishnudutas explain to the Yamadutas that Ajamila's sincere calling of the Lord's name at the time of death has purified him, and he should be spared from punishment.

The chapter is a powerful illustration of the significance of chanting the holy names of the Lord, especially at the time of death, as it can grant spiritual liberation. It emphasizes the mercy and compassion of Lord Vishnu and highlights the transformative power of devotion.

This chapter is part of the larger narrative in the Bhagavatam, which explores various aspects of devotion, morality, and spirituality through storytelling and philosophical discourse.

06-02 Ajamila Delivered by the Vishnudutas

In this chapter, the Yamadutas, messengers of Yamaraja, the god of death, question the Vishnudutas about their interference in Ajamila's case. The Vishnudutas eloquently explains the power of devotional service and the significance of chanting the holy names of the Lord, emphasizing that one's actions and intent at the moment of death are crucial.

The chapter also illustrates the contrast between the path of devotion and the passage of fruitive work or karma. It highlights the mercy and compassion of Lord Vishnu, who forgives Ajamila's sins and grants him spiritual liberation due to his sincere devotion.

This Chapter continues Ajamila's redemption and provides valuable insights into the concepts of karma, devotion, and the role of divine intervention in the lives of devotees.

06-03 Yamaraja Instructs His Messengers

In this chapter, Yamaraja, the god of death, addresses his messengers, the Yamadutas, after their unsuccessful attempt to bring Ajamila to the court of Yamaraja. Yamaraja chastises the Yamadutas for their lack of knowledge about the power of chanting the holy name of the Lord.

Yamaraja explains the importance of understanding the principles of religion and the concept of the soul's journey through various bodies based on karma. He emphasizes that the name of the Supreme Lord, especially the phrase "Narayana," is so potent that it can nullify the reactions of one's sinful actions and free a person from the cycle of birth and death.

This chapter is pivotal in the narrative, highlighting the significance of devotional service and the transformative effect of chanting the Lord's name. It also underscores the idea that genuine spiritual understanding is essential for anyone involved in matters related to the soul and the afterlife.

Overall, the Chapter provides a philosophical perspective on the power of devotion and the importance of divine knowledge in understanding the nature of the soul and its journey.

06-04 The Hamsa-guhya Prayers

In this chapter, Prajapati Daksha, the chief of the Prajapatis (progenitors of humankind), offers a series of profound prayers to Lord Vishnu, also known as the Supreme Personality of Godhead.

Daksha's prayers are heartfelt expressions of devotion and surrender to the Lord. He acknowledges the Lord as the universe's ultimate creator, maintainer, and destroyer. Daksha describes the various incarnations and forms of the Lord, recognizing His omnipotence and intangible qualities.

The chapter also narrates how Daksha initially had conflicts with his son-in-law, Lord Shiva, who understood the Lord's supreme position and the importance of spiritual knowledge and devotion.

This Chapter is a significant section of the Bhagavatam that emphasizes the importance of recognizing the divine nature of the Supreme Lord and the transformative power of devotion and prayer in one's spiritual journey. It serves as a reminder of the need for humility and surrender in pursuing spiritual realization.

06-05 Narada Muni Cursed by Prajapati Daksha

This chapter revolves around an incident involving two prominent personalities in Hindu mythology: Narada Muni and Prajapati Daksha.

In this chapter, Narada Muni, a celestial sage and devotee of Lord Vishnu, visits the assembly of Prajapati Daksha, who is conducting a grand sacrifice (yajna). However, Daksha is not particularly respectful or welcoming to Narada because Narada's teachings and actions often highlight the supremacy of devotion to the Supreme Lord over ritualistic sacrifices.

During the assembly, Narada expresses his devotion to Lord Vishnu and emphasizes the futility of mere ritualistic ceremonies without proper spiritual understanding and dedication. This angers Daksha, who accuses Narada of disrupting the sacrifice and even insults him.

In response to Daksha's insults, Narada Muni gracefully departs from the assembly, but he predicts that Daksha's arrogance and disrespect for devotees will lead to unfortunate consequences in the future.

This chapter illustrates the contrast between devotion and ritualism and the consequences of pride and disrespect toward spiritual personalities. It also foreshadows future events and conflicts in the Bhagavatam's narrative.

06-06 Daksha Curses Lord Shiva

This chapter continues the narrative from the previous chapters, focusing on the conflict between Prajapati Daksha and Lord Shiva.

After the incident with Narada Muni, Daksha proceeds with his grand sacrifice (yajna) and intentionally excludes his son-in-law, Lord Shiva, whom he strongly dislikes. Sati, Lord Shiva's wife and Daksha's daughter learns about this exclusion and becomes distressed. Despite Lord Shiva's advice, she attends the sacrifice without an invitation.

Upon her arrival at the sacrifice, Daksha insults Lord Shiva in front of the assembled sages and demigods, criticizing his unorthodox appearance and behaviour. Unable to bear her father's insults towards her husband, Sati becomes extremely upset and ultimately gives up her life by self-immolation through the power of her yogic meditation.

Learning about Sati's tragic death, Lord Shiva is filled with grief and rage. He creates the terrifying Virabhadra and Bhadrakali, who wreak havoc at Daksha's yajna, causing chaos and destruction.

This chapter highlights the consequences of pride, disrespect, and familial conflicts. It sets the stage for further events in the Bhagavatam, including the reconciliation between Lord Shiva and Daksha and the subsequent birth of Sati in a different form.

06-07 Indra Offends His Spiritual Master

141

In this chapter, the narrative shifts from the previous conflicts involving Daksha and Lord Shiva to a new story centred around Indra, the king of the heavenly demigods, and his spiritual teacher, Brihaspati.

The chapter begins with a background story: Indra had disrespected and neglected his guru, Brihaspati while celebrating his victory over the demons. As a result, Brihaspati decided to leave Indra's service and went to join the demigods' rivals, the demons.

With Brihaspati's absence, the demons, led by their new priest, Shukracharya, became powerful and eventually defeated Indra and the demigods. Realizing his mistake, Indra sought the advice of Lord Vishnu's devotees and took steps to rectify his relationship with Brihaspati.

The chapter emphasizes the importance of respecting and honouring one's spiritual teacher and the consequences of neglecting this duty. It also highlights the complexities of power and authority in the celestial realms.

The chapter serves as a moral lesson about humility, devotion, and the significance of maintaining a respectful relationship with one's guru, even in the realm of the gods.

06–08 The Narayana-kavaca Shield

This chapter introduces the powerful Narayana-Lavaca mantra and its significance in protecting those who chant it.

The chapter describes how Indra, the king of the demigods, becomes concerned about his vulnerability to demonic attacks after losing his guru, Brihaspati. In his distress, Indra approaches Lord Vishnu, who instructs him to seek the shelter of the Narayana-kavaca, a mantra that acts as a protective shield.

Indra learns this mantra from Lord Vishnu and, by chanting it with devotion, becomes invulnerable to the attacks of the demons. He regains his confidence and strength, defeating the monsters and restoring the demigods to their heavenly abode.

This chapter emphasizes the potency of divine mantras, particularly the Narayana-kavaca, in providing protection and strength to those who sincerely chant them. It reinforces the idea that devotion to the Supreme Lord is a source of power and security in times of adversity.

The chapter highlights the significance of the Narayana-kavaca mantra and its role in safeguarding Indra and the demigods from demonic threats, illustrating the power of devotion and divine intervention.

06-09 Appearance of the Demon Vritrasura

143

This chapter introduces the character of Vritrasura, a formidable demon with a unique disposition.

Vritrasura is born to the sage Twashtri and is initially a virtuous soul. However, he transforms into a demon due to events and a curse. Despite his demonic appearance and nature, Vritrasura remains deeply philosophical and demonstrates detachment and devotion to Lord Vishnu.

The chapter focuses on the background and character development of Vritrasura, setting the stage for future confrontations between him and the demigods, particularly Lord Indra.

Chapter 9 lays the foundation for the story of Vritrasura, a complex character combining demonic qualities and spiritual wisdom, making him a unique figure in the Bhagavatam's narrative.

06-10 The Battle - Demigods and Vritrasura

This chapter narrates a significant battle between the demigods, led by King Indra, and the formidable demon Vritrasura.

Vritrasura, despite his demonic nature, possesses great strength and bravery. He engages in fierce combat with the demigods, and a formidable fight ensues. Vritrasura displays his martial prowess and philosophical wisdom during the battle, even discussing spiritual topics with Indra.

The battle reaches a critical point when Vritrasura gains the upper hand and severely injures Indra. However, at the pivotal moment, Indra remembers the instructions of his spiritual master and prays to Lord Vishnu for help. Lord Vishnu intervenes, empowering Indra to continue the fight. Indra ultimately defeats Vritrasura with divine assistance, and the demon meets his demise.

This chapter highlights the interplay between good and evil, the importance of seeking divine intervention in times of crisis, and the significance of spiritual knowledge even amid battles. It also underscores the idea that devotion and prayer can lead to victory over seemingly insurmountable challenges.

Chapter 10 portrays a dramatic battle between the demigods and Vritrasura, showcasing themes of courage, wisdom, and divine support that can lead to triumph over adversity.

06-11 The Transcendental Qualities of Vritrasura

This chapter provides a detailed exploration of the remarkable character and spiritual qualities of Vritrasura, the demon who fought against the demigods in the previous chapters.

Despite being a demon, Vritrasura exhibited extraordinary qualities such as deep philosophical wisdom, humility, and devotion to the Supreme Lord. He displayed these virtues even in the heat of battle, engaging in profound conversations with Indra, the king of the demigods.

The chapter describes Vritrasura's remarkable demeanour and realization that the Supreme Lord is the ultimate controller of all events, even his death in battle. He views his imminent death as an opportunity to attain liberation through devotion to the Lord.

Vritrasura's character exemplifies that genuine spirituality transcends external appearances and that even a demon can attain spiritual enlightenment through sincere devotion and understanding divine truths.

Chapter 11 offers a deeper insight into the spiritual qualities and realization of Vritrasura, highlighting the Bhagavatam's broader message that true spirituality is not confined to any particular background or identity.

06-12 Vritrasura's Glorious Death

This chapter continues the narrative of Vritrasura, the demon with remarkable spiritual qualities and wisdom despite his demonic nature.

In this chapter, the battle between Vritrasura and the demigods, led by Indra, reaches its climax. Despite being severely wounded, Vritrasura remains undeterred in his devotion to the Supreme Lord. He continues to express his transcendental knowledge and surrender to the divine will.

As the battle unfolds, Vritrasura prays to Lord Vishnu, expressing his willingness to accept whatever outcome the Lord desires. He acknowledges that his life and death are ultimately under the control of the Supreme.

In a dramatic and spiritually significant moment, Vritrasura is finally defeated by Indra, and the demon is granted liberation. Lord Vishnu personally appears before Vritrasura, recognizing his devotion, and blesses him with a divine form suitable for entering the Lord's abode.

This chapter underscores the power of unwavering devotion, even in adversity, and the transformative effect of surrendering to the divine will. It portrays Vritrasura's glorious death as he attains liberation and the favour of the Supreme Lord through his devotion and wisdom.

Chapter 12 highlights the culmination of Vritrasura's spiritual journey, emphasizing themes of surrender, devotion, and the ultimate liberation of the soul.

06-13 The Behavior of a Perfect Person

This chapter guides the qualities and behaviour of a perfect person, primarily through the teachings of Narada Muni.

Narada Muni imparts wisdom to Maharaja Yudhishthira, one of the Pandava brothers, about the attributes that define an ideal human being. He emphasizes humility, compassion, truthfulness, austerity, and self-control. Narada Muni explains that one should not harm others and treat all living beings respectfully.

The chapter also discusses the importance of devotional service to the Supreme Lord, highlighting that genuine spirituality involves dedicating one's actions and thoughts to the divine. Narada Muni stresses that true perfection is achieved by lovingly serving the Lord with devotion and surrender.

Chapter 13 serves as a guide for living a righteous and spiritually fulfilling life. It encourages individuals to cultivate virtuous qualities and dedicate their lives to selfless service and devotion to the Supreme, ultimately leading to spiritual growth and enlightenment.

06-14 King Chitraketu's Lamentation

This chapter centres around King Chitraketu, who is overcome by profound grief and lamentation.

King Chitraketu, once childless, is blessed with a son named Harsha by the great sage Angira. However, when Harsha grows up, he dies unexpectedly due to a snake bite. Chitraketu is devastated by the loss of his beloved son and is overwhelmed with sorrow.

In his deep lamentation, Chitraketu questions the unfairness of life and the ways of destiny. He expresses his anguish and frustration, wondering why his joy has become such intense sorrow.

The chapter illustrates life's transient and unpredictable nature and the inevitable reality of suffering and loss. It serves as a reminder of the impermanence of material existence and the challenges of coping with grief and tragedy.

Ultimately, Chitraketu's lamentation becomes a backdrop for later teachings and spiritual insights that he receives from the sage Angira, which are explored in subsequent chapters of the Bhagavatam.

06-15 The Saints Narada and Angira

This chapter continues the narrative of King Chitraketu, who was grieving the loss of his son in the previous chapter.

In this chapter, the great sage Narada and the sage Angira come to console and instruct King Chitraketu, who is still overwhelmed by grief. They share profound spiritual wisdom and teachings to help him understand the nature of life, death, and the soul's journey.

Narada and Angira emphasize the soul's eternal nature, explaining that the material body is temporary, but the soul is immortal and beyond birth and death. They guide Chitraketu to transcend his attachment to the physical form of his son and recognize the spiritual essence within all living beings.

The chapter highlights the transformative power of spiritual knowledge and the importance of seeking guidance from wise sages during distress. It is a turning point for Chitraketu, helping him understand life's spiritual dimensions and ultimately find solace and enlightenment.

Chapter 15 focuses on the teachings of Narada and Angira, which provide King Chitraketu with profound insights into the nature of the soul and help him overcome his grief and attachment to the material world.

06-16 King Chitraketu Meets the Supreme Lord

This chapter marks a significant moment in King Chitraketu's spiritual journey.

After receiving teachings from the sages Narada and Angira, Chitraketu continues his meditation and deep introspection. As a result of his devotion and inner searching, he has a divine vision in which he meets Lord Sankarshana, an expansion of Lord Vishnu.

In this vision, Lord Sankarshana imparts further spiritual wisdom to Chitraketu, emphasizing the eternal nature of the soul, the illusory nature of the material world, and the importance of devotion to the Supreme Lord for liberation.

Chitraketu's encounter with Lord Sankarshana is a transformative experience, further solidifying his understanding of spiritual truths. The chapter highlights the significance of divine revelations and personal encounters with the Supreme in one's spiritual journey.

Chapter 16 portrays King Chitraketu's profound spiritual experience as he meets Lord Sankarshana and receives deeper insights into the nature of the soul and the path to liberation through devotion.

06-17 Mother Parvati Curses Chitraketu

In this chapter, the narrative shifts to an incident involving Chitraketu's encounter with Lord Shiva and Goddess Parvati.

King Chitraketu, after his spiritual awakening and the vision of Lord Sankarshana, returns to his kingdom and expresses his newfound wisdom. However, he remains childless, which causes concern and sadness for him and his queen, Kritadyuti.

Chitraketu decides to perform a yajna (sacrifice) to seek the blessings of Lord Shiva and Parvati for a child. He invites numerous sages, demigods, and divine beings to the yajna. During the event, Lord Shiva and Parvati appear. Still, Parvati becomes upset when she learns that Chitraketu already has a son from a previous birth and cannot have another child due to his past karma.

In her anger and frustration, Parvati curses Chitraketu to become a demon in his next life. Despite Lord Shiva's attempts to mitigate the curse, Parvati's words remain potent, and Chitraketu accepts his fate with equanimity.

This chapter illustrates the intricate workings of karma and destiny, highlighting that even spiritual wisdom does not exempt one from the consequences of past actions. It also portrays the importance of acceptance and humility in facing life's challenges.

Chapter 17 explores the story of Chitraketu's desire for a child, his encounter with Lord Shiva and Parvati, and the unexpected curse that shapes his future destiny.

06-18 Diti Vows to Kill King Indra

This chapter delves into the story of Diti, a daughter of Daksha and a mother of demons, and her determination to give birth to a powerful son who can defeat King Indra.

Diti is the mother of the demoniac brothers, Hiranyaksha and Hiranyakashipu. She desires to have a son who can avenge their deaths at the hands of Lord Vishnu's incarnations, Varaha and Narasimha. Diti follows a strict regimen of purification and austerity to ensure the birth of such a robust child.

However, Diti becomes impatient and makes a mistake by approaching her husband, Kashyapa, for union during an inauspicious time. Kashyapa, being a sage, had advised her to wait for an auspicious time. As a result of this impatience, Diti becomes pregnant with twin sons, but they are born prematurely and are not as powerful as she had hoped.

The chapter highlights the consequences of impatience and the importance of following divine instructions. It also foreshadows the birth of the famous demon king, Bali, who plays a significant role in later sections of the Bhagavatam.

Chapter 18 focuses on Diti's desire for a powerful son and her impatience, leading to her children's premature birth. It is a cautionary tale about the importance of patience and spiritual guidance.

06-19 Pumsavana Ritualistic Ceremony

This chapter explores how Lord Brahma instructed Daksha, one of his sons and a prominent Prajapati, to perform a special ritual known as the Pumsavana ceremony.

Pumsavana is a Vedic ritual performed during pregnancy to bless the child and ensure the well-being of both the mother and the unborn child. In this context, Daksha's daughter-in-law, Prasuti, is pregnant with her child, and Daksha, under Lord Brahma's guidance, arranges for this ceremony to be conducted.

The chapter describes the elaborate preparations and rituals involved in the Pumsavana ceremony. It emphasizes the importance of following religious traditions and conducting such practices with great care and devotion.

While this chapter may seem to focus on the details of the Pumsavana ritual, it also highlights the significance of religious customs and practices in the Vedic tradition, illustrating how they play a role in the lives of individuals and families, especially during significant events like pregnancy.

Chapter 19 provides insights into the Pumsavana ritual's performance as Lord Brahma instructed, emphasizing the role of tradition and spirituality in significant life events.

Canto 7

07-01 The Supreme Lord Is Equal to Everyone

Lord imparts profound spiritual wisdom to the king and his assembly as follows:

Equality of the Supreme Lord: The chapter emphasizes that the Supreme Lord, in this case, Lord Vishnu or Lord Krishna, is impartial and treats all living beings equally. He doesn't discriminate based on caste, creed, or social status. This idea is central to the Bhakti (devotional) philosophy, which teaches that God's love and grace are accessible to everyone, regardless of background.

Narada's Teachings: Narada Muni instructs King Yudhishthira on various aspects of devotion, righteousness, and the nature of the divine. He stresses the importance of surrendering to the Supreme Lord with faith and love.

Prahlada's Example: The chapter also introduces the story of Prahlada Maharaja, a young devotee of Lord Vishnu who remained steadfast in his faith despite facing extreme adversity. Prahlada's story is a significant part of the Bhagavatam and teaches the qualities of unwavering devotion and the protection the Lord provides to His sincere devotees.

The Glories of Devotion: Narada describes the immense benefits of devotion to the Supreme Lord. He explains that belief leads to liberation (moksha) and grants spiritual insight, inner peace, and divine protection.

Consequences of Sin: The chapter discusses the effects of sinful actions and how they can be mitigated through devotion and sincere repentance.

07-02 Hiranyakashipu, the King of the Demons

Here are the key themes and events of this chapter.

Hiranyakashipu's Ascendancy: The chapter begins by describing the rise of Hiranyakashipu, who is portrayed as a powerful demon king. He has gained immense strength through austerities and has become almost invincible. However, his growing power also leads to tyranny and oppression.

Prahlada's Birth: The chapter introduces Prahlada, the son of Hiranyakashipu, who is a devoted follower of Lord Vishnu right from birth. Despite being raised in a demoniac environment, Prahlada remains unwavering in his devotion to the Supreme Lord.

Conflict between Father and Son: The primary focus of this chapter is the conflict between Hiranyakashipu, who hates Lord Vishnu, and Prahlada, an ardent devotee of Lord Vishnu. Despite Hiranyakashipu's efforts to change his son's beliefs and even attempts to kill him, Prahlada remains steadfast in his devotion.

Prahlada's Teachings: Prahlada imparts spiritual wisdom to his demoniac classmates, teaching them about the supremacy of Lord Vishnu and the futility of material pursuits. His teachings starkly contrast the values of his father's kingdom. Hiranyakashipu's Anger: As Hiranyakashipu's efforts to dissuade Prahlada fail, he becomes increasingly angry and resorts to more extreme measures to eliminate his son. However, all his attempts are thwarted by the divine protection that Prahlada receives from Lord Vishnu.

Narada's Arrival: Narada Muni, the sage known for his divine knowledge and devotion to Lord Vishnu, plays a pivotal role in this chapter. He visits Hiranyakashipu's palace and imparts spiritual wisdom to the demon king, but Hiranyakashipu remains stubborn in his atheism.

07-03 Hiranyakashipu's Plan to Become Immortal

Here are the key themes and events.

Hiranyakashipu's Desperation: Hiranyakashipu has become increasingly frustrated and angered by his inability to control or change his son Prahlada's devotion to Lord Vishnu. Despite numerous attempts to kill Prahlada, the young devotee remains unharmed due to the divine protection of Lord Vishnu.

Consulting His Advisers: Realizing that his son cannot be quickly subdued, Hiranyakashipu turns to his demoniac advisers and strategists for guidance. He seeks their counsel on attaining immortality and becoming invincible to rule over the universe unopposed.

Boons from Lord Brahma: The demon advisers advise Hiranyakashipu to perform severe austerities to please Lord Brahma, who is considered the creator of the universe. Hiranyakashipu then goes into deep meditation and performs rigorous penance for many years, subjecting himself to extreme hardships.

Lord Brahma's Arrival: Impressed by Hiranyakashipu's determination and penance, he appears before him and offers to grant him a boon. Hiranyakashipu makes a series of requests, including the desire for immortality. However, Lord Brahma explains that immortality is not within his power to be granted.

Frustrated by Lord Brahma's inability to fulfil his primary desire, Hiranyakashipu formulates a cunning request. He asks for specific conditions that he believes would make him virtually immortal, such as not being killed by any living being, not being killed inside or outside any residence, not being killed during the day or night, and not being killed by any weapon.

Lord Brahma Grants the Boon: Lord Brahma, bound by his promise, grants Hiranyakashipu the requested boon, which includes these seemingly invulnerable conditions. This boon makes Hiranyakashipu believe he has achieved immortality and becomes even more tyrannical.

07-04 Hiranyakashipu Terrorizes the Universe

Hiranyakashipu's Abuse of Power: Following his belief that he has gained invincibility through the boon granted by Lord Brahma, Hiranyakashipu becomes increasingly oppressive and abuses his newfound power. He terrorises not only the celestial beings but also the sages and demigods, causing havoc throughout the universe. Suppression of Religious Practices: Hiranyakashipu actively suppresses all forms of religious worship, especially the worship of Lord Vishnu. He orders his demonic minions to prevent anyone from performing any rituals or prayers associated with Vishnu.

Prahlada's Devotion: Despite the widespread oppression and fear created by his father, Prahlada remains unwavering in his devotion to Lord Vishnu. He continues to preach the glories of the Supreme Lord and encourages others to turn towards a path of righteousness and faithfulness. Hiranyakashipu's hostility towards his son Prahlada intensifies as he perceives him as threatening his rule. He tries various means to dissuade Prahlada from his devotion, including threats, persuasion, and violence. However, Prahlada's faith remains steadfast.

Narasimha's Emergence: As Hiranyakashipu's cruelty escalates, Lord Vishnu intervenes. He appears in a fierce and unique form known as Narasimha, which is neither fully human nor wholly animal. Narasimha emerges from a pillar in Hiranyakashipu's palace, which fulfils the conditions of the boon granted to the demon king.

The Battle of Narasimha and Hiranyakashipu: A dramatic and intense battle ensues between Lord Narasimha and Hiranyakashipu. Narasimha embodies the divine fury and, being neither day nor night, neither inside nor outside, using His lion-like form, he ultimately defeats and vanquishes Hiranyakashipu. This confrontation showcases the divine's ability to uphold righteousness and protect His devotees. Prahlada's Grace, though initially concerned for his father's wellbeing, Prahlada recognizes the divine will in the form of Narasimha and continues to offer his prayers and devotion to the Lord throughout the battle.

07-05 Prahlada Maharaja

This chapter begins with a description of Prahlada's early life and his upbringing in the demoniac environment of his father's palace. Despite being surrounded by atheism and cruelty, Prahlada remains a dedicated devotee of Lord Vishnu from a very young age. Prahlada's profound devotion to Lord Vishnu inspires his classmates and other young demons in the kingdom. He imparts spiritual wisdom to them, teaching them about the supreme importance of commitment to the Supreme Lord and the futility of material pursuits.

Hiranyakashipu's Frustration: Hiranyakashipu's attempts to change or eliminate Prahlada's devotion have consistently failed, and this chapter highlights his growing frustration and anger towards his son. He believes that Prahlada's devotion is a direct challenge to his authority. Despite his severe adversity, Prahlada's faith in Lord Vishnu remains unwavering. He attributes his strength and knowledge to the grace of the Supreme Lord. Hiranyakashipu continues threatening Prahlada, trying to intimidate him into giving up his devotion. He even resorts to physical violence, but Prahlada remains resolute in his faith.

Narasimha's Appearance: The chapter describes in detail the dramatic and awe-inspiring appearance of Lord Narasimha, the half-man, half-lion incarnation of Lord Vishnu. Narasimha emerges from a pillar in Hiranyakashipu's palace, which fulfils the conditions of the boon granted to the demon king. The climax of the chapter is the intense battle between Lord Narasimha and Hiranyakashipu. Narasimha embodies divine fury and ultimately defeats and vanquishes Hiranyakashipu. This confrontation showcases the Holy's ability to uphold righteousness and protect His devotees. After defeating Hiranyakashipu, Lord Narasimha turns His attention to Prahlada. Prahlada humbly prays to the Lord, who is pleased with his devotion and grants him blessings and guidance.

07-06 Prahlada Instructs Schoolmates

Here are the key themes and events:

Prahlada's Influence: This chapter describes how Prahlada profoundly impacts his demoniac schoolmates despite being young. His unwavering devotion to Lord Vishnu and his teachings about the Supreme Lord's greatness inspire his classmates.

Prahlada's Compassion: Prahlada feels compassion for his demoniac friends, steeped in ignorance and worldly desires. He tries to enlighten them about the importance of devotion to Lord Vishnu and the futility of pursuing material pleasures.

The Nature of the Material World: Prahlada explains to his friends that the material world is temporary and filled with suffering. He teaches them that true happiness and liberation can only be attained through devotion to the Supreme Lord and detachment from material desires.

The Power of the Holy Name: Prahlada emphasizes the significance of chanting the holy names of the Lord, especially the Hare Krishna mantra, as a means of purifying the mind and achieving spiritual realization.

Demoniac Rejection of Wisdom: Despite Prahlada's wise teachings, most of his demoniac schoolmates reject his message and indulge in sinful activities and cruelty. They mock and criticize him for his faith and devotion.

Prahlada's Steadfastness: Throughout the chapter, Prahlada remains unwavering in his devotion and commitment to Lord Vishnu. He prays to the Lord to forgive his classmates for their ignorance and cruelty.

Divine Protection: Prahlada's unshakable faith and devotion to Lord Vishnu continue to be rewarded, as the Lord's divine protection ensures that no harm inflicted upon him by his father or classmates can take his life.

07-07 Killing the Demon Hiranyaksha

Here are the key themes and events:

The Context: The chapter begins with a description of the demon Hiranyaksha, a brother of the demon king Hiranyakashipu. Hiranyaksha's name means "golden- eyed," and he is known for his immense power and cruelty.

Hiranyaksha's Disturbance: Hiranyaksha becomes a menace to the universe as he submerges the Earth into the cosmic ocean, causing chaos and destruction. His actions disrupt the universe's balance, and the demigods approach Lord Brahma for help.

Lord Brahma's Meditation: Lord Brahma, the creator of the universe, meditates to seek Lord Vishnu's assistance in dealing with the threat posed by Hiranyaksha. In response, Lord Vishnu incarnates as Lord Varaha (the boar) to restore cosmic order.

Lord Varaha's Appearance: Lord Varaha emerges from the nostril of Lord Brahma as a massive boar, symbolizing the divine power that sustains the universe. His appearance is awe-inspiring, with a vast body and sharp tusks.

The Battle with Hiranyaksha: Lord Varaha confronts Hiranyaksha and engages in a fierce battle with the demon in the cosmic ocean. The action is described in vivid detail, highlighting Lord Varaha's divine prowess.

The Defeat of Hiranyaksha: After a prolonged and intense battle, Lord Varaha defeats Hiranyaksha by using His tusks to pierce the demon's abdomen. This victory restores the Earth from the depths of the cosmic ocean.

Recovery of the Earth: Lord Varaha rescues the Earth and places her back in her rightful position within the universe. This act symbolises the restoration of order and balance in the cosmos.

Praise and Gratitude: The demigods, sages, and celestial beings present in the heavenly realms offer prayers of gratitude and praise to Lord Varaha for His divine intervention and the restoration of the Earth.

07-08 Lord Nrisimhadeva Slays the Demons

Here are the key themes and events:

Hiranyakashipu's Wrath: This chapter describes Hiranyakashipu's intense anger and desire for revenge after his brother Hiranyaksha was killed by Lord Varaha. He blames Lord Vishnu for losing his brother and vows to avenge his death.

Prahlada's Devotion: Despite his father's fury and violent threats, Prahlada remains unwavering in his devotion to Lord Vishnu. He continues to pray and seek the blessings of the Lord for himself and his demoniac classmates.

Hiranyakashipu's Challenges: Hiranyakashipu tries various means to kill Prahlada, including poisoning him, trampling him with elephants, and throwing him from cliffs, but each time, Prahlada is miraculously unharmed due to Lord Vishnu's divine protection.

Lord Nrisimhadeva's Appearance: As Hiranyakashipu's anger and frustration peak, Lord Vishnu appears in His fierce form as Lord Nrisimhadeva, a half-man, half-lion incarnation. He emerges from a pillar in Hiranyakashipu's palace, fulfilling the conditions of Hiranyakashipu's boon.

The Battle with Hiranyakashipu: An intense and terrifying battle ensues between Lord Nrisimhadeva and Hiranyakashipu. Lord Nrisimhadeva does not fit any of the conditions specified in the boon—neither man nor beast, neither inside nor outside, and the battle takes place at dusk, on the threshold of the palace. He places Hiranyakashipu on His lap, which is neither land nor air and uses His sharp nails to tear apart the demon's chest and end his life.

Prahlada's Prayers: After defeating Hiranyakashipu, Lord Nrisimhadeva's fierce form becomes calm, and He blesses Prahlada. Prahlada, in a mood of devotion and gratitude, offers prayers to the Lord, expressing his awe and love for the Supreme.

The Return of Peace: With the defeat of Hiranyakashipu, the universe is relieved of the terror and oppression caused by the demon king. Lord Nrisimhadeva's victory restores cosmic balance and order.

07-09 Prahlada Pacifies Lord Nrisimhadeva

The key themes and events:

Prahlada's Prayers: This chapter begins with Prahlada offering heartfelt prayers to Lord Nrisimhadeva after the Lord's fierce battle with and victory over his demoniac father, Hiranyakashipu. Prahlada's prayers are a beautiful expression of devotion and gratitude for the Lord's mercy and protection. Prahlada displays profound humility in his prayers, acknowledging his insignificance and the greatness of the Supreme Lord. He refers to himself as the lowest of all beings and expresses his unworthiness to pray to the Lord. Prahlada's prayers describe the awe-inspiring form of Lord Nrisimhadeva, who is simultaneously fearsome and merciful. He praises the Lord's transcendental qualities, such as omnipotence, omniscience, and omnipresence.

Devotion's Triumph: Prahlada's prayers emphasise that commitment to the Supreme Lord transcends material power and luxury. He was defeated despite Hiranyakashipu's immense material strength, while Prahlada's simple but unwavering devotion triumphed. Prahlada acknowledges the Lord's compassion in personally appearing to protect him and destroy the demon Hiranyakashipu. He also praises the Lord for His mercy in freeing him from the cycle of birth and death (samsara).

Lessons of Detachment: Prahlada's prayers contain teachings on detachment from material desires and attachments. He emphasises that the material world is temporary and full of suffering, and true happiness lies in devotion to the Supreme Lord.

Prahlada's Ultimate Surrender: In the concluding part of his prayers, Prahlada surrenders himself entirely to the Lord, expressing his desire to be an eternal servant of the Lord's devotees and to continuously engage in the Lord's service.

The Lord's Response: Lord Nrisimhadeva, pleased with Prahlada's heartfelt prayers and devotion, showers His blessings upon Prahlada. He assures Prahlada of His protection and promises that Prahlada's descendants will rule the earth for many generations.

07-10 Best Among Exalted Devotees

This chapter begins with Prahlada continuing his heartfelt prayers to Lord Nrisimhadeva. He praises the Lord's divine qualities, metaphysical nature, and supreme position in the universe. Prahlada's prayers serve as a source of inspiration for devotees and highlight the power of unwavering devotion. Prahlada emphasizes that the Supreme Lord is the ultimate well-wisher of all beings.

Detachment from Material Desires: Prahlada instructs that true wisdom lies in recognizing the impermanence of material pleasures and possessions. He encourages separation from worldly desires and attachments, which lead to suffering and bondage in the cycle of birth and death (samsara). Prahlada underscores the significance of chanting the holy names of the Lord, especially the Hare Krishna mantra, as a potent means of purifying the mind and achieving spiritual realization. He describes the benefits of nama-sankirtana (chanting the names of the Lord in a congregational setting).

Prahlada advises that one should engage in truthful and pleasing speech free from harsh words and criticism. Such an address is pleasing to the Lord and conducive to spiritual growth. Prahlada recognizes the importance of serving devotees and offering them respect. He explains that one can gain the Lord's favour and blessings by honouring and serving his devotees. In the concluding part of his prayers, Prahlada expresses his complete surrender to the Lord's will and seeks the Lord's guidance and protection throughout his life. Lord Nrisimhadeva is pleased with Prahlada's prayers and devotion. He acknowledges Prahlada as His greatest devotee and blesses him with a long and prosperous life in this world and the spiritual realm.

07-11 The Perfect Society: Four Social Classes

The key themes and events:

The Four Social Classes: This chapter describes the varnas or social classes that traditionally made up ancient Indian society. The Brahmanas were considered the priestly class responsible for performing religious rituals, teaching scriptures, and guiding society in spirituality and morality. The Kshatriyas were the warrior and ruling class. They were responsible for protecting the kingdom, maintaining law and order, and governing the land. The Vaishyas were the merchant and agricultural class. They engaged in trade, commerce, agriculture, and animal husbandry to sustain the economy. The Shudras were the labourer and servant class. They performed various services, including manual labour, to support the other three varnas. Each varna had specific duties and responsibilities, and working together harmoniously contributed to social stability.

Roles and Dharma (Duty): The Brahmanas were regarded as society's intellectual and spiritual leaders. They were responsible for teaching and preserving the Vedic scriptures, conducting rituals, and guiding individuals in their spiritual pursuits. The Kshatriyas were tasked with protecting the kingdom and its citizens. They upheld justice, maintained law and order, and ensured the safety and security of the people. The Vaishyas played a crucial role in economic activities. They engaged in agriculture, trade, and commerce, contributing to the material prosperity of society. The Shudras, while considered the servant class, were also integral to culture. They provided essential services and labour that supported the functioning of the other varnas. Individuals are believed to progress spiritually and contribute positively to society by fulfilling their prescribed obligations with devotion and integrity.

Equality in Spirituality: While the varna system outlines societal roles and responsibilities, it underscores the idea that all individuals, regardless of their varna, have equal potential for spiritual growth and liberation through devotion to the Supreme Lord.

07-12 The Perfect Society: Four Spiritual Classes

Spiritual Hierarchy: This chapter delves into the spiritual hierarchy within society, emphasising the importance of the four varnas in facilitating the spiritual growth of individuals. The varnas are explained in their spiritual context, highlighting their roles in aiding people on their path to self-realisation and God's realisation.

Brahmanas (Spiritual Teachers): The chapter underscores the significance of Brahmanas as spiritual guides and teachers. They are expected to possess qualities such as purity, self-control, knowledge of scriptures, and devotion to the Supreme. Their primary duty is to impart spiritual wisdom and perform rituals for the benefit of society.

Kshatriyas (Warriors and Rulers): Kshatriyas are responsible for maintaining law and order in society. In the spiritual context, they must protect the righteous and uphold justice. They should exhibit courage, righteousness, and a sense of responsibility to safeguard dharma (right).

Vaishyas (Merchants and Agriculturists): Vaishyas are responsible for economic activities and commerce. In the spiritual context, they are encouraged to perform their duties honestly and ethically, support spiritual causes, and contribute to the welfare of society.

Shudras (Servants and Laborers): Shudras are regarded as the working class. In the spiritual context, they must assist the other three varnas in their respective roles. Their service is considered valuable when it is rendered with humility and devotion.

Equality in Spiritual Pursuit: While the varna system outlines societal roles and responsibilities, the chapter emphasises that all individuals, regardless of their varna, have the potential for spiritual growth and liberation through devotion to the Supreme Lord. Spiritual realisation is not restricted by caste or social status.

The Importance of Dharma: The chapter highlights the significance of dharma, or righteous duty, in one's spiritual journey. Following one's prescribed duties with sincerity, devotion, and integrity means attaining spiritual elevation and realisation.

07-13 The Behavior of a Perfect Person

Here are the key themes and teachings:

This chapter describes the ideal qualities and characteristics that a spiritually advanced and virtuous individual should cultivate. These qualities are often called "dharma" and include honesty, compassion, humility, self-control, and a sense of justice. The chapter emphasizes the importance of separation from material desires and possessions. A perfect person is not excessively attached to the fleeting pleasures and controls of the material world but is focused on spiritual growth and service to others. Equality and compassion are highlighted as essential attributes of a perfect person. Such an individual treats all living beings with kindness and empathy, recognizing the divine presence in everyone.

Honesty and truthfulness are emphasized as fundamental virtues. A perfect person speaks the truth, upholds honesty in all dealings, and maintains integrity in their actions and words. Humility is regarded as a crucial quality. A perfect person remains modest and does not become arrogant or proud, even if they possess excellent knowledge or accomplishments. The chapter discusses the practice of abstinence and self-control as a means to discipline one's desires and senses. By controlling the mind and senses, one can progress toward spiritual realization.

A perfect person does selfless service without expecting personal gain. Service is seen as a way to please the Supreme and uplift fellow beings. The chapter emphasizes that the ultimate perfection is attained through dedication to the Supreme Lord. By cultivating a loving relationship with the Divine, one can transcend material limitations and achieve spiritual enlightenment. Contentment with one's present circumstances and possessions signifies spiritual advancement. A perfect person does not constantly crave more material wealth or comforts. The chapter highlights the need to renounce ego and pride and obstacles to spiritual growth. An ideal person recognizes the divine as the ultimate source of all achievements and does not take credit for themselves. Avoidance of Envy: Envy and jealousy are detrimental qualities that hinder spiritual progress. A perfect person is free from such negative emotions and harbours goodwill toward others.

07-14 Ideal Family Life

The key themes and teachings:

The Importance of Family Life: The chapter begins by emphasizing the significance of family life in the context of the Vedic culture. It acknowledges that family life is fundamental to human society and allows individuals to practice dharma (righteousness) and spirituality. The chapter outlines the roles and responsibilities of various family members, including parents, children, and relatives. It emphasizes each family member's duties toward maintaining a harmonious and virtuous household. One of the essential teachings is showing respect and reverence to elders in the family. Respecting parents and grandparents is considered a fundamental duty in Hindu culture.

The Role of Grihastha (Householder): Grihastha refers to the householder or family person. The chapter highlights that a Grihastha should provide for the family's material needs while fostering spiritual growth among family members. Parents are encouraged to impart spiritual wisdom and cultural heritage to their offspring. Maintaining harmony and love within the marriage relationship is emphasized. Mutual respect, fidelity, and support between husband and wife are essential for a successful family life. Regular spiritual practices, such as daily prayers and ceremonies, are recommended to infuse the home with spiritual vibrations. While family life is essential, the chapter advises individuals not to become overly attached to material possessions or relationships. Detachment and a sense of renunciation are encouraged to focus on spiritual growth.

The Purpose of Family Life: As emphasised in the chapter, the ultimate purpose of family life is to create an environment conducive to spiritual advancement. Family members are encouraged to cultivate devotion to the Supreme Lord and engage in selfless service. The chapter includes the story of Dhruva Maharaja, a young prince who attained spiritual realisation through his determination and devotion and became a renowned saint. Dhruva's example illustrates how one can use family life as a platform for spiritual growth.

07-15 Instructions for Civilized Human Beings

The key themes and teachings:

The Purpose of Life: The chapter begins by addressing the fundamental question of the purpose of human life. It emphasises that the ultimate goal of life is spiritual realisation and union with the Supreme Lord. The chapter outlines human beings' primary duties and responsibilities in a civilised society. These duties include honesty, truthfulness, compassion, self-control, and adherence to dharma (righteousness). Education is essential for understanding their spiritual nature and moral responsibilities. A well-rounded education should include academic knowledge, spiritual wisdom, and moral values. The chapter emphasises the importance of respecting and respecting elders and teachers. Appreciating the wisdom and experience of elders is regarded as a virtue. Charity and selfless service are encouraged to purify the heart and uplift society. Giving to those in need is considered an essential duty. Truthfulness in speech and action is highlighted as a foundational virtue. Truthfulness is seen as a means to establish trust and maintain social harmony.

Adherence to Dharma: Dharma, or righteous duty, is central to leading a virtuous life. Humans are encouraged to fulfil their prescribed societal obligations while upholding moral and ethical values.

Detachment from Material Desires: The chapter underscores the importance of detachment from excessive material desires. Detachment is seen as a way to avoid entanglement in the birth and death cycle and focus on spiritual growth.

The Role of Women: Women are recognised as equal societal partners and encouraged to participate in spiritual and cultural activities. The chapter highlights the importance of respecting and protecting women.

The chapter advises against lying, stealing, violence, and deceit. Such negative behaviours are seen as detrimental to individual and societal well-being. Moderation in all aspects of life, including eating, sleeping, and recreation, is advocated to maintain physical and mental health and support spiritual practices.

Canto 8

08-01 The Manus, Administrators of the Universe

Here are the key themes and events:

The Context: This chapter takes place within the broader context of the cosmic creation and destruction cycle, a recurring theme in Hindu cosmology. It is time to dissolve the current cosmic design in the narrative.

Lord Brahma's Anxiety: Lord Brahma, the creator of the universe, becomes anxious as he witnesses the approaching end of the current creation. He realizes it's time for the cosmic dissolution (pralaya) and the withdrawal of all manifested universes.

The Role of Manus: Manus are ancient and enlightened beings whom Lord Brahma appoints to serve as administrators and progenitors during the different phases of cosmic creation. They guide and govern various aspects of life in the material world.

The Appearance of Swayambhuva Manu: This chapter introduces Swayambhuva Manu, the first Manu of the present cosmic cycle. He is born from Lord Brahma's body and is endowed with great wisdom and qualities. Swayambhuva Manu and his wife, Shatarupa, play a vital role in populating the world with living beings.

The Creation of Offspring: Swayambhuva Manu and Shatarupa are blessed by Lord Brahma to create offspring. They follow austerities and rituals and, in due course, produce children who become the progenitors of various species and classes of beings. The Duties of Manus: Manus is responsible for procreation and establishing and upholding dharma (righteousness) in society. They impart spiritual and moral guidance to their descendants and set an example for virtuous living.

Manu's Obedience to Lord Brahma: Swayambhuva Manu demonstrates excellent humility and obedience to Lord Brahma, who guides him in his responsibilities as the progenitor of humanity and the maintainer of order in the universe.

08-02 The Elephant Gajendra's Crisis

Here are the key events and themes:

The Setting: The chapter begins by describing a beautiful lake named Trikuta. In this lake lived a magnificent elephant named Gajendra, the king of elephants. Gajendra was known for his strength and majesty.

The Plight of Gajendra: While enjoying a playful bath in the lake with his elephant herd, Gajendra is suddenly attacked by a mighty crocodile. He cannot free himself from the crocodile's grip despite his strength and efforts. Gajendra realizes his helplessness and imminent death.

Gajendra's Prayer: As Gajendra struggles for his life, he offers a heartfelt prayer to Lord Vishnu, the Supreme Lord. Gajendra calls out to the Lord in his prayer, seeking His protection and salvation. He expresses his surrender and devotion, recognizing the Lord's omnipotence.

The Crocodile's Past Life: The crocodile in the lake was a Gandharva (celestial being) named Huhu in his previous life. Due to a curse, he had been transformed into a crocodile and lived in the lake. The crocodile had the boon that he could only be liberated by the touch of Lord Vishnu.

Lord Vishnu's Arrival: Moved by Gajendra's sincere devotion and prayer, Lord Vishnu, riding on the back of Garuda (His eagle carrier), arrives at the scene. The Lord's appearance is described as awe-inspiring and divine.

The Divine Intervention: Lord Vishnu, with His Sudarshana Chakra (a spinning disc weapon), immediately severs the crocodile's head, liberating Huhu. Gajendra is freed from the crocodile's grip, and his soul is released from the cycle of birth and death.

Gajendra's Transformation: Gajendra undergoes a divine transformation as he is liberated. His elephant body is transformed into a celestial form, and he ascends to the spiritual realm, accompanied by Lord Vishnu and His sacred associates.

The Lesson of Devotion and Surrender: This story is a powerful lesson on the importance of unwavering devotion and surrender to the Supreme Lord. Gajendra's sincere prayer and complete sacrifice led to his rescue and liberation by the Lord.

08-03 Gajendra's Prayers of Surrender

Here are the key events and themes:

Gajendra's Relief: Having been saved from the crocodile's attack and liberated by Lord Vishnu, Gajendra feels immense gratitude and relief. He realizes the divine presence of the Lord and understands the importance of surrendering to Him.

Gajendra's Humility: despite his majestic appearance as an elephant king, Gajendra humbly acknowledges his insignificance in the grand cosmic order. He recognizes that all living beings, including great demigods and sages, are ultimately subordinate to the Supreme Lord.

Gajendra's Prayer: Gajendra offers a heartfelt prayer to Lord Vishnu, praising His divine attributes, qualities, and ethereal form. His prayer is filled with devotion and surrender as he seeks shelter and protection in the Lord's lotus feet.

Description of Lord Vishnu: In his prayer, Gajendra describes Lord Vishnu's various forms, including His four-armed form holding the conch, discus, mace, and lotus. He acknowledges the Lord as the source of all creation and the ultimate goal of life.

Gajendra's Spiritual Realization: Through his prayer, Gajendra achieves a profound spiritual realization. He understands the futility of material pursuits and the impermanence of the material world. He longs for liberation from the cycle of birth and death (samsara) and seeks a place in the Lord's eternal abode.

The Lord's Response: Pleased with Gajendra's sincere prayers and surrender, Lord Vishnu, known as Hari, descends from His divine abode to protect and bless Gajendra. The Lord's appearance is resplendent and merciful.

Gajendra's Liberation: Lord Vishnu touches Gajendra with His divine conch, and Gajendra is immediately liberated from his elephant body. His soul attains a spiritual form suitable for eternal service to the Lord.

The Witnessing Devas: The demigods and heavenly beings, witnessing this divine event, shower flowers and praises upon Lord Vishnu for His mercy and compassion toward His devotee.

08-04 Gajendra Returns to the Spiritual World

Here are the key events and themes:

Gajendra's Liberation: After offering heartfelt prayers of surrender to Lord Vishnu, Gajendra is liberated from his elephant body and attains a spiritual form suitable for eternal service to the Lord. He is freed from the cycle of birth and death (samsara).

Entering the Spiritual Realm: Gajendra, now in his spiritual form, is carried by Lord Vishnu to His divine abode, Vaikuntha. This heavenly realm is beyond the material world and is characterized by spiritual opulence, bliss, and eternal life.

Divine Attendants: As Gajendra enters Vaikuntha, he is welcomed by religious attendants, including celestial nymphs and heavenly beings. He experiences the joy and ecstasy of the spiritual realm.

Meeting with the Lord: Gajendra has the privilege of meeting Lord Vishnu in Vaikuntha. The Lord embraces Gajendra and showers His blessings upon him. This reunion is a moment of immense spiritual fulfilment for Gajendra.

Gajendra's Transformation: Gajendra's form becomes radiant and divine in the spiritual realm. He is freed from the limitations of his previous earthly existence and is now fully immersed in spiritual consciousness.

Witnessing Other Devotees: Gajendra observes other liberated souls and devotees in Vaikuntha, all engaged in divine service and devotion to the Supreme Lord. This further deepens his understanding of the spiritual realm and the bliss of love.

Transcendence of Material Attachments: Gajendra's journey and liberation highlight the excellence of material attachments and the ultimate goal of human life—to return to the spiritual world and engage in loving service to the Supreme Lord.

Lesson of Devotion and Surrender: The chapter underscores the importance of devotion, surrender, and unwavering faith in the Lord. Gajendra's sincere prayers and sacrifice led to his liberation and return to the spiritual realm, emphasizing the transformative power of devotion.

08-05 The Demigods Appeal to the Lord for Protection

Here are the key events and themes:

The Demon Hiraṇyākṣa: The chapter introduces Hiraṇyākṣa, a powerful demon who emerges from the ocean and begins tormenting the celestial beings and the Earth itself. He symbolizes the disruptive and destructive forces of the material world.

The Demigods' Plight: The demigods, including Lord Indra, the king of the heavenly realm, and other celestial beings, cannot withstand Hiraṇyākṣa's might and aggression. They realize that they need divine intervention to deal with this formidable adversary.

The Demigods' Prayer: Recognizing Lord Vishnu as their ultimate protector and saviour, the demigods gather and offer heartfelt prayers to Him. They seek His assistance in subduing Hiraṇyākṣa and restoring order in the universe.

Descriptions of Lord Vishnu: The demigods' prayers vividly describe the intangible qualities, forms, and attributes of Lord Vishnu. They acknowledge Him as the source of creation, the sustainer of the universe, and the ultimate refuge of all living beings.

The Lord's Compassion: Lord Vishnu, known for His compassion toward His devotees, responds to the sincere prayers of the demigods. He assures them of His protection and expresses His willingness to incarnate on Earth to confront Hiraṇyākṣa.

The Incarnation of Lord Vishnu: The chapter foreshadows Lord Vishnu's upcoming incarnation as Lord Varaha, a divine boar. The Lord's incarnation, Varaha, will be instrumental in subduing Hiraṇyākṣa and rescuing the Earth from the depths of the cosmic ocean.

08-06 The Demigods Appeal

Here are the key events and themes:

Continuation of the Threat: Hiraṇyākṣa, the mighty demon, continues his rampage and poses a severe threat to the demigods and the Earth. His oppressive rule and destruction disrupt the cosmic balance.

The Demigods' Desperation: The demigods, including Lord Indra and other celestial beings, find themselves in a desperate situation. They realize they cannot defeat Hiraṇyākṣa alone and turn to Lord Vishnu for help.

The Demigods' Sincere Prayers: The demigods have expressed their devotion to Lord Vishnu. They glorify the Lord's transcendental qualities, forms, and attributes and acknowledge Him as the ultimate protector and maintainer of the universe.

Praise of Lord Vishnu's Incarnations: The demigods recount the Lord's past incarnations, emphasizing His willingness to descend to the material world whenever there is a threat to dharma (righteousness) and the balance of the cosmos. They recall His divine incarnations, such as Lord Matsya (the fish) and Lord Kurma (the tortoise).

The Lord's Assurance: Lord Vishnu, who is compassionate and responsive to the prayers of His devotees, hears the demigods' heartfelt plea. He assures them of His protection and promises to incarnate on Earth to deal with Hiraṇyākṣa and restore order in the universe.

The Upcoming Incarnation: The chapter anticipates the Lord's forthcoming incarnation as Lord Varaha, the divine boar. Lord Varaha will play a pivotal role in subduing Hiraṇyākṣa and rescuing the Earth from its clutches.

08-07 Lord Śiva Saves the Universe by Drinking Poison

Here are the key events and themes:

The Churning of the Milk Ocean: The chapter begins with the demigods and demons coming together to churn the Milk Ocean to obtain the nectar of immortality (amrita). They use Mount Mandara as the churning rod and the serpent Vasuki as the rope.

Emergence of Poison: During the churning, the first substance that emerges from the ocean is a deadly poison known as "halahala" or "Kalakuta." This poison is so potent that it threatens to destroy all of creation.

The Gods' Dilemma: Faced with the danger of the poison spreading across the universe, the demigods and demons become distressed. They realize the need for immediate intervention to save the universe from destruction.

Lord Shiva's Arrival: Lord Shiva, the powerful and compassionate deity, arrives at the scene. He understands the gravity of the situation and decides to take action to prevent the poison from wreaking havoc.

Lord Shiva's Heroic Act: out of his deep concern for the welfare of all living beings, Lord Shiva voluntarily drinks the deadly poison. He holds the poison in his throat, turning it blue, often called "Neelkanth" (the one with a blue throat).

Deities' Gratitude: The gods and demons are immensely relieved and express their gratitude to Lord Shiva for saving the universe from the catastrophic effects of the poison. They praise him for his selfless and fearless act.

Lord Shiva's Renunciation: Lord Shiva's act of drinking the poison highlights his qualities of self-sacrifice, compassion, and detachment from worldly comforts. He places the welfare of the universe above his well-being.

Lord Shiva's Divine Nature: The chapter emphasises Lord Shiva's divine nature as both a powerful deity and a benevolent protector of the universe. He is regarded as a symbol of spiritual realisation and the destroyer of ignorance.

08-08 The Churning of the Milk Ocean

Here are the key events and themes:

Resumption of the Churning: After the emergence and handling of the deadly poison (halahala) by Lord Shiva, the churning of the Milk Ocean resumes. With the help of Mount Mandara and Vasuki the serpent, the demigods and demons continue their efforts to extract valuable treasures from the ocean.

Emergence of Divine Treasures: As the churning continues, various divine treasures and entities emerge from the ocean. These include the goddess of fortune, Lakshmi Devi; the celestial physician, Dhanvantari, holding the pot of amrita; the divine cow, Surabhi; and the wish-fulfiling tree, Kalpavriksha.

The appearance of Kamadhenu: Kamadhenu, the celestial cow, also emerges from the ocean during the churning. Kamadhenu possesses the ability to grant any material desire and is highly revered.

The Goddess of Fortune's Choice: The goddess of fortune, Lakshmi Devi, emerges from the ocean and chooses her eternal residence. She chooses Lord Vishnu as her husband and eternal abode, affirming her position as the goddess of wealth and prosperity.

Dhanvantari and Amrita: Dhanvantari, the divine physician, appears carrying the pot of amrita (nectar of immortality). The demigods and demons eagerly desire the nectar, believing it will grant them immortality and great power.

The Conflict Over Amrita: A conflict ensues between the demigods and demons over possession of the amrita. They argue about who should have the nectar, leading to a significant struggle. Lord Vishnu intervenes to ensure that the nectar of immortality is distributed fairly and justly. He takes the form of Mohini, a beautiful enchantress, to distract and soothe the warring demigods and demons. As Mohini, Lord Vishnu distributes the amrita to the demigods seated separately from the demons. However, Lord Vishnu tactfully serves the demons an inferior substance that resembles nectar but lacks its life-giving properties. The demons, deceived by Mohini's illusion, believe they have consumed the amrita and become invincible. In their arrogance, they underestimate the demigods.

08-09 The Lord Incarnates as Mohinī-Mūrti

Here are the key events and themes:

The Continued Conflict: The chapter begins with the ongoing conflict between the demigods and demons over possessing the amrita (nectar of immortality) obtained from the churning of the Milk Ocean. Both groups are determined to secure the nectar for themselves.

Lord Vishnu's Intervention: To resolve the dispute and ensure the fair distribution of the amrita, Lord Vishnu incarnates as Mohinī-Mūrti, a captivating and intriguing female form. Her beauty is beyond description, and her grace enchants all who behold her.

The appearance of Mohinī-Mūrti: Mohinī-Mūrti gracefully enters the scene, captivating the attention of both the demigods and the demons. Her enchanting presence temporarily pacifies their fighting spirit.

Negotiating with Mohinī-Mūrti: Both the demigods and demons are mesmerized by Mohinī-Mūrti's appearance. They eagerly approach her and request her assistance in distributing the amrita. Mohinī-Mūrti agrees to help and takes on the role of the amrita distributor.

The Deceptive Strategy: As the demigods and demons sit separately in preparation to receive the amrita, Mohinī-Mūrti tactfully serves the demigods first, beginning with Lord Indra. She distributes the real amrita to them while serving an illusionary substance to the demons.

Demon Deception: The demons, fooled by Mohinī-Mūrti's illusion, believe they are consuming the amrita and become overconfident. They lose their desire to fight and are convinced of their invincibility.

The Demons' Downfall: After the distribution, Mohinī-Mūrti disappears, leaving the demigods fully empowered by the amrita. The demons, realizing they have been deceived and weakened, become disheartened and defeated.

The Victory of Virtue: The chapter underscores the victory of virtue and righteousness over deception and arrogance. It highlights the importance of divine intervention in ensuring justice and preserving cosmic order.

08-10 Battle Between the Demigods and the Demons

This chapter continues the narrative of the conflict between the demigods (celestial beings) and the demons (asuras) that arose during the churning of the Milk Ocean (Samudra Manthan) over the nectar of immortality (amrita). Following Lord Vishnu's incarnation as Mohinī-Mūrti, this chapter describes the resumption of hostilities between the two groups.

Despite the deception and defeat of the demons in the previous chapters, their hostility towards the demigods remains strong. They are determined to reclaim the nectar of immortality and regain their power. Tensions escalate as the demons, led by their influential leaders, gather their forces and prepare for battle against the demigods. The demigods also brace themselves for the impending conflict. The chapter describes the preparations made by both sides for the war. The demigods are aligned with Lord Indra, while the demons are led by their formidable commanders, including Balimaharaja and others. The battle between the demigods and demons unfolds intensely. The celestial beings and the demon armies clash, using various divine weapons and strategies.

Though previously deceived, the demons remain steadfast in pursuing power and immortality. Their decision to overpower the demigods and seize the nectar is unshaken. Amid the fierce battle, Lord Vishnu, the protector of the demigods, arrives on the scene to ensure the victory of virtue. He takes on the form of Lord Nṛsimha, a half-man, half-lion incarnation.

The Appearance of Lord Nṛsimha: Lord Nṛsimha's appearance is both fearsome and divine. He emerges from a pillar and strikes terror into the hearts of the demons. Lord Nṛsimha engages in a fierce battle with the demons, showcasing His incredible power and prowess. He ultimately defeats the demon armies and punishes the evil king, Hiraṇyakaśipu. Lord Nṛsimha's intervention and victory symbolise the defence of virtue and the destruction of evil forces. He assures the demigods of His continuous protection and the maintenance of cosmic order.

08-11 Lord Kṛṣṇa's Entrance into Dwārakā

Dwārakā is an essential city in Hindu mythology and is often associated with Lord Krishna's divine activities. Here are the key events and themes:

The Battle's Conclusion: The chapter begins by summarising the events that occurred in the previous chapters, including the battle between the demigods and demons, Lord Vishnu's intervention as Lord Nṛsiṁha, and the defeat of the demon forces.

Lord Krishna's Departure: After the battle, Lord Krishna decides to leave the Earth and return to His eternal abode, Dwārakā. He is accompanied by many demigods who are eager to witness His departure.

Travel to Dwārakā: Lord Krishna, with His queens, ministers, and soldiers, embarks on a magnificent chariot journey to Dwārakā. His divine presence and the sight of His chariot bring joy and relief to the residents of the Earth.

Reuniting with Loved Ones: As Lord Krishna reaches Dwārakā, His loved ones, including His parents, Vasudeva and Devakī, and His dear friend Uddhava, eagerly welcome Him. Their joy and devotion are palpable as they reunite with the Lord.

Dwārakā's Grandeur: The chapter vividly describes the opulence and grandeur of Dwārakā, which is a splendid city adorned with beautiful palaces, gardens, and lakes. The town reflects the magnificence of Lord Krishna's divine rule.

Krishna's Universal Form: Lord Krishna reveals His universal form to those assembled in Dwārakā, demonstrating His all-encompassing divine nature. His universal form is a breathtaking and awe-inspiring sight. The residents of Dwārakā, including His queens, express their deep love and devotion to Lord Krishna. They are overjoyed by His return and relish the opportunity to serve Him.

Establishing Dharma: Lord Krishna's presence in Dwārakā symbolises the establishment of dharma (righteousness) and the protection of His devotees. He rules as a just and benevolent king.

08-12 The Birth of Emperor Parīkṣit

Here are the key events and themes:

Curse of the Brahmana: The chapter begins with the background story of how Parīkṣit's birth came about. There was a Brahmana (priest) named Śṛṅgī who became infuriated when he saw King Parīkṣit placing a dead snake on his shoulders. In a fit of anger, the Brahmana cursed the king to die from the bite of a serpent within seven days.

King Parīkṣit's Response: Upon realizing the severity of the curse and the inevitability of his death, King Parīkṣit displayed exemplary humility and wisdom. He decided to renounce his kingdom and journey to holy places, seeking spiritual enlightenment in the remaining days of his life.

Seeking Shelter: King Parīkṣit travelled to various sacred places and eventually arrived at the banks of the Yamuna River, where he decided to fast and meditate in preparation for his imminent departure from the world.

Appearance of Śukadeva Gosvāmī: As King Parīkṣit was absorbed in meditation, the great sage Śukadeva Gosvāmī, who was known for his deep knowledge of spiritual wisdom and the Bhagavatam, arrived at the scene. His arrival marked the turning point in the narrative.

Śukadeva's Blessing: Śukadeva Gosvāmī recognized King Parīkṣit's virtuous qualities and deep desire for spiritual knowledge. Instead of cursing him, Śukadeva offered his blessings and counsel, explaining that Parīkṣit's inquiry into spiritual matters would benefit all of humanity.

Divine Intervention: The sages and celestial beings present at the scene were impressed by Śukadeva Gosvāmī's words and the humility of King Parīkṣit. They saw this as a divine arrangement and realized that the king's curiosity would lead to the discussion of transcendental knowledge, eventually compiled as the Srimad Bhagavatam.

Parīkṣit's Question: Encouraged by Śukadeva Gosvāmī, King Parīkṣit posed a crucial question related to the ultimate duty and well-being of human beings as they face the inevitability of death.

08-13 Description of Future Manus

This chapter provides a glimpse into the universe's future by describing the future Manus, who are the progenitors and lawgivers for each cycle of creation in Hindu cosmology. Manus plays a crucial role in the governance of the world and the dissemination dharma (righteousness).

Here are the key events and themes:

Introduction to the Manus: The chapter begins by explaining the concept of Manus, who are semi-divine beings entrusted with presiding over a specific period (Manvantara) during the creation cycle. Each Manu establishes and propagates the codes of conduct and laws (dharma) for humanity during their rule.

Details of the Manus: The chapter lists the names of future Manus who will appear in the upcoming cycles of creation. These Manus are associated with different periods and yugas (ages) within the cosmic process.

Characteristics of the Yugas: The text describes the features and durations of the four yugas that repeat cyclically—Satya Yuga (the age of truth and righteousness), Treta Yuga, Dvapara Yuga, and Kali Yuga (the age of discord and spiritual decline).

The Role of Manus: Manus are the custodians of dharma and are responsible for upholding moral and ethical values during their respective Manvantaras. They guide humanity and maintain order in the universe.

Repetition of Creation: The chapter emphasizes the cyclical nature of creation, with the universe going through periods of creation, maintenance, and dissolution in a continuous cycle. Each Manu presides over a portion of this cycle.

The Importance of Dharma: Throughout the chapter, the importance of dharma is underscored. It is stated that adherence to dharma is the key to leading a righteous and purposeful life, even amid the changing yugas.

08-14 The System of Universal Management

Here are the key events and themes:

Universal Structure: The chapter begins by explaining the hierarchical structure of the universe. It describes how Lord Brahma, the creator, is at the top of this cosmic hierarchy. Below Brahma are various celestial beings with specific duties and responsibilities.

Brahma's Role: Lord Brahma is described as the first created being and the chief engineer of the universe. He is responsible for developing and managing the cosmos during his day, lasting billions of Earth years.

Demigods and Their Functions: The chapter elaborates on the demigods (devas) who govern different aspects of the universe. For example, Indra is responsible for rain and weather, Yama for death and justice, and Agni for fire. Each demigod has a specific portfolio and role in cosmic administration.

The Four Kumāras: The chapter introduces the four Kumaras—Sanaka, Sanandana, Sanātana, and Sanat-kumāra. These highly elevated beings are renowned for their devotion and knowledge. They remain eternally young and celibate, representing the aspect of universal renunciation.

Duty of the Kumāras: The Kumaras travel throughout the universe and maintain a vow of celibacy and renunciation. They serve as teachers of transcendental knowledge and exemplify the qualities of purity and detachment.

Lord Shiva's Role: The chapter also discusses Lord Shiva's position as one of the primary cosmic administrators. Lord Shiva is the destroyer and is pivotal in the creation, maintenance, and dissolution cycle.

Lord Vishnu as the Sustainer: Lord Vishnu is described as the ultimate sustainer of the universe. He maintains cosmic balance and intervenes whenever there is a threat to dharma (righteousness).

Maintaining Cosmic Harmony: The chapter emphasises the harmonious functioning of all these celestial beings and their respective roles in preserving cosmic order. It highlights the interdependence and cooperation among them.

08-15 Bali Mahārāja Conquers the Heavenly Planets

In this chapter, Bali Mahārāja embarks on a journey to conquer the heavenly planets, challenging the authority of Lord Indra, the king of the demigods.

Bali Mahārāja's Resolve: Bali Mahārāja desires to expand his influence and power despite being a benevolent and virtuous king. He decides to perform a grand sacrifice (yajña) to gain the strength needed for his ambitious conquest.

Preparations for the Sacrifice: Bali Mahārāja prepares for the sacrificial ceremony with great pomp and grandeur. He invites various Brahmanas (priests) and assembles a formidable army.

Lord Vāmana's Arrival: During the sacrifice, an extraordinary incident occurs. Lord Vāmana, an incarnation of Lord Vishnu as a dwarf Brahmana boy, arrives at Bali Mahārāja's ceremony. Lord Indra and other demigods in disguise accompany Lord Vāmana.

The Request for Alms: Lord Vāmana approaches Bali Mahārāja and makes an unusual request. He asks for three paces of land, measured by His steps. Despite the counsel of his spiritual teacher, Śukrācārya, and his family, Bali Mahārāja agrees to grant Lord Vāmana's request.

The Extraordinary Act: Lord Vāmana, in His small form, expands to cover the entire universe with His first two steps. For His third step, He asks Bali Mahārāja where to place it. Bali Mahārāja humbled and recognizing the Lord's divinity, offers his head as a place for the third step.

Lord Vāmana's Blessings: Lord Vāmana, pleased with Bali Mahārāja's humility and devotion, grants him a boon and promises to protect and guide him. He then returns the heavenly kingdom to Lord Indra and instructs Bali Mahārāja on the principles of dharma and devotion.

Bali Mahārāja's Exile: Despite losing his kingdom, Bali Mahārāja is content and grateful for the Lord's presence and blessings. He is exiled to the lower planetary systems but remains devoted to Lord Vāmana.

08-16 Executions of the Royal Order by the Lord

This chapter continues the narrative of Lord Vāmana's interactions with Bali Mahārāja and describes how the Lord protected Bali Mahārāja while ensuring the restoration of cosmic order and dharma.

Here are the key events and themes from Srimad Bhagavatam Canto 8, Chapter 16:

Bali Mahārāja's Service: Despite losing his kingdom and being exiled to the lower planetary systems, Bali Mahārāja remains devoted to Lord Vāmana. He serves the Lord with great reverence and sincerity.

Bali's Request: Bali Mahārāja expresses his desire to see Lord Vāmana in His complete, universal form. The Lord, pleased with Bali's devotion, agrees to reveal His cosmic form.

The Appearance of Lord Vāmana: Lord Vāmana displays His cosmic form, which encompasses the entire universe. Bali Mahārāja is awe-struck by the majestic sight of the Lord's universal manifestation.

The Lord's Explanation: Lord Vāmana explains to Bali Mahārāja that He is the ultimate source and controller of the entire creation. He is present in all beings and is the ultimate goal of all spiritual paths.

The Assurance of Protection: Lord Vāmana assures Bali Mahārāja that despite losing the kingdom and exile, the Lord will always protect him and his dynasty. He also blesses Bali with a particular boon.

Bali's Release from Bondage: The chapter describes how Bali Mahārāja, due to his unwavering devotion and humility, is released from the bondage of material desires and liberated from the cycle of birth and death.

The Return of the Demigods: Lord Vāmana instructs Bali Mahārāja to return the heavenly kingdom to Lord Indra and the demigods. Bali Mahārāja fulfils the Lord's instructions, and the demigods regain their celestial abodes.

Lord Vāmana's Departure: Lord Vāmana takes leave of Bali Mahārāja and returns to His abode, expressing His pleasure with Bali's devotion and his fulfilment of dharma.

08-17 The Supreme Lord Agrees to Become Aditi's Son

This chapter focuses on the celestial goddess Aditi's intense desire to have Lord Vishnu as her son and her austere penance to achieve this divine goal.

Aditi's Desire: Aditi, the mother of the demigods (devas), is distressed because her sons, the demigods, are oppressed by the demons (asuras). She desires a powerful protector and requests a solution for her husband, Kaśyapa Muni.

Kaśyapa's Advice: Kaśyapa Muni, a renowned sage, and her husband advise Aditi to perform a special ritual called "payo-vrata" to please Lord Vishnu. They hope to gain His favour and have Him as their son by propitiating the Supreme Lord.

Aditi's Austerity: Aditi begins her austere penance with great determination. She performs the ritual, strictly observing all the prescribed rules and regulations, and meditates upon Lord Vishnu.

Lord Vishnu's Appearance: Impressed by Aditi's devotion and penance, Lord Vishnu appears before her in a dazzling and luminous form. He praises her dedication and assures her that He will fulfil her desire.

The Boon Request: Aditi expresses her desire for Lord Vishnu to incarnate as her son and protect the demigods from the oppression of the demons. Lord Vishnu agrees to this request and promises to descend to the Earth as her son in His form as Lord Vāmana.

Brahmā's Approval: Lord Brahmā, the creator, and other celestial beings who witness this divine exchange between Aditi and Lord Vishnu are delighted and offer their blessings. They understand that the Lord's incarnation as Vāmana will bring prosperity and protection to the universe.

The Advent of Lord Vāmana: The chapter concludes with the assurance that Lord Vishnu will indeed take birth as Lord Vāmana, the dwarf Brahmana, in Aditi's womb to fulfil her desire and restore balance in the cosmos.

08-18 Lord Vāmanadeva, the Dwarf Incarnation

Here are the key events and themes:

Lord Vāmanadeva's Descent: Lord Vāmanadeva, an incarnation of Lord Vishnu, takes birth as a dwarf Brahmana in the family of the sage Kaśyapa and Aditi, as per their desire. He aims to subdue the demon king Bali Mahārāja and restore the heavenly kingdom to the demigods.

The Appearance of Lord Vāmanadeva: Lord Vāmanadeva's divine appearance is enchanting. He radiates brilliance and grace. His presence is a source of great joy and auspiciousness to those who witness it.

The Yajña of Bali Mahārāja: Bali Mahārāja, as part of his devotion and generosity, is performing a grand yajña (sacrifice) where he has vowed to give charity to anyone who approaches him. He seeks to extend his hand in charity even to the dwarf Brahmana.

Vāmanadeva's Request: Lord Vāmanadeva, in His guise as a dwarf Brahmana, approaches Bali Mahārāja during the yajña and humbly asks for a small piece of land, which He can cover with three of His steps. Bali Mahārāja, moved by the Brahmana's humility and innocence, agrees to the request.

The Miracle of Lord Vāmanadeva: Lord Vāmanadeva's first step covers the entire Earth, and His second step spans the heavenly planets. With His third step, He places His foot on Bali Mahārāja's head. This incredible display reveals the Lord's omnipotence and the vastness of the cosmos.

Bali Mahārāja's Surrender: Bali Mahārāja, recognizing the divine identity of the dwarf Brahmana, offers his head as the third step. He accepts defeat gracefully and expresses his willingness to serve the Lord.

Blessings for Bali: Lord Vāmanadeva, pleased by Bali Mahārāja's surrender and devotion, offers benefits to him. He grants Bali the position of the ruler of the lower planetary systems, known as Sutala, and assures him of protection and eternal service.

Return of the Heavenly Kingdom: With Bali's surrender and humility, the heavenly kingdom is returned to the demigods, led by Lord Indra. The balance in the cosmic order is restored.

08-19 Lord Vāmanadeva Begs Charity

Here are the key events and themes:

Background of Bali's Sacrifice: Bali Mahārāja is conducting a grand yajña (sacrificial ceremony) as part of his holy and generous nature. He has vowed to give charity to anyone approaching him during the yajña.

Lord Vāmanadeva's Arrival: Lord Vāmanadeva, in the form of a dwarf Brahmana, arrives at Bali Mahārāja's sacrificial arena during the yajña. His appearance is humble, and He carries a waterpot (kamaṇḍalu) and a staff (danda).

Bali's Welcome: Recognizing the divine nature of the Brahmana boy, Bali Mahārāja welcomes Him with great respect and offers to fulfil any request He may have.

Vāmanadeva's Request: Lord Vāmanadeva makes a seemingly modest request. He asks for three paces of land, which He can measure with His feet. Bali Mahārāja, pleased with the boy's humility, agrees without hesitation.

Bali's Guru's Concern: Bali Mahārāja's spiritual teacher, Śukrācārya, suspects that the dwarf Brahmana is none other than Lord Vishnu and warns Bali that granting this request may lead to disaster. However, Bali Mahārāja remains firm in his commitment to honour his vow.

Lord Vāmanadeva's Expanding Form: To the astonishment of all present, Lord Vāmanadeva's form begins to expand. His slight frame transforms into a cosmic size, and with His first two steps, He covers the entire earthly realm and the heavenly planets.

The Third Step: Lord Vāmanadeva asks Bali Mahārāja where to place His third step.

True to his word, Bali offers his head as a place for the Lord's third step.

Lord's Blessings: Pleased with Bali Mahārāja's unwavering devotion and adherence to his vow, Lord Vāmanadeva grants him a particular boon. He becomes Bali's eternal protector and promises to reside in Bali's kingdom.

08-20 Bali Mahārāja Surrenders the Universe

This chapter continues the story of Bali Mahārāja and his interactions with Lord Vāmanadeva. It focuses on Bali's surrender and willingness to give up everything, including his life, to honour his promise to the Lord.

Here are the key events and themes from Srimad Bhagavatam Canto 8, Chapter 20:

Lord Vāmanadeva's Expanding Form: In the previous chapter, Lord Vāmanadeva had requested three paces of land from Bali Mahārāja, and His small form had expanded to cover the entire universe with His first two steps. He had just placed His foot on Bali's head for the third step.

Bali's Surrender: Despite the enormous size of the Lord's foot, Bali Mahārāja remains calm and surrendered. He recognizes the Lord's divinity and realizes that this situation tests his devotion and promise to grant the Lord's request.

Bali's Offer: Bali Mahārāja, in a mood of self-surrender and devotion, offers his head as the resting place for the Lord's third step. He expresses his readiness to fulfil his vow at any cost.

Lord Vāmanadeva's Pleasure: Lord Vāmanadeva, pleased with Bali's unwavering devotion and surrender, grants him His divine blessings and protection. The Lord assures Bali that He will permanently reside in Bali's heart and be present in his dynasty.

Praise from Celestial Beings: The celestial beings, including Lord Brahmā and Lord Shiva, witness this extraordinary act of devotion and selflessness. They shower praises on Bali Mahārāja for his dedication and truthfulness.

Bali's Exile: Following the Lord's request, Bali Mahārāja is sent to the lower planetary system known as Sutala, where he rules as a great king. Despite being exiled from the heavenly planets, Bali remains content due to his devotion to the Lord.

Conclusion of the Pastime: The chapter concludes with the understanding that Bali Mahārāja's surrender and humility have earned him the Lord's eternal grace and protection.

08-21 The Demon Maya Danava Defeated

This chapter narrates the conflict between the demon Maya Danava and the demigods, highlighting the cunning and deceptive nature of Maya Danava and his eventual defeat by the celestial beings.

Here are the key events and themes from Srimad Bhagavatam Canto 8, Chapter 21:

Maya Danava's Deception: Maya Danava, a powerful demon with exceptional architectural and engineering skills, had constructed a splendid city named Tripura for the monsters. He had designed this city to fly in the sky and remain invulnerable to attack.

The distress of the Demigods: The flying city of Tripura caused pain to the demigods, who sought the help of Lord Shiva to destroy it. Lord Shiva agreed to help but warned the demigods to wait for an opportune moment.

Lord Shiva's Plan: Lord Shiva devised a plan to destroy Tripura. He waited for the proper planetary alignment, known as "yoga-pīṭha," which would make the city vulnerable.

The Battle: When the celestial planets are aligned correctly, Lord Shiva, riding on his bull Nandi and armed with his bow and arrow, attacked Tripura. Despite Maya Danava's clever design, Lord Shiva's hand penetrated the city and caused it to disintegrate.

Maya Danava's Escape: Realizing that the city was destroyed, Maya Danava, who was inside the city, fled to the lower planetary systems to save his life.

Demigods' Victory: The demigods celebrated their victory over Tripura and praised Lord Shiva for his assistance.

Srimad Bhagavatam Canto 8, Chapter 21, serves as a cautionary tale about the consequences of misuse of power and the deceptive nature of demonic forces. It highlights the role of Lord Shiva in assisting the demigods and the ultimate triumph of divine principles over demonic influences. The story of Maya Danava's defeat showcases the importance of righteous actions and divine intervention in the face of adversity.

08-22 Bali Mahārāja Surrenders His Life

Here are the key events and themes:

Bali Mahārāja's Surrender: Bali Mahārāja offering his head as a resting place for Lord Vāmanadeva's third step in the previous chapters, is ready to fulfil his promise to the Lord. He is prepared to offer anything, including his life, to honour his vow.

Lord Vāmanadeva's Praise: Lord Vāmanadeva, pleased with Bali's unwavering surrender and devotion, praises Bali Mahārāja for his extraordinary sacrifice and selflessness.

The Return of the Demigods: Lord Vāmanadeva instructs Bali Mahārāja to return the heavenly kingdom to Lord Indra and the demigods. Bali Mahārāja willingly complies with the Lord's command, demonstrating his humility and dharma (righteousness) adherence.

Bali's Offer: Bali Mahārāja expresses his heartfelt gratitude to the Lord for the opportunity to serve Him despite losing everything. He acknowledges the Lord's supreme position and offers his life as a humble gift to the Lord.

The Blessings: Lord Vāmanadeva, touched by Bali Mahārāja's surrender and devotion, grants him a particular boon. He assures Bali Mahārāja of a glorious future and the opportunity to personally witness the Lord's pastimes in the heavenly planets in the future.

Bali's Exile to Sutala: Bali Mahārāja, as per the Lord's instructions, is exiled to the lower planetary system of Sutala, where he rules as a virtuous and devoted king. Despite being in a lower realm, he continues to be protected and blessed by the Lord.

08-23 The Demigods Regain the Heavenly Planets

This chapter describes the demigods' victorious return to the heavenly planets after their defeat by the demon Bali Mahārāja and his subsequent surrender to Lord Vāmanadeva.

Here are the key events and themes from Srimad Bhagavatam Canto 8, Chapter 23: Bali Mahārāja's Surrender: The previous chapters detailed the story of Bali Mahārāja's confrontation with Lord Vāmanadeva, where Bali offered his head as the Lord's third step. Lord Vāmanadeva granted Bali blessings and exiled him to the lower planetary system of Sutala.

The Demigods' Request: With Bali Mahārāja's surrender and departure to Sutala, the demigods, led by Lord Indra, approached Lord Vāmanadeva and expressed their desire to regain the heavenly planets. Lord Vāmanadeva agreed to their request.

Preparing for Battle: Lord Vāmanadeva and the demigods are ready for a battle to reclaim the heavenly kingdom from the demons. The Lord mounted His chariot, which the son of Indra drove, and they proceeded to confront the demon forces.

The Battle Commences: A fierce battle between the demigods and demons ensued. Lord Vāmanadeva displayed His divine prowess and bravery, leading the demigods to defeat the demon armies.

Demon Defeat: Despite the demons' initial resistance, Lord Vāmanadeva's superior strength and strategy led to their defeat. The demigods regained control of the heavenly planets.

Praise and Gratitude: The demigods praised Lord Vāmanadeva for His invaluable assistance and blessings. They acknowledged His supreme power and offered their gratitude for His divine intervention.

Bali Mahārāja's Continued Rule: Lord Vāmanadeva assured the demigods that Bali Mahārāja would continue to rule in Sutala, where he would be an ideal king, and the Lord Himself would protect him.

08-24 Matsya, the Lord's Fish Incarnation

This chapter introduces one of the incarnations of Lord Vishnu, known as Matsya, the divine fish incarnation. It describes the events surrounding Matsya's appearance and how He saves humanity and knowledge during a great deluge.

Here are the key events and themes:

The Appearance of Lord Matsya: The chapter begins with the sage Maitreya narrating the story of Lord Matsya's appearance. Lord Vishnu incarnates as a giant fish (Matsya) to rescue the Earth and its inhabitants during a cosmic deluge (pralaya).

The Deluge's Origin: The great deluge is initiated by Lord Brahmā, the creator, at the end of the previous kalpa (cosmic cycle) to cleanse and renew the universe. The world is submerged in water, and all life forms are endangered.

King Satyavrata's Devotion: During the deluge, King Satyavrata (Vaivasvata Manu) finds himself in a boat and worships the fish he encounters. Unbeknownst to him, this fish is the Supreme Lord in His Matsya incarnation.

The Fish's Request: The Matsya (fish) incarnation proliferates and becomes gigantic. It informs King Satyavrata of the impending deluge and asks for protection. The fish also instructs the king to collect various seeds of plants, herbs, and the seven great sages (Saptarishi) to preserve knowledge.

King Satyavrata's Duties: King Satyavrata dutifully follows Lord Matsya's instructions. He gathers the necessary items and the sages, ensuring the survival of life and knowledge during the catastrophic deluge.

The Arrival of Matsya: As the waters rise and the deluge begins, Lord Matsya's great form navigates the cosmic ocean. He pulls the king's boat to safety, thus saving him and the seeds of life and knowledge.

Lord Matsya's Grace: The chapter concludes with Lord Matsya, the fish incarnation, displaying His divine form to King Satyavrata and imparting spiritual knowledge. The king becomes a saintly ruler and carries out his duties as a devotee of the Lord.

Canto 9

09-01 The Dynasty of Amsuman

In this chapter, the text continues the narrative of the dynasty of King Priyavrata, one of the sons of Lord Brahma, who ruled over the earthly realms and decided to retire from worldly life to engage in ascetic practices. His son, Agnidhra, succeeded him as king.

Introduction of King Priyavrata: The chapter introduces King Priyavrata and his ruling of the earthly planets. It describes how he was initially reluctant to rule and sought guidance from his spiritual master, Narada Muni, who advised him to fulfil his duties as a ruler and then retire for spiritual pursuits.

Description of Priyavrata's Ascetic Practices: After ruling for a certain period, King Priyavrata handed over his kingdom to his sons and engaged in severe ascetic practices, which included meditation and penance. He sought spiritual enlightenment and liberation from the cycle of birth and death.

Description of His Sons: The chapter also mentions Priyavrata's sons and their names. Among his sons, Agnidhra is highlighted as a prominent character in the subsequent chapters.

Description of Earth's Structure: The text briefly describes the cosmic geography, including the arrangement of planetary systems, continents, oceans, and mountains. It mentions the seven seas and seven islands on the Earth.

Glorification of King Priyavrata: The chapter praises King Priyavrata's devotion and determination in pursuing spiritual realization. His story serves as an example of how even rulers can balance their worldly responsibilities with spiritual aspirations.

09-02 The Dynasties of the Sons of Manu

Introduction of Manu: The chapter begins by introducing Manu, who is considered the progenitor of humankind in Hindu cosmology. Manu is a pious and virtuous ruler entrusted with the responsibility of preserving and propagating dharma (righteousness) during the various cycles of creation and dissolution.

Sons of Manu: The chapter lists the names of Manu's sons and describes their respective roles and contributions. These sons include Priyavrata (previously mentioned in Canto 9, Chapter 1), Uttanapada, and Devahuti.

Priyavrata's Lineage: The text provides a more detailed account of the descendants of Priyavrata, mainly focusing on his son Agnidhra, who became the ruler of Jambudvipa (one of the continents on Earth). Agnidhra's sons and their division of Jambudvipa into nine varshas (subdivisions) are described.

Uttanapada's Lineage: The chapter also discusses the descendants of Uttanapada, another son of Manu, and particularly highlights the life of Dhruva, who was a renowned devotee of Lord Vishnu. Dhruva's story is well-known for his intense penance and devotion to attain Lord Vishnu's divine vision.

Devahuti's Marriage to Kardama Muni: The text briefly narrates the story of Devahuti, one of Manu's daughters, who married Kardama Muni, a sage known for his spiritual wisdom and asceticism. Their union led to the birth of Lord Kapila, an incarnation of Lord Vishnu, who would later impart spiritual knowledge to Devahuti.

Moral and Spiritual Lessons: Throughout the chapter, ethical and spiritual lessons are conveyed through the stories of these illustrious personalities. Devotion, dharma, and the pursuit of spiritual knowledge are emphasized.

Canto 9, Chapter 2 connects the lineage of Manu and his descendants, such as Dhruva and Kapila, to the broader narrative of the Srimad Bhagavatam, which culminates in the teachings and pastimes of the Lord Krishna. It highlights the significance of righteous rulers and devoted individuals in preserving and propagating dharma and spirituality in the world.

09-03 The Marriage of Sukanya and Cyavana Muni

This chapter narrates a unique and intriguing story involving a princess named Sukanya and the sage Cyavana Muni. It contains valuable lessons about devotion, duty, and the significance of inner qualities over external appearances.

Sukanya's Plight: The chapter introduces Princess Sukanya, the daughter of King Saryati, who was known for her beauty and virtue. Despite her noble birth and beauty, Sukanya faced a challenge as her chosen husband, Ashvapati, a king from a neighbouring kingdom, was blind.

Sage Cyavana Muni: One day, while Sukanya was in the forest, she mistakenly pricked the eyes of a meditating sage named Cyavana Muni, who was deep in meditation. Disturbed by her actions, the sage opened his eyes and cursed her, saying she would lose her youth and beauty.

Sukanya's Devotion: Despite the curse, Sukanya remained devoted to her husband, Ashvapati. She took good care of him and never complained about their situation. Her unwavering devotion and virtuous character shone through, even in adversity.

Cyavana Muni's Transformation: Seeing Sukanya's devotion and virtue, Cyavana Muni was moved. He offered her a boon, allowing her to choose when her youth and beauty would be restored. Sukanya requested that her husband, Ashvapati, be given back his sight, which Cyavana Muni granted.

Reunion and Marriage: With her husband's sight restored, Sukanya's devotion was rewarded, and they lived happily together. The chapter concludes by restoring Sukanya's youth and beauty, demonstrating that inner qualities and passion are more significant than external appearances.

Canto 9, Chapter 3, teaches essential lessons about devotion, fidelity, and the power of inner qualities. Sukanya's unwavering commitment to her husband and her virtuous character are celebrated in this story. It also illustrates the concept of dharma (duty), as Sukanya's dedication to her husband and virtue were integral to her righteous path. The narrative emphasizes that true beauty lies in one's character and actions rather than external physical attributes.

09-04 Ambarisha Maharaja Offended by Durvasa Muni

Introduction of King Ambarisha: The chapter introduces King Ambarisha, a pious and devoted ruler known for his unwavering devotion to Lord Vishnu. He was well- respected for his righteous rule and his dedication to religious practices.

Durvasa Muni's Visit: Sage Durvasa Muni, known for his quick temper, decided to visit King Ambarisha. The king warmly welcomed the sage and offered him a seat, intending to receive his blessings.

Ekadashi Vrata: King Ambarisha had been observing a sacred Ekadashi fast, a vow to fast on the eleventh day of the lunar cycle in honour of Lord Vishnu. As part of this vow, the king did not take any food for the day and planned to break his fast only after offering food to Durvasa Muni. As the day wore on, Sage Durvasa Muni's meditation deepened, and hours passed without him realizing it. The appointed time for breaking the fast was approaching, and King Ambarisha was in a dilemma about what to do.

Durvasa's Wrath: To avoid any offence, King Ambarisha took a sip of water to sustain himself while waiting for Durvasa's return. When Durvasa Muni finally emerged from his meditation and saw what had happened, he became infuriated. He perceived this act as a slight against him and his ascetic practices.

Lord Vishnu's Intervention: In his anger, Durvasa Muni created a demon to harm King Ambarisha. In response, Lord Vishnu immediately sent His Sudarshana Chakra (divine discus) to protect the king. The Sudarshana Chakra pursued Durvasa Muni relentlessly.

Durvasa's Humility: Realizing the severity of the situation and the omnipresence of Lord Vishnu, Durvasa Muni sought refuge with King Ambarisha, who prayed to Lord Vishnu to recall His Sudarshana Chakra. The Lord obliged, and Durvasa Muni learned the lesson of humility and the supremacy of devotion.

Resolution and Lessons: The incident deepened the king's devotion to Lord Vishnu, and Durvasa Muni recognized the power of a devotee's humility and dedication. Both the king and the sage reconciled, and Durvasa Muni departed.

09-05 Durvasa Muni's Life Spared

Here is a summary of the key points:

Durvasa Muni's Humiliation: This chapter describes how Durvasa Muni, realizing his mistake in trying to harm King Ambarisha, felt deep remorse and humiliation. He recognized that the king's devotion to Lord Vishnu was unparalleled and that his actions had been inexcusable.

Seeking Forgiveness: Sage Durvasa decided to go to Lord Brahma and Lord Shiva to seek their counsel and forgiveness for his misconduct. However, both Brahma and Shiva informed Durvasa that only Lord Vishnu had the power to forgive him and remove the sins he had incurred.

Durvasa Muni's Pilgrimage: Understanding that he needed to approach Lord Vishnu directly, Durvasa embarked on an extensive pilgrimage to various holy places and performed severe austerities to gain the Lord's favour.

Return to King Ambarisha: Durvasa Muni returned to King Ambarisha after completing his pilgrimage and austerities and humbly sought his forgiveness. The king, displaying his kindness and forgiveness, warmly received Durvasa and assured him that all was forgiven.

Durvasa's Realization: With a heart full of gratitude and realization, Durvasa Muni acknowledged the power of devotion, humility, and the grace of Lord Vishnu. He understood that devotion to the Lord was the ultimate path to spiritual liberation.

Lord Vishnu's Benediction: Lord Vishnu, who is pleased with Durvasa Muni's transformation and sincere repentance, blessed him and assured him of His protection in the future.

This chapter demonstrates how sincere repentance and a change of heart can lead to spiritual growth and redemption. Durvasa Muni's journey from anger and arrogance to humility and devotion serves as a powerful lesson in the transformative power of recognizing one's mistakes and seeking forgiveness from both the offended party and the divine.

09-06 The Downfall of Saubhari Muni

The key points:

Saubhari Muni's Austerities: The chapter introduces Saubhari Muni, a highly ascetic and celibate sage known for his deep meditation and penance. He lived underwater in the River Yamuna and was renowned for his spiritual prowess.

Temptation and Desires: While meditating underwater, Saubhari Muni saw fish engaged in amorous activities, which aroused his curiosity and desires. He realized he had neglected his worldly desires for too long and longed for a more earthly life. Marrying Fifty Women: Overwhelmed by his newfound desires, Saubhari Muni decided to marry. Astonishingly, he married fifty princesses and began living a life of family responsibilities, much to the surprise of the celestial beings and other sages.

Frustration and Regret: Saubhari Muni soon found himself entangled in the complexities of married life, dealing with the demands and expectations of his fifty wives. He became increasingly frustrated and regretted his decision to abandon his ascetic practices.

Return to Asceticism: Realizing the emptiness of his desires and the entanglement of family life, Saubhari Muni ultimately renounced his married life and returned to his ascetic practices. He engaged in severe penance, focusing on controlling his desires and attachments.

Lessons and Teachings: The chapter highlights the futility of indulging in desires and the importance of self-control in spiritual life. Saubhari Muni's story is a cautionary tale about the dangers of succumbing to desires and distractions on the spiritual path.

The Srimad Bhagavatam explores the themes of desire, attachment, and the challenges accomplished ascetics face when they momentarily lose sight of their spiritual goals. It underscores the need for self-control, renunciation, and a balanced approach to life's desires and responsibilities. Saubhari Muni's story ultimately teaches that pursuing spiritual wisdom and inner peace should always remain paramount, even in worldly temptations.

09-07 The Descendants of King Mandhata

Introduction of King Mandhata: The chapter introduces King Mandhata, a righteous and powerful monarch renowned for his devotion to Lord Vishnu and his commitment to dharma (righteousness). He was considered one of the most illustrious kings in the lineage of Manu.

Mandhata's Exploits and Virtues: The text describes King Mandhata's many accomplishments, including his victories in various battles and his successful rule, which brought prosperity and peace to his kingdom. He was also known for his generosity and compassion towards his subjects.

Descendants of Mandhata: The chapter lists the names of Mandhata's sons and their contributions. His descendants were equally virtuous and made significant contributions to society. Among his sons, Susandhi was particularly praised for his qualities and deeds.

Story of Ambarisha: The chapter also mentions Ambarisha, one of Mandhata's descendants, known for his unwavering devotion to Lord Vishnu. The tale of Ambarisha's devotion is briefly recounted, emphasising his steadfast observance of Ekadashi fasting.

Details of the Dynasty: The chapter details the various branches of Mandhata's dynasty, including the rulers of different regions and their virtuous qualities. It highlights the lineage's commitment to upholding dharma and fostering spiritual knowledge.

Moral and Spiritual Significance: Throughout the chapter, there are ethical and spiritual lessons emphasising the importance of virtuous rule, devotion to God, and the role of kings in setting examples for their subjects. The chapter underscores the idea that righteous and ethical leadership can bring prosperity and harmony to society.

09-08 The Sons of Sagara Meet Lord Kapila

King Sagara's Sacrifice: The chapter begins by recounting the story of King Sagara, a noble ruler who sought to perform the Ashvamedha (horse sacrifice) to assert his sovereignty over the universe. However, during the ceremony, the sacrificial horse was stolen by Lord Indra, the king of the demigods, and taken to the netherworld.

Descendants of King Sagara: King Sagara had two wives, Kesini and Sumati. Sumati gave birth to 60,000 sons, while Kesini bore only one, Asamanjasa. Sagara's descendants were known as the Sagara princes.

Quest to Retrieve the Horse: King Sagara's 60,000 sons embarked on a mission to retrieve the stolen horse and complete their father's sacrifice. They dug a vast pit (later known as the Sagara Ocean), searching for the horse.

Discovery of the Horse: As the princes dug deeper into the earth, they eventually discovered the sacrificial horse near the ashram of the sage Kapila. However, the sage was in deep meditation and unaware of their activities.

The Sons' Disrespect: The princes, impatient and unaware of Kapila's spiritual stature, wrongly accused him of stealing the horse and disrespected him. Their disrespectful actions incurred the sage's wrath.

Kapila's Curse: Lord Kapila, an incarnation of Lord Vishnu and a highly realized sage, opened His eyes and cast a powerful curse on the sons of Sagara. As a result, all 60,000 sons were instantly reduced to ashes.

Anshuman and Dilipa: After the tragedy, Sagara's grandson, Anshuman, continued the search for the sacrificial horse. His son, Dilipa, also tried to retrieve it but was unsuccessful. Dilipa's sincerity and devotion to the mission earned him the grace of Lord Kapila.

Lord Kapila's Teachings: Recognizing Dilipa's devotion, Lord Kapila appeared before him and imparted spiritual knowledge. He explained the principles of devotional service, the significance of detachment from material desires, and the path to attaining liberation.

09-09 The Dynasty of Amsuman

In this chapter, the text continues the narrative of King Sagara's descendants. It provides an account of the dynasty of Amsuman, one of the sons of Sagara, who continued the quest to retrieve the sacrificial horse that Lord Indra stole.

Here is a summary of the key points from Canto 9, Chapter 9:

Introduction of Amsuman: The chapter begins by introducing Amsuman, the grandson of King Sagara. Amsuman was known for his virtuous character and commitment to completing the Ashvamedha sacrifice that his grandfather Sagara had started.

Amsuman's Quest: Amsuman, like his predecessors, was determined to retrieve the stolen sacrificial horse and complete the yajna (sacrifice). He followed the path his father, Dilipa, and his grandfather, Anshuman, took in search of the horse.

Discovery of the Horse: Amsuman, with his unwavering devotion and dedication to the mission, finally found the sacrificial horse grazing near the ashram of Kapila Muni, who was none other than an incarnation of Lord Vishnu.

Lord Kapila's Blessings: Recognizing Amsuman's sincerity and devotion, Lord Kapila appeared before him and praised his determination. Lord Kapila explained the significance of the Ashvamedha sacrifice and blessed Amsuman, assuring him that his gift would be successful.

Completion of the Sacrifice: Amsuman returned to his kingdom with the sacrificial horse and performed the Ashvamedha sacrifice according to Vedic rituals and under the guidance of learned Brahmanas (priests). The successful completion of the gift brought great fame and prosperity to his kingdom.

Subsequent Generations: The chapter details the descendants of Amsuman and their contributions to society. It highlights their adherence to dharma (righteousness) and the preservation of Vedic traditions.

09-10 The Pastimes of the Lord, Ramachandra

This chapter narrates the pastimes of Lord Rama, an incarnation of Lord Vishnu, during His time on Earth, mainly focusing on the episode of His marriage to Sita and the events leading up to it.

Here is a summary of the key points from Canto 9, Chapter 10:

Introduction to Lord Rama: The chapter begins by introducing Lord Rama as the seventh incarnation of Lord Vishnu. Lord Rama is described as the embodiment of dharma (righteousness) and is revered for His exemplary character, humility, and devotion to truth.

Dasharatha's Concern: The chapter narrates the concern of King Dasharatha, Lord Rama's father, regarding his lack of a male heir. In his desire for an heir, Dasharatha decides to perform a yajna (sacrifice) to seek the blessings of the celestial beings.

Sage Vishwamitra's Request: Sage Vishwamitra, a revered sage known for his spiritual power, visits Dasharatha's kingdom and requests the king's assistance in protecting a yajna he intends to perform. Vishwamitra seeks Lord Rama's help in safeguarding the yajna from the disruptions caused by demons.

Rama's Accompaniment: Dasharatha, happy to oblige the sage, agrees to send Lord Rama and his younger brother, Lakshmana, to accompany Vishwamitra. The young princes are known for their valour and virtue.

Lord Rama's Feats: As Lord Rama and Lakshmana accompany Vishwamitra, they encounter various challenges and demons. Lord Rama displays His divine prowess by defeating the monsters, earning the sage's admiration.

Arrival at Mithila: Lord Rama and Lakshmana, along with Sage Vishwamitra, eventually arrive in the city of Mithila, where King Janaka is holding a grand assembly and a svayamvara (a ceremony where the bride chooses her groom) for his daughter, Sita.

Lord Rama's Marriage: In the assembly, Lord Rama effortlessly lifts the divine bow of Lord Shiva and wins the hand of Sita in marriage. This event marks the union of Lord Rama and Sita, which is celebrated as one of the most significant moments in Hindu mythology.

09-11 Description of Lord Ramachandra

Chapter provides a concise and respectful summary of the life and divine pastimes of Lord Rama, who is considered one of the incarnations of Lord Vishnu. Lord Rama's story, known as the Ramayana, is one of Hindu mythology's most revered and beloved narratives.

Lord Rama's Advent: The chapter begins by acknowledging the intangible nature of Lord Rama's appearance on Earth. It highlights that Lord Rama descends to the material world to protect dharma (righteousness) and annihilate the forces of evil.

Lord Rama's Divine Family: The text briefly mentions Lord Rama's family, including His father, King Dasharatha, His mother, Queen Kausalya, and His brothers Lakshmana, Bharata, and Shatrughna. It also notes His divine consort, Sita Devi.

The Marriage of Rama and Sita: The chapter describes the divine wedding of Lord Rama and Sita during the svayamvara ceremony in Mithila. Lord Rama's exceptional feat of stringing Lord Shiva's bow and winning Sita's hand is emphasised.

Lord Rama's Exile: The narrative briefly mentions the unfortunate circumstances that led to Lord Rama's exile to the forest. He willingly lived for fourteen years to honour His father's promise to Queen Kaikeyi.

Sita's Abduction: The chapter touches upon the episode of Sita's abduction by the demon king Ravana, who disguised himself as a sage to deceive Sita.

Lord Rama's Quest: It describes Lord Rama's relentless search for Sita, His alliance with the monkey army led by Hanuman and the construction of the bridge to Lanka to rescue Sita.

Battle Against Ravana: The chapter briefly mentions Lord Rama's epic battle against Ravana, the demon king of Lanka, and Ravana's eventual defeat and death.

Reunion with Sita: The narrative highlights Lord Rama's reunion and the joyous return to Ayodhya, where the citizens welcome them.

Lord Rama's Benevolent Rule: The chapter underscores Lord Rama's righteous rule as the king of Ayodhya, where the citizens enjoyed prosperity and happiness.

09-12 The Dynasty of Kusa

This chapter continues the narrative from the previous chapter. It delves into the lineage and history of Lord Rama's sons, mainly focusing on the dynasty of Kusa, the eldest son of Lord Rama and Sita.

Here is a summary of the key points from Canto 9, Chapter 12:

Introduction of Kusa: The chapter begins by introducing Kusa, the eldest son of Lord Rama and Sita. Kusa was known for his exemplary qualities, including his virtuous character and devotion to Lord Vishnu.

Lava and Kusa: The text mentions that Kusa had two sons named Lava and Kusa. Both sons inherited their father's virtues and became illustrious rulers in their own right.

The Kingdom of Ayodhya: After the return of Lord Rama and Sita to Ayodhya, Lord Rama ruled the kingdom with great righteousness and justice. The citizens of Ayodhya enjoyed a period of prosperity and harmony during His reign.

Lava and Kusa's Upbringing: The chapter describes how Lava and Kusa were raised with love and care by Lord Rama and Sita in Ayodhya. They received proper education and were trained in various arts, including music and archery.

Lord Rama's Disappearance: It is mentioned that after some time, Lord Rama decided to conclude His earthly pastimes and return to His spiritual abode, Vaikuntha. He instructed Lava and Kusa to carry His legacy and rule the kingdom.

Lava and Kusa's Rule: Following Lord Rama's departure, Lava and Kusa ascended the throne and ruled Ayodhya with the same principles of righteousness, dharma, and devotion their father upheld. They continued the legacy of their ancestors.

Lava and Kusa's Contribution: The chapter highlights some of the notable achievements of Lava and Kusa during their rule, including their commitment to dharma and the welfare of their subjects.

Dynasty of Kusa: The chapter details the lineage of Kusa, tracing the descendants who continued to rule Ayodhya and uphold the principles of dharma and righteousness.

09-13 The Dynasty of Maharaja Nimi

This chapter provides an account of the lineage of Maharaja Nimi, a virtuous and righteous ruler, and the circumstances surrounding his life and dynasty.

Here is a summary of the key points from Canto 9, Chapter 13:

Introduction of Maharaja Nimi: The chapter introduces Maharaja Nimi as a highly virtuous and righteous king who ruled the kingdom of Videha. Maharaja Nimi was known for his dedication to dharma (righteousness) and his commitment to the welfare of his subjects.

Nimi's Sacrifice and Cursed by Sages: Maharaja Nimi decided to perform a grand yajna (sacrifice) to benefit his kingdom and subjects. However, the sages he invited to conduct the gift, led by the sage Vasishtha, were delayed due to their engagement in another yajna. In their absence, Maharaja Nimi's impatience led him to perform the yajna without them, which was considered disrespectful.

Creation of Nimi's Son: In response to Maharaja Nimi's actions, the sages pronounced a curse on him, causing his physical body to perish. However, the philosopher Angira, who was present at the scene, created a son for Maharaja Nimi by his mystic potency. This son was named Mithila.

Mithila's Dynasty: The chapter traces the lineage of Mithila and his descendants who ruled the kingdom of Videha. Mithila's dynasty continued to follow the principles of dharma and uphold the righteous rule initiated by Maharaja Nimi.

Birth of Janaka: King Janaka emerged as a prominent ruler among Mithila's descendants. King Janaka, also known as Videha Janaka, is renowned for his association with Lord Rama, particularly in the Ramayana, where he is depicted as the father of Sita, who becomes Lord Rama's consort.

09-14 King Puranjana Goes to the Forest

Puranjana is a king who becomes entangled in the cycle of birth and death due to his material desires and attachments. King Puranjana is described as profoundly attached to his queen, who symbolizes the physical body, and his various queens, who represent the senses. His desires for material enjoyment and understanding gratification keep him bound in the earthly realm. The chapter describes Puranjana's wealthy city, representing the physical body and its various components, including the senses and the mind. The town is protected by a formidable wall, symbolizing the false ego that keeps the soul trapped in illusion.

The Queen's Complaint: Queen Puranjani, representing the physical body, becomes dissatisfied with the king's constant pursuit of material desires and attachments. She chastises the king for neglecting his duties and engaging in unnecessary activities. In response to the queen's complaints, King Puranjana decides to go to the forest to hunt for a better life, representing the relentless pursuit of material desires. The forest represents the unpredictable and dangerous nature of material existence. In the forest, King Puranjana encounters a band of Yavanas (savage tribesmen), symbolizing time and the inevitability of old age and death. In his attempt to defend himself, Puranjana's body becomes severely wounded, signifying the physical deterioration accompanying ageing.

Severely wounded and defeated in the forest, King Puranjana finally realizes the futility of his material pursuits and the impermanence of his earthly body. He returns to the city, symbolizing the soul's eventual realization of the transitory nature of worldly life.

09-15 Parasurama, the Lord's Warrior Incarnation

This chapter narrates the story of Lord Parasurama, one of the incarnations of Lord Vishnu, known for his martial prowess and mission to rid the world of corrupt and oppressive Kshatriya rulers.

Introduction of Lord Parasurama: The chapter begins by introducing Lord Parasurama as the sixth incarnation of Lord Vishnu. He was born in the Brahmin lineage of the sage Jamadagni and was known for his extraordinary skill in warfare and archery. Parasurama's Origin: The text describes the background of Lord Parasurama's incarnation. He was born to avenge the mistreatment of his father, Jamadagni, by the Kshatriya (warrior) rulers who oppressed the Brahmins and caused harm to his family. Parasurama's Axe: Lord Parasurama became famous for carrying an axe (parasu) that he used to rid the world of corrupt Kshatriya rulers. He waged wars against these oppressive kings and defeated them in battle.

Annihilation of Kshatriyas: Lord Parasurama's mission to protect the Brahmins and restore dharma has led to the devastation of the Kshatriya class on multiple occasions. He filled five lakes with the blood of the slain warriors, earning him the title "Bhargava Rama" (Rama, the descendant of Bhrigu).

Parasurama's Guru Dakshina: The chapter recounts the story of Lord Parasurama's Guru Dakshina (teacher's fee) to his father's spiritual teacher, the sage Richika. He fulfils his father's promise by offering the sage a special Ramadhan (wish-fulfiling cow). Lord Parasurama's Renunciation: After fulfilling his mission of cleansing the Earth of corrupt rulers and avenging the wrongs against his family, Lord Parasurama decided to renounce his warrior life and pursue spiritual knowledge and meditation. He approached the sage Dattatreya as his spiritual guide.

Significance of Parasurama's Incarnation: The chapter underscores the divine mission of Lord Parasurama to protect dharma and uphold righteousness. His life and actions embody Lord Vishnu's intervention when the world is plagued by adharma (unrighteousness).

09-16 Parasurama Destroys the World's Ruling Class

This chapter continues the narrative of Lord Parasurama's activities and mission to rid the world of oppressive Kshatriya rulers.

Parasurama's Continuing Mission: The chapter begins by emphasizing Lord Parasurama's relentless mission to eliminate corrupt and oppressive Kshatriya rulers. He continued to wage wars against them and challenge their dominance.

Appearance of Lord Rama: The text mentions the arrival of Lord Rama, another incarnation of Lord Vishnu, in the lineage of King Raghu. Lord Rama is celebrated for His adherence to dharma and role in the epic Ramayana, where He defeats the demon king Ravana and rescues His consort, Sita.

Sage Vasishtha's Advice: Recognizing the destructive nature of Lord Parasurama's activities and the importance of Lord Rama's divine mission, the sage Vasishtha advised Lord Parasurama to stop his warfare and retire to the Mahendra Mountains for meditation and penance.

Lord Parasurama's Compliance: Following Vasishtha's counsel, Lord Parasurama agreed to lay down his weapons and retire to the Mahendra Mountains. His compliance marked the end of his mission to rid the world of oppressive Kshatriya rulers.

Lord Rama's Mission: The chapter briefly mentions Lord Rama's mission to defeat the demon king Ravana and restore dharma. Lord Rama's life and actions exemplify adherence to righteousness, duty, and the protection of the virtuous.

Lord Parasurama's Meditation: Lord Parasurama, now retired from warfare, engaged in deep meditation and penance in the Mahendra Mountains. He focused on his spiritual practices and sought inner realization.

Conclusion: The chapter concludes by emphasizing the significance of Lord Parasurama's activities in restoring dharma and the divine nature of his mission. It also acknowledges the importance of Lord Rama's appearance and His role in upholding righteousness.

09-17 The Dynasties of the Sons of Pururava

This chapter provides a genealogical account of the descendants of King Pururava, who was an important figure in ancient Indian mythology. Pururava was renowned for his association with the celestial nymph Urvashi.

Here is a summary of the key points from Canto 9, Chapter 17:

Introduction of King Pururava: The chapter introduces King Pururava, a virtuous and mighty ruler. He was a descendant of the lunar dynasty (Chandravamsa) and was known for his devotion to Lord Vishnu.

King Pururava's Association with Urvashi: The chapter recounts how Pururava encountered Urvashi, a celestial nymph from the heavenly realms. Their association led to the birth of several sons.

Birth of Ayu: Urvashi and Pururava's union delivered a son named Ayu, who eventually became a king and continued the lunar dynasty.

Dynasty of Ayu: The chapter provides a list of kings in the dynasty of Ayu, which includes Nahusha, Yayati, and Yadu, among others. Yayati's story is particularly notable for his youth exchange with his sons.

Yadu's Dynasty: The chapter continues by tracing the lineage of Yadu, one of Pururava's descendants. Yadu's descendants became known as the Yadavas, who played a significant role in ancient Indian history and mythology.

The Birth of Puru: The narrative shifts to the birth of another son of Pururava and Urvashi named Puru. Puru's dynasty also played a crucial role in the history of India.

Birth of Dushyanta: The chapter mentions the birth of Dushyanta, a well-known king who appears in the Mahabharata. He was a descendant of Puru and played a role in the story of Shakuntala.

09-18 King Yayati Regains His Youth

This chapter continues the narrative of King Yayati, a significant figure in Hindu mythology, and recounts how he regained his youth through a divine boon.

Here is a summary of the key points from Canto 9, Chapter 18:

Yayati's Story: The chapter briefly recounts the background of King Yayati, the son of King Nahusha and a descendant of King Pururava. Yayati's story is notable for his desire for youthful vigour and the events that transpired.

Yayati's Request: As Yayati grew older, he became dissatisfied with old age and sought to regain his youth and physical strength. He approached his five sons and asked them to exchange their youth for his old age.

Sons' Responses: Yayati's sons initially hesitated to grant his request, but ultimately, his youngest son, Puru, agreed to exchange his youth with his father, while the others declined.

Regaining Youth: With Puru's consent, Yayati regained his youthful appearance and strength. He enjoyed the pleasures of youth for a thousand years.

Realization of Futility: Yayati realised the futility of material desires and sensual enjoyment after indulging in worldly pleasures for a thousand years. He understood that true happiness and spiritual growth lay beyond physical appearances and bodily pleasures.

Yayati's Advice to Puru: Yayati then returned his youth to Puru and advised him on the importance of dharma (righteousness) and the pursuit of spiritual knowledge. He recognized Puru's virtuous character and declared him the rightful heir to the throne.

Puru's Dynasty: Puru's descendants became known as the Puru dynasty and played a significant role in the history and lineage of Indian kings.

09-19 King Yayati Achieves Liberation

This chapter continues the narrative of King Yayati and explores his spiritual journey towards liberation after realizing the transient nature of material pleasures.

Here is a summary of the key points from Canto 9, Chapter 19:

Yayati's Reflection: King Yayati, having experienced the fleeting nature of youth and sensual pleasures, realized the emptiness and impermanence of worldly enjoyment. He understood that material desires could never lead to true satisfaction or happiness.

Yayati's Renunciation: Yayati decided to renounce his kingdom and worldly attachments to pursue a life of spiritual realization. He entrusted the rule of his kingdom to his sons and retired to the forest for meditation and austerities.

Penances and Austerities: Yayati engaged in rigorous penances and austerities to purify his heart and consciousness in the forest. He practised self- control and sought inner realization.

Realization of the Self: Through his dedicated spiritual practices, Yayati achieved self-realization and recognized his eternal nature as an atman (soul) distinct from the physical body. He gained a deeper understanding of the Supreme Truth.

Returning to the Kingdom: After attaining spiritual wisdom and liberation from the cycle of birth and death, Yayati decided to return to his kingdom. However, he did not return to the pleasures of the material world but instead chose to rule as a spiritually enlightened king.

Yayati's Legacy: Yayati ruled his kingdom with wisdom, compassion, and a focus on dharma (righteousness). He ensured the welfare of his subjects and upheld moral values.

Departure to the Forest: Yayati eventually left the kingdom and returned to the forest to continue his spiritual pursuits. He handed over the kingdom to his son Yadu and embarked on a life of meditation and devotion.

09-20 The Dynasty of Puru

This chapter provides a genealogical account of the descendants of King Puru, one of the sons of King Yayati. It focuses on the Puru dynasty and its role in the history and lineage of Indian kings.

Here is a summary of the key points from Canto 9, Chapter 20:

Introduction of King Puru: The chapter begins by introducing King Puru, one of the sons of King Yayati. Puru was known for his virtuous character and righteousness.

Puru's Dynasty: The text traces the lineage of King Puru and his descendants, highlighting their contributions to the history of India. The Puru dynasty significantly influenced the region's political and cultural development.

Yadu's Dynasty: The chapter also mentions King Yadu, another son of Yayati, and his descendants, who became known as the Yadavas. The Yadu dynasty became a prominent ruling dynasty in ancient India.

Role of Yadu and Puru Dynasties: The text briefly touches upon the part of both the Yadu and Puru dynasties in shaping the history and culture of ancient India. These dynasties are considered to be important in the lineage of kings and warriors.

Connection to Lord Krishna: The chapter lays the historical foundation for the appearance of Lord Krishna, born in the Yadu dynasty. Lord Krishna is a central figure in Hinduism and plays a pivotal role in the Mahabharata and other sacred texts.

09-21 The Dynasty of Bharata

This chapter provides a genealogical account of the descendants of King Bharata, who was a notable figure in Indian mythology. Bharata's dynasty is significant as it is from this lineage that the name "Bharata" was derived as another name for India.

Here is a summary of the key points from Canto 9, Chapter 21:

Introduction of King Bharata: The chapter introduces King Bharata, a virtuous and illustrious ruler who was a descendant of King Puru. King Bharata was known for his righteous rule and devotion to Lord Vishnu.

Bharata's Dynasty: The text traces the lineage of King Bharata and his descendants, who continued to rule different regions in ancient India. The dynasty of Bharata played a significant role in the history and culture of the Indian subcontinent.

The Naming of Bharata: The chapter explains that India became known as "Bharata" in this dynasty. This name is still used today to refer to the country.

Role in Indian History: The chapter briefly mentions the contributions and historical significance of the Bharata dynasty in shaping the socio-political landscape of ancient India. Various kings and rulers from this dynasty played vital roles in the region's history.

Connection to Lord Rama: The text highlights that Lord Rama, an incarnation of Lord Vishnu, also appeared in the lineage of King Bharata. Lord Rama's life and actions are chronicled in the epic Ramayana, and He is revered as a symbol of righteousness and dharma.

Canto 9, Chapter 21, serves as a genealogical account that establishes the historical lineage of King Bharata and his descendants. It underscores the importance of the name "Bharata" as a reference to India and its connection to ancient Indian history and culture. Additionally, the chapter acknowledges the significance of Lord Rama's appearance in this dynasty, emphasizing His role as a divine incarnation and a beacon of righteousness and virtue in Hindu tradition.

09-22 The Descendants of Ajamidha

This chapter provides a genealogical account of the descendants of King Ajamidha, a historical figure in Indian mythology. The chapter traces the lineage of various kings and dynasties in ancient India.

Here is a summary of the key points from Canto 9, Chapter 22:

Introduction of King Ajamidha: The chapter introduces King Ajamidha, a virtuous and righteous ruler. He is listed as one of the descendants of King Bharata, whose dynasty has been discussed in previous chapters.

Ajamidha's Dynasty: The text traces the lineage of King Ajamidha and his descendants, who ruled different regions in ancient India. The chapter provides a chronological account of the rulers and dynasties from this lineage.

Role in Indian History: The chapter briefly mentions the contributions and historical significance of the dynasty of King Ajamidha in shaping the political and cultural landscape of ancient India. Various kings from this lineage played roles in the history of the subcontinent.

Connection to Lord Rama: The text highlights that Lord Rama, an incarnation of Lord Vishnu, also appeared in the lineage of King Ajamidha. Lord Rama's life and actions are celebrated in the epic Ramayana, and He is revered as a symbol of righteousness and dharma.

Canto 9, Chapter 22, serves as another genealogical account within the Srimad Bhagavatam, providing historical context and connecting the lineage of King Ajamidha to the broader narrative of Indian history and culture. The chapter acknowledges the significance of Lord Rama's appearance in this lineage, reinforcing His divine role in upholding dharma and virtuous living in Hindu tradition.

09-23 The Dynasties of the Sons of Yayati

This chapter provides a detailed genealogical account of the descendants of King Yayati, who was a prominent figure in Hindu mythology. As described in earlier chapters, Yayati's story is well-known for his youth exchange with his sons.

Here is a summary of the key points from Canto 9, Chapter 23:

Introduction of King Yayati: The chapter briefly reintroduces King Yayati, the son of King Nahusha and a descendant of King Pururava. Yayati's life and actions are mentioned as context for understanding his descendants and their roles in Indian history.

Yayati's Five Sons: The text recounts how King Yayati had five sons—Yadu, Turvasu, Druhyu, Anu, and Puru. These sons are central figures in the genealogy and history of ancient Indian dynasties.

Descendants of Yadu: The chapter provides a comprehensive account of the descendants of Yadu, one of Yayati's sons. The Yadu dynasty played a significant role in Indian history and produced notable rulers.

Descendants of Turvasu, Druhyu, Anu, and Puru: The text also traces the lineages of Yayati's other sons—Turvasu, Druhyu, Anu, and Puru. Each of these dynasties produced its line of kings and had a role in shaping the cultural and political landscape of ancient India.

Lord Krishna's Connection: The chapter mentions that Lord Krishna, an incarnation of Lord Vishnu, appeared in the Yadu dynasty, highlighting His significance in the context of this genealogy.

Canto 9, Chapter 23, serves as a detailed genealogical account that helps establish the historical lineage of King Yayati and his sons. It connects the broader narrative of Indian history and culture by tracing the descendants of Yayati and their respective contributions to the region's socio-political landscape. The chapter also acknowledges the importance of Lord Krishna's appearance in the Yadu dynasty, reinforcing His divine role in Hindu tradition.

09-24 Krsna the Supreme Personality of Godhead

This chapter provides a transcendental and philosophical description of Lord Krishna, regarded as the Supreme Personality of Godhead in Hinduism. It offers insights into His divine nature, activities, and significance in the spiritual realm.

Here is a summary of the key points from Canto 9, Chapter 24:

Glorification of Lord Krishna: The chapter begins with the praise and glorification of Lord Krishna as the ultimate source and controller of all existence.

The Form of the Lord: It describes Lord Krishna's transcendental form, which is beyond the material creation and is characterized by eternal bliss, knowledge, and beauty. His form is the embodiment of divine grace and charm.

Lord Krishna's Pastimes: The chapter discusses the various pastimes and activities of Lord Krishna during His incarnations on Earth. It highlights His role in uplifting humanity and reestablishing dharma (righteousness).

The Purpose of Krishna's Incarnations: It explains that Lord Krishna descends to the material world to protect the righteous, annihilate the wicked, and reestablish the principles of religion. His incarnations are acts of divine compassion and mercy.

Devotion to Lord Krishna: The text emphasizes the significance of devotional service (bhakti) to Lord Krishna as the most direct and effective path to spiritual realization and liberation. It describes how the love and devotion of His devotees bring Him great pleasure.

The Importance of Hearing about Krishna: The chapter highlights the importance of hearing and reading about the pastimes and glories of Lord Krishna. Hearing purifies the heart and strengthens one's devotion to the Supreme Lord.

Lord Krishna's Universal Form: It briefly mentions Lord Krishna's universal form, which encompasses the entire cosmos and reveals His omnipotent and all- encompassing nature.

Canto 10

10-01 The Advent of Lord Krishna

Canto 10, Chapter 1, also known as "Sri Krishna Janma" or "The Advent of Lord Krishna," narrates the divine birth of Lord Krishna. It is often called the Janmashtami episode, as it describes the circumstances surrounding Krishna's appearance.

The chapter begins with a description of the challenging circumstances in the kingdom of Mathura under the oppressive rule of King Kamsa. Kamsa was a cruel and unjust ruler destined to be killed by the eighth child of his sister, Devaki. As a result, he imprisoned Devaki and her husband Vasudeva to prevent this prophecy from coming true. Each time Devaki gave birth to a child, Kamsa would kill the baby.

The chapter then describes the momentous night when Lord Krishna, chose to descend to the earthly realm. At the stroke of midnight, Devaki gave birth to Krishna, and a series of miraculous events occurred. The prison doors opened independently, and Vasudeva, following divine guidance, carried the newborn Krishna across the river Yamuna to Gokul, where he would be raised by Nanda and Yashoda, his foster parents.

Upon reaching Gokul, Vasudeva exchanged baby Krishna with Yashoda's daughter, who had just been born. When he returned to the prison, the doors closed, and Kamsa remained unaware of Krishna's birth.

This chapter sets the stage for the subsequent chapters and cantos of the Srimad Bhagavatam, which detail the various enchanting and divine pastimes of Lord Krishna during his childhood and youth. It is a beloved section for devotees of Krishna and is often recited and celebrated during Janmashtami, the annual festival marking Krishna's birth.

10-02 Prayers by the Demigods

The chapter begins with a description of the circumstances following Lord Krishna's miraculous birth in the prison of King Kamsa. After the birth of Krishna and the subsequent exchange of babies, Vasudeva, filled with immense gratitude and devotion, returns to the prison with Yashoda's daughter, who is Krishna's sister, Yogamaya. As soon as Vasudeva returns with the baby girl, the prison doors close, and Kamsa remains unaware of the birth of Lord Krishna. Vasudeva offers prayers to Lord Krishna, recognizing him as the Supreme Lord and the source of all existence. He marvels at Krishna's transcendental nature and thanks him for appearing in the world to fulfil his divine mission.

The celestial demigods, who had been observing the events on Earth, were overjoyed at Krishna's appearance. They understood that Krishna had incarnated to relieve the Earth from the burden of demonic oppression and to protect the righteous. In their excitement and devotion, they descended to the prison cell and offered heartfelt prayers to the unborn Lord within Devaki's womb.

The prayers offered by the demigods are filled with praises for Krishna's various divine qualities and pastimes. They recognize him as the ultimate goal of all spiritual seekers and as the Supreme Personality of the Godhead who sustains and maintains the universe.

Prayers by the Demigods for Lord Krishna in the Womb

10-03 The Birth of Lord Krishna

Chapter 3 of the tenth canto begins with the continuation of the story after the demigods had offered their prayers to Lord Krishna in Devaki's womb. In response to the demigods' prayers, the Supreme Lord Krishna instructed Yogamaya (His divine energy) to transfer Him from Devaki's womb to that of Rohini, another wife of Vasudeva who lived in Gokul. This divine transfer happened seamlessly, ensuring Krishna's safety and enabling Him to grow up in Gokul under the loving care of Nanda and Yashoda.

Back in the prison cell in Mathura, Kamsa was still unaware of the birth of Lord Krishna due to the extraordinary events that had occurred. Instead, he believed that Devaki had suffered a miscarriage. He remained apprehensive about the prophecy that Devaki's eighth child would be his destroyer but remained ignorant of Krishna's existence.

Meanwhile, in Gokul, the residents celebrated the birth of Nanda and Yashoda's son, believing him to be their child. They were overjoyed and engaged in various festivities and rituals to welcome the newborn, who was none other than Lord Krishna. The chapter vividly describes the celebrations, the rituals performed by the cowherd community, and the sheer bliss that enveloped Gokul.

The divine nature of Krishna's appearance is emphasized in this chapter, as even the people of Gokul were unaware of His celestial origin. They saw Him as an ordinary child, unaware of His divinity. This aspect of Krishna's life is a recurring theme in his earthly pastimes, where he often behaves like an average human being while simultaneously displaying his divine powers.

10-04 The Atrocities of King Kamsa

The chapter begins with King Kamsa being informed about the birth of Devaki and Vasudeva's eighth child, destined to be his killer. Despite his earlier attempts to kill Devaki's children, all of them had been either miscarriages or stillborn, and he remained unaware of the divine nature of the child who was transferred to Gokul (Krishna).

Kamsa was deeply troubled by the prophecy, and fear consumed him. He called for his advisors, who warned him that the child he feared had already taken birth and was living in Gokul. In a fit of rage and anxiety, Kamsa summoned a wicked demoness named Putana and ordered her to kill all newborn babies in the kingdom, believing that one could be Lord Krishna. Putana, a formidable and deceptive demoness, followed Kamsa's orders. She assumed a beautiful form to deceive the residents of Gokul and gain access to their homes. She poisoned her breast and went from house to house, offering breast milk to the babies. When she reached the home of Nanda and Yashoda, she attempted to do the same to Krishna.

However, Lord Krishna, omniscient and all-powerful, recognized Putana's evil intentions. He revealed His divine nature as the Supreme Lord and protected the innocent. As Putana tried to feed Krishna her poisoned milk, He sucked the milk and her very life force. Putana, unable to escape Krishna's divine power, assumed her proper horrific form and collapsed, meeting her demise at the hands of the infant Krishna. The news of Krishna's sacred act quickly spread, leaving everyone in awe of His divine powers.

10-05 The Meeting of Nanda and Vasudeva

chapter begins with describing the ongoing atrocities of King Kamsa and his relentless attempts to eliminate Lord Krishna. After the failure of Putana's attempt to kill Krishna, Kamsa sent various other demons to Gokul to carry out his evil plans, all of whom were ultimately defeated by the divine infant.

While Krishna was successfully thwarting these demonic attacks, Vasudeva, Krishna's biological father, remained imprisoned in Mathura by Kamsa. Vasudeva was yearning to see his beloved son, whom he had not seen since the moment of Krishna's birth. He was also concerned about Krishna's safety and well-being in Gokul.

Meanwhile, in Gokul, Nanda Maharaja, Krishna's foster father, was aware that Krishna was not his biological son but had been entrusted to him by Vasudeva for protection. Nanda felt great affection and responsibility for Krishna and was concerned about the dangers of Kamsa's relentless pursuit.

The situation reached a critical point when Vasudeva was granted a brief release from his imprisonment to participate in a sacrifice organized by Kamsa. During this time, Nanda visited Mathura, hoping to meet Vasudeva and express his concern for Krishna's safety.

In Mathura, Nanda and Vasudeva had an emotional and heartwarming reunion. They shared their experiences and their deep love for Krishna. Vasudeva praised Nanda for his devoted care of Krishna and thanked him for protecting their divine child.

Vasudeva then revealed Krishna's true identity as the Supreme Lord, informing Nanda that Krishna had been sent to Earth to fulfil a divine mission. Nanda, overwhelmed by the realization that Krishna was the Supreme Lord Himself, offered prayers and respects to Vasudeva and Lord Krishna.

After their heartfelt meeting, Vasudeva returned to his imprisonment in Mathura, and Nanda returned to Gokul with a deeper understanding of Krishna's divine nature.

10-06 The Killing of the Demon Putana

The chapter begins with a continuation of the narrative about the tyrannical King Kamsa's relentless efforts to eliminate the infant Krishna. Learning that his previous attempts to kill Krishna had failed, Kamsa decided to employ more powerful and cunning demons to accomplish the task.

In this context, he summoned Putana, a formidable and deceitful demoness known for her ability to assume various forms and deceive people. Kamsa ordered Putana to kill all newborn babies in the kingdom, believing that one of them might be Lord Krishna.

Putana eagerly accepted Kamsa's mission and transformed herself into a beautiful young woman to deceive the residents of Gokul. She entered the village and went to the house of Nanda and Yashoda, where Krishna was living as their foster child.

Putana maliciously picked up the baby Krishna and offered her poisoned breast milk to Him. She hoped that this poison would kill Him. However, Lord Krishna, who is omniscient and all-powerful, recognized Putana's evil intentions and decided to reveal His divine nature.

As Putana attempted to feed Krishna, He sucked out the poisoned milk and her life force. Unable to escape Krishna's divine power, Putana revealed her proper horrific form and expanded in size. Still an infant, Krishna held onto her tightly, and she could not escape. Eventually, Putana met her demise as her gigantic form fell lifeless.

The residents of Gokul, who witnessed this extraordinary event, were both astonished and terrified. They realized that Krishna was no ordinary child and that He possessed divine powers far beyond their comprehension.

Canto 10, Chapter 6, underscores the divine nature of Lord Krishna from a very early age. It demonstrates His ability to protect His devotees and defeat evil forces effortlessly. The story of Putana's demise is an example of Krishna's divine mission to safeguard dharma (righteousness) and eliminate adharma (unrighteousness), as well as the extraordinary events that marked His presence on Earth.

10-07 The Killing of the Demon Trinavarta

The chapter begins with a description of the ongoing activities of Lord Krishna in Gokul, where He was living with His foster parents, Nanda and Yashoda, and performing various enchanting pastimes.

Meanwhile, in Mathura, King Kamsa grew increasingly desperate to eliminate Lord Krishna, who was destined to be his killer. Kamsa continued to send demons to Gokul with the hope of killing Krishna.

One such demon was Trinavarta, who was a powerful whirlwind demon. Trinavarta assumed a gigantic form and descended upon Gokul to take Krishna high into the sky and then drop Him to His death. The demon disguised himself as a whirlwind and approached the village.

Krishna, ever alert, recognized the danger posed by Trinavarta. As the demon approached, Krishna allowed Trinavarta to pick Him up. However, Krishna's divine powers immediately came into play. He expanded His body so Trinavarta could not carry Him far into the sky. Instead, Trinavarta was dragged down to the ground due to the weight of Krishna's divine form.

In the end, the demon Trinavarta met his demise as he crashed to the ground, his evil intentions thwarted by the divine power of Lord Krishna. The villagers rushed to the scene, astonished to see Krishna playing calmly atop the fallen demon's body.

10-08 Lord Krishna Shows the Universal Form

The chapter begins by describing Lord Krishna's playful activities as a young boy in Vrindavan. He is known for His charming and mischievous nature, and He often engages in pranks with His friends and fellow cowherd boys.

One day, Krishna and His friends enter the forest near Vrindavan to graze their cows. As they do so, Krishna's divine play takes a unique turn. While in the woods, the boys become hungry and consume their lunch. Krishna suggests that they eat their meal near the bank of the Yamuna River.

As they sit down to eat, Krishna and His friends notice that the trees and creepers in the forest have taken on a mystical appearance, and a sweet fragrance fills the air. Intrigued, they explore further and enter a grove that appears to be glowing with divine light.

Inside the grove, Krishna reveals His universal form (Vishvarupa) to His friends and the cowherd boys. This form is vast, all-encompassing, and contains countless universes, planets, and cosmic manifestations. It is a heavenly display of His divine nature as the Supreme Lord, showcasing His omnipotence and omnipresence.

Krishna's friends, initially bewildered and awestruck by this transcendental vision, are both amazed and fearful. They witness the universe, with its galaxies, gods, and celestial beings, all within Krishna's universal form. The boys see themselves and everything they know as part of Krishna's divine display.

Despite their fear, Krishna's friends are comforted when they see that Krishna's beautiful, childlike form is present within this universal manifestation. They realize their beloved Krishna, whom they love and play with daily, is indeed the Supreme Lord.

Amid this divine revelation, the cowherd boys experience awe, reverence, and love for Krishna. After a period, Krishna withdraws His universal form, returning to His usual, charming appearance. Deeply affected by this experience, the boys continue their playful activities with Krishna, now with an even greater understanding of His divine nature.

10-09 Mother Yashoda Binds Lord Krishna

The chapter begins with describing Lord Krishna's playful activities in the village of Vrindavan, where He grew up in the care of His foster parents, Nanda and Yashoda. Krishna is known for His mischievous and endearing behaviour, and He often engages in pranks with His friends and fellow cowherdboys.

On one particular day, the young Krishna and His friends enter a neighbour's courtyard to steal yoghurt, butter, and other sweets. Other villagers warned Yashoda about Krishna's antics, and she decided to take preventive measures.

Yashoda approached Krishna with a loving and affectionate demeanour and tried to discourage Him from entering the neighbour's house. She offered Him various delicious sweets and tried to divert His attention, but Krishna was determined to enjoy the butter and yoghurt hidden in the neighbour's home.

Eventually, Yashoda realized that her attempts to dissuade Krishna were in vain, and she decided to tie Him up with a rope, believing that this would prevent Him from causing further mischief. Yashoda fetched a rope from her house and approached Krishna, who was unaware of her intentions.

As Yashoda attempted to bind Krishna, she found that no matter how much she extended the rope, it was always just two fingers too short to encircle His waist fully. This action mystified Yashoda and filled her with wonder and love for her divine son.

In His playful and loving mood, Krishna allowed Himself to be bound by Yashoda, not with the rope of her effort but with the bond of her motherly love and devotion. The chapter describes the touching scene of Yashoda's loving attempt to bind Krishna and the profound realization that He is not an ordinary child but the Supreme Lord Himself.

Canto 10, Chapter 9, captures the essence of the divine play of Lord Krishna in Vrindavan and His unique relationship with His devotees, especially His mother, Yashoda. It showcases the beauty of unconditional love and devotion that transcends all external barriers and limitations.

10-10 The Deliverance of the Yamala-Arjuna Trees

On one occasion, Krishna and His friends, including Balarama, were herding cows in the woods. As they wandered deep into the forest, Krishna and Balarama noticed two gigantic Yamala-Arjuna trees. These trees had been cursed to remain in their current immobile form due to the result of their past deeds. Their souls were trapped within the trees, and they had been suffering for a very long time.

Krishna, being the Supreme Lord and the embodiment of compassion, was moved by the plight of these two souls. He decided to free them from their curse and grant them liberation. Krishna instructed His friends to bring a rope, and with the help of Balarama and the other cowherd boys, He attempted to pull down the trees.

Despite the massive size and weight of the trees, Krishna effortlessly uprooted them, causing a tremendous commotion. As the trees fell, two extraordinarily effulgent beings emerged from them. These beings were the original souls of the trees and were now free from their cursed condition.

These liberated souls, recognizing Lord Krishna as offered Him their heartfelt prayers and sought His blessings. They expressed gratitude for Krishna's mercy and asked Him to grant them a place in His eternal abode. In His divine compassion, Krishna assured the souls that they would attain a spiritual form suitable for entering His abode. He then disappeared into the forest, leaving the souls in spiritual bliss.

This chapter illustrates several essential themes in the Srimad Bhagavatam:

Krishna's compassion, devotion and divinity: It highlights Lord Krishna's boundless mercy and His willingness to go to great lengths to alleviate the suffering of His devotees and grant them liberation. The story emphasizes the significance of prayer and surrenders to the Supreme Lord. The Yamala-Arjuna trees were delivered from their cursed state due to their encounter with Krishna and devotion to Him. The incident reaffirms Krishna's divinity as the Supreme Lord, capable of performing miraculous acts even as a child.

10-11 The Childhood Pastimes of Krishna

This Chapter is a collection of several delightful and heartwarming stories from Krishna's childhood. These stories showcase the unique and intimate bond between Krishna and the residents of Vrindavan.

Binding of Krishna by Mother Yashoda: The chapter begins by describing how Mother Yashoda, out of love and concern for Krishna's safety, would often try to bind Him with ropes while He played. However, Krishna cleverly evades her efforts by running away or manifesting forms of other deities to confuse her. This endearing pastime highlights the playful and mischievous nature of Krishna.

Krishna's Complaints: On one occasion, Krishna approached Yashoda and complained that His playmates, the cowherd boys, were disturbing Him and spreading false accusations about His misdeeds. Krishna's innocent and playful complaints reflect His deep attachment to His friends.

Krishna's Imitation: The chapter narrates an incident where Krishna imitated the demigods and cows. He skillfully transformed Himself into a captivating representation of the universe, displaying all the planets and heavenly bodies. His astonishing display left the residents of Vrindavan astounded.

Krishna's Disappearance: In one playful episode, Krishna, along with His friends, would often hide and then reappear. Krishna would disguise Himself as someone else, leaving His friends puzzled. This pastime demonstrates Krishna's divine ability to captivate the hearts and minds of His devotees.

Krishna's Dancing: The chapter describes how Krishna would perform charming and captivating dances, often in the company of the cowherd girls, known as gopis. His dances and flute-playing would enchant the entire forest of Vrindavan, and the residents would gather to witness these divine performances.

Krishna's Stealing of Butter: Krishna's love for butter is well-known, and He would often sneak into the houses of the cowherd women to steal butter. The chapter narrates the delightful interactions between Krishna and the gopis as they playfully tried to protect their butter from Him.

10-12 The Killing of the Demon Aghasura

On one particular day, Krishna and His cowherd friends decided to explore the forests along the Yamuna River. As they ventured deeper into the woods, they came across a gigantic python-like demon named Aghasura. Aghasura was a brother of Putana, another demoness who had previously attempted to kill Krishna but was defeated by Him. Aghasura, having heard of his sister's defeat, harboured intense anger and malice towards Krishna and the cowherd boys. He assumed a massive form, lying in wait along their path. He planned to devour Krishna and His friends in one swift motion. As the boys entered the demon's open mouth, they noticed an unbearable foul odour and realized something was amiss. However, they continued walking deeper into the demon's mouth, thinking it was a cave or tunnel. They were shocked to see Aghasura's gigantic form, his mouth wide open and filled with rows of sharp teeth.

Krishna, understanding the danger, remained calm and fearless. He decided to deliver both His friends and Aghasura. He expanded Himself within Aghasura's body, causing the demon extreme pain and discomfort. Unable to bear the agony, Aghasura's life force was extinguished, and he fell lifeless. Krishna then assumed His original form and, with His divine potency, released His friends unharmed from Aghasura's body. Initially frightened, the cowherd boys soon realised that Krishna had saved them and were filled with gratitude and wonder.

This chapter illustrates several essential themes in the Srimad Bhagavatam: Krishna's compassion, divinity and Devotee relationships: It showcases Lord

Krishna's deep concern for His devotees and His ability to protect them from all dangers. Krishna's actions in this episode reaffirm His divine nature as the Supreme Lord who can effortlessly conquer even the most formidable demons. The episode emphasizes the loving and intimate bond between Krishna and His devotees, as the Cowherd boys completely trusted Him.

10-13 The Stealing of the Boys and Calves by Brahma

The chapter begins by describing a beautiful day in Vrindavan, where Lord Krishna and His friends (the cowherd boys) and their calves would often roam freely in the forest. His playful and mischievous nature marked Krishna's endearing childhood pastimes.

One day, Lord Brahma, the creator of the universe and a mighty demigod, decided to test Krishna's divinity. Brahma observed Krishna's enchanting pastimes and became intrigued that Krishna's friends and calves appeared to be mere expansions of Krishna Himself.

To test Krishna's divinity, Brahma decided to steal both the cowherd boys and the calves. He used his mystic powers to remove them from the earthly realm and conceal them temporarily. Brahma thought this action would bewilder Krishna and cause Him to reveal His true identity.

However, Lord Krishna, Godhead's Supreme Personality and the controller of all mystic powers, immediately understood Brahma's actions. Rather than becoming bewildered, Krishna responded with His divine potency. He expanded Himself into multiple forms, replicating each of the stolen boys and calves with an exact copy.

Krishna's replicated forms were so perfect that even the boys and calves could not distinguish them from their friends. This action continued for an entire year, according to earthly time, while Brahma kept the originals hidden in a cave.

After a year had passed, Brahma became increasingly perplexed and concerned about the welfare of the boys and calves. He returned to Vrindavan and was astounded to see that Krishna was still playing with the identical boys and calves as if nothing had happened. Brahma realized the extent of Krishna's divinity and understood He was the Supreme Lord, controlling everything within the universe.

Brahma, filled with humility and devotion, offered prayers to Lord Krishna and acknowledged his mistake. Krishna mercifully forgave Brahma and revealed His original forms, allowing Brahma to see the cowherd boys and calves still safe and sound in the cave.

10-14 Brahma's Prayers to Lord Krishna

The chapter begins with Lord Brahma, the creator of the universe and a mighty demigod, returning to Vrindavan after his year-long absence. Brahma was filled with awe and humility upon realizing the divinity and omnipotence of Lord Krishna, who had effortlessly duplicated the cowherd boys and calves when Brahma had temporarily hidden them. As Brahma arrived in Vrindavan, he saw Lord Krishna playing with the identical boys and calves as if nothing had happened. Krishna's divine nature was unmistakable, and the sight deeply moved Brahma.

Overwhelmed with devotion, Brahma offered Lord Krishna heartfelt and eloquent prayers. In these prayers, he acknowledged Krishna as the source of all creation and the ultimate universe controller. Brahma praised Krishna's divine qualities, including His compassion, mercy, and love for His devotees.

Brahma recognized that Krishna had expanded Himself into innumerable forms to perform His earthly pastimes while maintaining His position as the Supreme Lord in the spiritual world. He expressed gratitude for Krishna's merciful revelation and sought forgiveness for his audacious attempt to test the Lord's divinity.

Krishna acknowledged Brahma's devotion and understanding in His loving and compassionate manner. He assured Brahma that His divine pastimes in Vrindavan were meant to attract and bring spiritual realization to those who sincerely seek Him.

As a result of Krishna's will, Brahma's bewilderment was dispelled, and he realized that everything in the material and spiritual realms is ultimately controlled by Lord Krishna. He understood that Krishna's expansions, whether in the spiritual or material worlds, are entirely under His divine control.

The chapter concludes with Krishna, the cowherd boys, and the calves returning to their original forms, revealing their transcendental identities. Brahma witnessed this transformation and marvelled at Krishna's unparalleled supremacy.

10-15 The Killing of Dhenuka, the Ass Demon

The chapter begins by describing the serene and picturesque landscapes of Vrindavan, where Lord Krishna, along with His cowherd friends, would often graze their cows. The forests were filled with the sweet fragrance of blooming flowers, and the atmosphere was joyous.

One day, as Krishna and His friends roamed the forests of Vrindavan, they reached an area known as Talavana. This place was infested with demons who had taken the form of donkeys, and their leader was Dhenuka, a powerful and wicked demon.

As Krishna and His friends entered Talavana, they were immediately confronted by Dhenuka and his demon companions. In his donkey form, Dhenuka began to attack Krishna's friends, kicking them with great force. However, Lord Krishna, the Supreme Lord with unmatched strength, quickly overpowered Dhenuka.

Krishna grabbed Dhenuka by his hind legs and whirled him around, causing the demon to lose consciousness. Krishna then threw Dhenuka against a palm tree with such force that the demon's life was extinguished, and the tree was uprooted and shattered into pieces.

Upon witnessing Krishna's feat, the other demons in the form of donkeys charged at Him in anger. However, Krishna effortlessly defeated them individually, just as He had with Dhenuka. The demon attack left Krishna's friends and the residents of Vrindavan in awe of His divine powers.

After the battle, Krishna and His friends enjoyed the delicious fruits of Talavana without fear of the demon inhabitants. They relished the ripe fruits and considered their victory over Dhenuka and his associates a delightful pastime.

Canto 10, Chapter 15, is yet another example of Lord Krishna's divine prowess and His role as the protector of His devotees. It illustrates how Krishna fearlessly defeated the demons and brought peace and joy to the residents of Vrindavan. The episode adds to the rich tapestry of Krishna's childhood pastimes in Vrindavan, where He displayed His divine nature through playful interactions and heroic acts.

10-16 Krishna Chastises the Serpent Kaliya

The chapter begins with Lord Krishna, His friends, and the cows enter the Yamuna River to play. However, the water of the Yamuna becomes poisonous due to the presence of the evil serpent Kaliya.

When Krishna and His friends enter the river, they become affected by the poison, and the residents of Vrindavan become distressed.

Seeing the danger, Lord Krishna jumps into the river and begins to dance on the hoods of the multi-headed serpent Kaliya.

A fierce and dramatic battle takes place between Krishna and Kaliya. Krishna eventually subdues the serpent by dancing on its head and chastising it.

Kaliya's wives come forward to plead for mercy on behalf of their husbands. In His compassionate form, Krishna decides to spare Kaliya's life but banishes him from the Yamuna.

The chapter concludes with Kaliya and his family leaving the Yamuna River and the river's waters becoming pure and beneficial once again.

This chapter is a profound allegory for the triumph of divine intervention over evil forces and the importance of surrendering to the sacred. It is a significant episode in the life of Lord Krishna, illustrating His divine powers and His role as a protector of His devotees.

Please note that the Srimad Bhagavatam is a vast text; this summary only covers a small part. The entire scripture contains many stories and teachings that delve into various aspects of devotion and spirituality.

10-17 The Supreme Lord Agrees to Become Aditi's Son

The chapter begins with Aditi, the mother of the demigods (devas), approaching her husband, Kashyapa Muni. She expresses her concern about the oppression and suffering faced by the demigods due to the demon king Bali, who has become very powerful.

Aditi is distressed and seeks a solution to help the demigods regain their celestial kingdom and power. She desires to have Lord Vishnu as her son to protect and assist the demigods.

Kashyapa Muni, understanding her devotion and desire to serve Lord Vishnu, advises her to perform an extraordinary penance called "Payovrata." This penance involves observing austerities and worshipping Lord Vishnu with great devotion.

Aditi faithfully follows Kashyapa Muni's instructions and begins her penance. She engages in deep meditation and worship of Lord Vishnu, offering Him various prayers and offerings.

Pleased with Aditi's devotion and penance, Lord Vishnu appears before her. Aditi wants Him to become her son to protect the demigods.

Lord Vishnu agrees to Aditi's request and assures her that He will descend as her son to assist the demigods and restore their glory.

This chapter highlights the concept of divine intervention and the compassionate nature of Lord Vishnu. It also emphasizes the power of devotion and penance in seeking the protection and blessings of the sacred. Lord Vishnu promises to incarnate as Aditi's son, setting the stage for the subsequent narratives in the Srimad Bhagavatam, particularly the appearance of Lord Krishna on Earth.

As with many chapters in the Srimad Bhagavatam, this story carries deeper spiritual and philosophical meanings, illustrating the importance of seeking divine help and surrendering to the Supreme Lord in times of adversity.

10-18 Lord Balarama Slays the Demon Pralamba

The chapter begins with Lord Balarama and Lord Krishna, along with their friends and cowherd companions, playing near the Yamuna River. They are enjoying their childhood in the idyllic setting of Vrindavan.

While playing, they decide to have a friendly game of "who can jump the highest." In this game, they jump and delight in each other's feats.

Pralamba, a deceitful demon disguised as a cowherd boy, joins their group. He plans to harm Lord Balarama and take advantage of the situation.

When it's Lord Balarama's turn to jump, He takes a gigantic leap into the sky. At this moment, the demon Pralamba, who carries Lord Balarama on his shoulders, reveals his proper form. Pralamba's real intention is to kidnap Lord Balarama.

Lord Balarama realizes the demon's treachery and becomes furious. He increases His size and strength and proceeds to kill the monster.

Lord Balarama defeats Pralamba in a fierce battle. He strikes Pralamba with such force that the demon collapses to the ground, lifeless.

The demigods and the residents of Vrindavan witness this divine pastime and offer their prayers to Lord Balarama.

This chapter showcases the extraordinary strength and courage of Lord Balarama, an avatar of Lord Vishnu and the source of spiritual power and guidance. It also illustrates how the Supreme Lord, even in His childhood pastimes, deals with and defeats the forces of evil.

The Srimad Bhagavatam uses such stories to entertain and convey profound spiritual teachings, emphasizing the importance of seeking divine protection and guidance. This incident is one of many in Lord Krishna and Lord Balarama's childhood adventures, each carrying unique lessons and messages.

10-19 The Killing of the Demon Aghasura

The chapter begins with Lord Krishna and His cowherd friends, including His brother Balarama, entering the forest of Vrindavan with their cows to enjoy a picnic.

Aghasura, a powerful demon in the form of a giant serpent, had assumed the appearance of a massive, long-hooded python. He lay in wait in the forest with an evil intention.

As the children and cows proceed into the forest, they come across the massive form of Aghasura, which has created an illusion of appearing as an enticing cave. Unaware of the danger, the children enter the cave to play and enjoy their meal.

Aghasura, with his mouth wide open like a cave, swallows all the children, along with their cows, into his belly.

Inside Aghasura's belly, the children and cows find themselves in a dark and terrifying place. They are, however, under the loving and protective gaze of Lord Krishna.

Realizing the danger, Lord Krishna decides to reveal His divine form. He expands Himself within Aghasura's body, causing the demon great pain.

Unable to bear the agony, Aghasura succumbs to Lord Krishna's divine presence. He dies, and his enormous body falls to the ground.

Lord Krishna then unharmed all the children and cows from Aghasura's belly. They emerge safely and are overjoyed to see Krishna's miraculous feat.

This chapter illustrates the boundless mercy and divine power of Lord Krishna. It also emphasizes the importance of surrendering to the Supreme Lord despite insurmountable challenges. The story of Aghasura's defeat serves as a reminder of the protection and guidance that can be sought from the Lord during times of peril.

The Srimad Bhagavatam is rich in stories and teachings, each with spiritual significance and moral lessons.

10-20 The Rainy Season and Autumn in Vrindavan

The chapter begins with a description of the rainy season in Vrindavan. Rainy clouds fill the sky, and the peacocks and other birds sing melodiously in response to the rain. The rivers, lakes, and ponds are all full, and the entire land is lush and green.

Lord Krishna and His friends enjoy the rainy season in Vrindavan. They play various games, such as water sports, swinging on swings made of vines, and participating in mock battles.

The chapter also describes how Lord Krishna decorates Himself with peacock feathers and enjoys the sound of the peacocks' calls.

As the chapter progresses, it transitions into the autumn season, which is equally enchanting in Vrindavan. The trees are laden with fruits and flowers in autumn, filling the atmosphere with a sweet fragrance.

Lord Krishna continues His playful activities during autumn. He dances with the gopis (cowherd girls) and engages in the Rasa Lila, a divine dance with the gopis, a central theme in Lord Krishna's pastimes.

The chapter emphasizes the deep love and devotion the residents of Vrindavan have for Lord Krishna. Their interactions and activities show their pure affection and attachment to Him.

This chapter serves as a vivid portrayal of the natural beauty of Vrindavan and the blissful pastimes of Lord Krishna and His devotees during the rainy and autumn seasons. It underscores the idea that the Lord's presence enhances the beauty and joy of all seasons and that devotion and love for God can be expressed through various playful and devotional activities.

In the broader context of the Srimad Bhagavatam, these chapters depict the intimate and loving relationship between Lord Krishna and His devotees, highlighting the profound spiritual lessons embedded in His divine pastimes.

10-21 The Gopis Attracted by the Flute

The chapter begins by describing the setting of Vrindavan during the night. The moonlight bathes the land in a soft, silvery glow, and the air is filled with the sweet fragrance of blooming flowers.

Lord Krishna, known for His melodious flute playing, begins to play His flute in the forest. The sound of His flute is so captivating and enchanting that it draws the gopis' hearts.

The gopis, who are entirely devoted to Lord Krishna, hear the divine music of His flute and are immediately entranced. They leave their homes and families in the middle of the night to meet Krishna in the forest.

Overwhelmed by their love for Krishna, the gopis abandon all social norms and responsibilities to be with Him. Their passion for Krishna is described as selfless and all-consuming.

As the gopis reach the forest, they find Krishna and engage in the Rasa Lila, a divine dance with Him. This dance is not merely a physical act but a profound expression of their spiritual love and union with the Lord.

The gopis and Krishna dance together in the moonlit night, creating a celestial spectacle. Their love and devotion for Krishna are beyond worldly comprehension.

Lord Krishna, fully aware of the gopis' devotion, reciprocates with His divine love and grace. He expands Himself to be with each Gopi individually, making every one of them feel special.

This chapter of the Srimad Bhagavatam highlights divine love and devotion. The gopis' unwavering love for Lord Krishna and willingness to give up everything for His company demonstrate dedication. It teaches that true faith transcends worldly attachments and societal norms and is based on the intense desire to be close to the Divine.

The Rasa Lila, depicted in this chapter, is a profoundly spiritual and symbolic dance, illustrating the union of the individual soul (represented by the gopis) with the Supreme Soul (represented by Lord Krishna). It is considered one of the most profound and esoteric aspects of Lord Krishna's pastimes in Vrindavan.

10-22 Krishna Steals the Garments of the Unmarried Gopis

The chapter begins with Lord Krishna and the gopis participating in the traditional "Rasa Dance" during a full moon night. This dance is a divine and ecstatic expression of love and devotion between Krishna and the gopis. As the dance progresses, Krishna engages in a playful and mischievous pastime. He hides Himself from the gopis, who become anxious and search for Him in the moonlit forest. While hiding, Krishna reappears before the gopis, who are relieved to find Him. In His charming and charismatic manner, he gently addresses and teases them.

Then, Krishna playfully suggests that the gopis should surrender their clothes to Him as a sign of complete surrender and devotion. At first, the gopis hesitate but eventually agree, recognizing Krishna as the Supreme Lord and their beloved. The gopis remove their garments and hand them to Krishna. He mystically multiplies Himself to be present before each gopi individually and accepts their offerings. The gopis, now standing completely exposed, feel a mixture of embarrassment and devotion. Gopis fully surrender their hearts and selves to Krishna, recognizing that their love for Him transcends all social norms and modesty. After this playful exchange, Krishna returns the garments to the gopis, who dress themselves again.

The chapter concludes with Krishna and the gopis continuing their divine Rasa Dance, enveloped in the bliss of their spiritual union.

This chapter of the Srimad Bhagavatam is often seen as a symbolic representation of the soul's longing for union with the Divine. The gopis' willingness to give up everything, even their modesty, in their pursuit of Krishna symbolizes the idea that true devotion transcends worldly concerns and social conventions. It emphasizes the concept of complete surrender to the Supreme Lord out of pure love. The Rasa Dance is a profound and mystical expression of divine love and spiritual ecstasy, illustrating the intimate relationship between the individual soul and the Supreme Soul.

10-23 The Brahmanas' Wives Blessed

The chapter begins with the Brahmanas of Vrindavan performing a Vedic sacrifice known as the "yajna" with their wives. They are deeply devoted to Lord Krishna and have come to offer their prayers and seek His blessings.

During the yajna, the Brahmanas' wives ardently pray to Lord Krishna for His divine presence. They are eager to see Him and receive His blessings.

Lord Krishna, along with His friends, decides to fulfil the pure desires of these devoted women. He arrives at the sacrificial arena, and His presence immediately captivates everyone present.

The wives of the Brahmanas become ecstatic upon seeing Lord Krishna. They abandon formal rituals and social norms and rush to greet Him with great devotion and love.

Lord Krishna, recognizing the sincerity of their devotion, blesses the women by granting them His divine vision. He allows them to see Him in His universal, all-encompassing form, encompassing the entire cosmos.

The Brahmanas' wives behold this extraordinary vision of Krishna's universal form. They witness the entire creation within His body, experiencing a profound sense of oneness with the Supreme.

After this divine revelation, Lord Krishna blesses the women with the assurance that they will never forget and meditate upon this vision.

The chapter concludes with the Brahmanas' wives feeling immense gratitude and devotion toward Lord Krishna. They return to their homes with a deep sense of spiritual fulfilment.

This chapter of the Srimad Bhagavatam underscores the power of sincere devotion and the boundless compassion of the Lord. Lord Krishna, out of His love for His devotees, fulfils their deepest desires and grants them a vision of His universal form, revealing the interconnectedness of all beings and the divine nature of creation.

It emphasizes that devotion and love for God can transcend formal rituals and societal norms and that the Lord is always ready to bestow His blessings upon those who approach Him with a pure heart.

10-24 Worshiping Govardhana Hill

chapter begins with the residents of Vrindavan, mainly cowherds and farmers, preparing for their annual worship of the rain god, Lord Indra. It is customary to perform a grand sacrifice to Indra, believing it would ensure a bountiful harvest and protection from natural calamities.

Lord Krishna advises the residents that their devotion should be directed towards Govardhana Hill, abundant with natural resources and ample pasture for their cows. Krishna explains that instead of appeasing Lord Indra, they should perform a puja (ritual) to Govardhana Hill, who is non-different from Himself. He emphasizes that the hill deserves their worship as part of His divine creation. The residents of Vrindavan, guided by Krishna's words and their deep faith in Him, decide to follow His instructions. They gather various foods and offerings and arrange a grand festival to worship Govardhana Hill.

In a magnificent ceremony, the residents offer prayers and food to Govardhana Hill and seek its blessings for their well-being. Angered by abandoning his traditional worship, Lord Indra retaliates by sending a devastating rainfall and thunderstorm to flood Vrindavan. Lord Krishna, witnessing the distress of His devotees and the impending disaster, lifts Govardhana Hill with His little finger to provide shelter to the residents, cows, and other beings of Vrindavan. Lord Krishna holds Govardhana Hill aloft for seven days and nights, protecting everyone beneath it from the torrential rain and winds. Recognizing the futility of his actions and Lord Krishna's supremacy, Lord Indra eventually stops the rain and withdraws the storm.

The residents of Vrindavan, filled with gratitude and awe, understand the true divinity of Lord Krishna and His power over the demigods. They return to their daily lives with enhanced faith and devotion.

This chapter is a profound lesson in surrendering to the Supreme Lord and recognizing that true worship should be directed towards Himself rather than intermediary deities. It illustrates Lord Krishna's boundless love and protection to His devotees. The lifting of Govardhana Hill by Krishna symbolizes His role as the ultimate shelter and protector of those who take refuge in Him.

10-25 The Three Worlds Merged in Gokula

chapter begins with Lord Krishna instructing the residents of Vrindavan to perform the Govardhana Puja, a festival to worship Govardhana Hill. This chapter continues the events from the previous chapter, where Krishna advised them to worship the hill instead of the demigod Indra. Following Krishna's guidance, the residents prepare an elaborate feast and offer it to Govardhana Hill with great devotion. They perform rituals and prayers to express gratitude and love for the hill and Krishna.

Pleased with the residents' devotion, Lord Krishna expands Himself into a gigantic, all-encompassing form. In this divine form, He accepts the offerings made to Govardhana Hill. Lord Krishna then manifests the entire Govardhana Hill within Himself. He merges the hill into His form, signifying His all-pervading presence and the oneness of the material and spiritual worlds. As the residents of Vrindavan gaze upon this astonishing spectacle, they witness the entire universe, including the three worlds (heaven, earth, and the netherworld), merged within the body of Krishna.

This divine vision reveals the absolute truth about Lord Krishna's supreme position as the source and controller of all creation. It emphasizes His intangible nature and the interconnectedness of everything within Him.

The residents of Vrindavan, overwhelmed with wonder and love for Krishna, realize that their beloved Lord is none other than the Supreme Personality of Godhead. Their faith and devotion deepen further.

After some time, Lord Krishna resumes His original, intimate form and returns the offerings to the residents. The festival continues with joy and festivity; everyone partakes in the prasad (blessed food) with spiritual fulfilment.

This chapter underscores the central theme of devotion and surrenders to Lord Krishna. It highlights His omnipotence and His ability to manifest the entire cosmos within Himself. The merging of the three worlds into Krishna's divine form symbolizes that everything is ultimately interconnected and sustained by the Supreme Lord. The Govardhana Puja episode demonstrates Krishna's divine identity and the importance of recognizing and surrendering to the Supreme Lord in all aspects of life.

10-26 Wonderful Krishna

The chapter begins with the residents of Vrindavan marvelling at the wondrous feats of Lord Krishna. They discuss and celebrate His extraordinary abilities and divine nature.

The cowherd boys, Krishna's friends, enthusiastically share stories of His miraculous deeds. These include instances where Krishna effortlessly lifted Govardhana Hill and saved the residents from Indra's wrath and other incidents demonstrating His superhuman strength.

As the stories unfold, the residents of Vrindavan express their profound amazement and love for Krishna. They recognize Him as the Supreme Lord who has descended to bless and protect them.

The gopis (cowherd girls), in particular, express their awe and devotion to Krishna. They recounted incidents where Krishna demonstrated love and affection for them, such as playful pranks and the Rasa Lila dance.

The chapter highlights Krishna's role as the ultimate object of devotion and love, drawing everyone in Vrindavan closer to Him through their admiration and astonishment at His divine pastimes.

It also emphasizes the deep bond of friendship and love among the cowherd boys and the gopis, who cherish their relationship with Krishna and consider Him the most precious treasure in their lives.

Throughout the chapter, Lord Krishna's extraordinary qualities, including His compassion, beauty, and charm, are celebrated by the residents of Vrindavan.

This chapter serves as a celebration of Lord Krishna's divinity and His role as the Supreme Personality of Godhead. It illustrates the power of love and devotion in drawing individuals closer to God and recognizing His divine nature. The stories and experiences shared by the residents of Vrindavan reinforce the Bhagavatam's central message: to seek a deep, loving relationship with the Supreme Lord, Krishna, and to understand His transcendental nature through His pastimes and attributes.

10-27 Lord Indra and Mother Surabhi Offer Prayers

The chapter begins with Lord Indra realizing his mistake of becoming prideful and angry when the residents of Vrindavan, under Lord Krishna's guidance, stopped worshipping him and honoured Govardhana Hill.

Lord Indra acknowledges his arrogance and the futility of his actions. He understands that Lord Krishna is the Supreme Personality of Godhead and the ultimate controller of all cosmic affairs.

Feeling remorseful and humbled, Lord Indra approaches Lord Krishna in Vrindavan to seek His forgiveness and blessings.

Lord Indra arrives in Vrindavan and offers heartfelt prayers to Lord Krishna, acknowledging His divine qualities and supreme power. He seeks forgiveness for his offences and asks for Krishna's mercy.

Mother Surabhi, a celestial cow, arrives in Vrindavan and offers her prayers to Lord Krishna. She glorifies Krishna as the source of all nourishment, the protector of cows, and religious principles.

Lord Krishna accepts and forgives Lord Indra's prayers in His compassionate and forgiving nature. He also appreciates Mother Surabhi's devotion and praises her.

The residents of Vrindavan witness this exchange between Lord Krishna, Lord Indra, and Mother Surabhi, recognizing the supreme position of Lord Krishna and the futility of material pride and ego.

This chapter highlights the themes of humility, forgiveness, and devotion. Lord Indra's realization of his pride and sincere prayers to Lord Krishna serve as a lesson in humility and surrender before the Supreme Lord. Mother Surabhi's prayers emphasize cows' sacredness and association with the divine.

It also underscores the importance of recognizing Lord Krishna as the ultimate protector and sustainer of all life forms, including cows, and the significance of devotion and surrender in one's spiritual journey.

10-28 Lord Krishna Rescues Nanda Maharaja

chapter begins with the residents of Vrindavan preparing for a great festival to worship Lord Indra. They have decided to resume the tradition of offering sacrifices to Indra after Lord Krishna convinced them to focus their devotion on Govardhana Hill in a previous chapter.

Nanda Maharaja, Krishna's foster father, organises the festival in honour of Lord Indra. The residents of Vrindavan, following tradition, make elaborate arrangements for the worship. However, Lord Krishna reveals His supreme power by knowing the true nature of Indra's pride and desire to protect His devotees from unnecessary rituals.

Lord Krishna lifts Govardhana Hill with the little finger of His left hand. He holds it aloft like an umbrella to protect the residents of Vrindavan from the torrential rains and thunderstorms sent by Lord Indra in response to the cessation of his worship. Lord Indra's attempts to inundate Vrindavan are futile in the face of Krishna's divine power. Realizing his mistake and the supremacy of Lord Krishna, Indra withdraws the storm.

The residents of Vrindavan are filled with awe and gratitude for Lord Krishna's protection. They understand that Krishna is the Supreme Lord, the ultimate shelter and protector of His devotees.

After some time, Lord Krishna returns Govardhana Hill to its original position. The festival continues, but now, the residents of Vrindavan worship Krishna as the Supreme Lord and their ultimate refuge. Although Lord Indra feels embarrassed by his previous actions, he acknowledges Lord Krishna's greatness and supremacy and seeks forgiveness.

This chapter emphasizes the supremacy of Lord Krishna and the importance of surrendering to Him. It illustrates that true devotion is not tied to ritualistic practices but is rooted in love and dependence on the Supreme Lord.

The lifting of Govardhana Hill demonstrates Krishna's divine power and willingness to protect His devotees from all adversities. It also serves as a lesson in humility for Lord Indra, who comes to recognize the futility of his pride and ego in the presence of the Supreme Lord.

10-29 Krishna and the Gopis Meet

The chapter begins with Lord Krishna playing His flute on the banks of the Yamuna River during a moonlit night. His melodious music captivates the gopis' hearts, who sincerely love Him. The gopis, unable to resist Krishna's call, leave their homes and families behind to join Him in the forest. Their love for Krishna is so intense that it compels them to follow the sound of His flute, transcending all worldly considerations. When the gopis reach Krishna, they are filled with ecstasy and love. They express their longing and devotion to be with Him and engage in the Rasa Lila, a divine dance that symbolizes the soul's quest for union with the Supreme.

Lord Krishna, fully aware of the gopis' love and devotion, participates in the Rasa Lila with them. He expands Himself into multiple forms to dance individually with each gopi, simultaneously fulfilling their desire for personal connection.

The gopis experience a profound spiritual union with Krishna as the Rasa Lila progresses. Their love for Him is pure and selfless, devoid of material desires. It represents the highest form of devotion, known as bhakti. The entire Rasa Lila transcends time, and it seems the night extends endlessly, providing the gopis and Krishna with an eternal experience of divine love and bliss.

The chapter emphasizes that Lord Krishna, Godhead's Supreme Personality, reciprocates with His devotees' love and devotion. He manifests Himself in countless forms to engage in intimate relationships with each of them.

This chapter of the Srimad Bhagavatam is considered one of the text's most profound and spiritually significant portions. It illustrates the pinnacle of devotion and the intimate relationship between the individual soul (represented by the gopis) and the Supreme Soul (represented by Lord Krishna). The Rasa Lila is a powerful symbol of the soul's longing for union with the divine and the boundless love and compassion that the Supreme Lord bestows upon His devotees.

10-30 The Gopis' Songs of Separation

chapter begins with Lord Krishna enjoying the Rasa Lila dance with the gopis on the banks of the Yamuna River during a moonlit night. The dance is filled with love and devotion, and Krishna reciprocates with the gopis' feelings. Suddenly, Lord Krishna mysteriously disappears from the dance. The gopis, deeply absorbed in His divine presence, are left in shock and anguish.

In Krishna's absence, the gopis express their profound love and longing for Him through beautiful songs and prayers. They sing of their intense separation and yearning to be reunited with Krishna. The gopis' songs convey their deep emotions, describing how their lives have become meaningless without Krishna's presence. They express their willingness to give up everything for Him.

The gopis recall their earlier encounters with Krishna and the joy they experienced in His company. They express their feelings of abandonment and bewilderment at His disappearance. These songs of separation reveal the depths of the gopis' love for Krishna and their complete surrender to Him. Their intense devotion and longing exemplify the highest form of spiritual love and affection, "vipralambha bhava."

Lord Krishna, who is always aware of the gopis' feelings, eventually reappears before them, and their joy knows no bounds. The divine dance continues with even greater intensity and devotion.

This chapter highlights the concept of "Vipralambha-Seva," the devotional service characterized by intense feelings of separation from the beloved Lord. It emphasizes that devotion, union and separation from God are crucial in deepening one's love and attachment to the Supreme.

The gopis' songs and expressions of separation underscore the idea that longing and pining for God can intensify one's devotion and ultimately lead to a more profound spiritual connection with the Divine. It serves as a reminder that true passion transcends material desires and attachments, focusing solely on the yearning for union with the Supreme Lord.

10-31 The Gopis' Song of Separation

In this chapter, the cowherd women of Vrindavan, known as the gopis, express their deep love and longing for Lord Krishna when He leaves the village to go to Mathura.

The Setting: The chapter takes place in the pastoral village of Vrindavan, where Lord Krishna grew up. The gopis of Vrindavan, who were deeply devoted to Krishna, are the central characters.

Krishna's Departure: Lord Krishna, spending his childhood and early youth in Vrindavan, departs for Mathura to fulfil his divine mission. This departure causes immense grief and separation anxiety among the gopis, who are deeply attached to Him.

The Gopis' Expressions of Love: The gopis gather together and sing a heartfelt song of separation. Their music describes their love for Krishna, the pain of His absence, and their yearning to be reunited with Him. Their emotions are so intense that they are considered the epitome of devotion and love in the Bhakti tradition.

The Philosophical Significance: The Gopis' Song of Separation is not just a depiction of intense emotional love but also carries profound philosophical and spiritual messages. It illustrates the concept of "bhakti" (devotion) and the idea that the most profound spiritual connection with the Divine is through intense love and yearning for God.

Krishna's Response: Lord Krishna eventually returns to Vrindavan, and the gopis are overjoyed to be reunited with Him. This episode emphasizes the reciprocity of divine love, where the devotee's love for God and God's love for the devotee are inseparable.

Canto 10, Chapter 31 of the Srimad Bhagavatam is a poignant and profound portrayal of divine love, devotion, and the intense longing for the Supreme Being. It is considered a pinnacle of devotional literature and is often recited and studied by devotees seeking to deepen their spiritual connection with Lord Krishna.

10-32 The Reunion

In this chapter, there is a joyful and emotional reunion between Lord Krishna and the gopis.

Krishna's Return to Vrindavan: Lord Krishna left Vrindavan to fulfil various divine missions in the previous chapters. He had gone to Mathura, where he killed many demons and ultimately established the Yadu dynasty. However, the gopis of Vrindavan were heartbroken and in deep separation from Krishna.

The Gopis' Longing: The gopis of Vrindavan had intensely yearned for Krishna's return during His absence. Their love and devotion for Him were unwavering, and their hearts were filled with the pain of separation.

Krishna's Compassion: Understanding the depth of the gopis' devotion and the anguish of their separation, Lord Krishna, known for His boundless compassion, decides to return to Vrindavan.

The Gopis' Joyful Reunion: As Lord Krishna returns to Vrindavan, the gopis are overjoyed. Their joy knows no bounds as they see their beloved Krishna once again. They run to Him with great excitement and love. This reunion is a poignant and emotional moment in the Bhagavatam, symbolizing the bliss of a devotee's union with the Divine.

Krishna consoles them for the pain of His separation. He appreciates their unwavering devotion and assures them of His eternal love and presence in their hearts.

Dance of Divine Love: In their ecstatic joy, Lord Krishna and the gopis engage in a divine dance known as the "Rasa Lila." This dance symbolises the godly play and the intimate relationship between God and the devotee. It transcends the physical and represents the union of the individual soul with the Supreme Soul.

The Mysterious Nature of God: The chapter also highlights the mysterious nature of the Divine. Lord Krishna, can simultaneously expand Himself to dance individually with each gopi during the Rasa Lila, demonstrating God's infinite and omnipresent nature.

10-33 The Rasa Dance

This chapter continues the narrative surrounding Lord Krishna's pastimes in the village of Vrindavan. Specifically, it focuses on one of Hindu mythology's most famous and spiritually significant episodes: the Rasa Lila.

Setting: The chapter takes place in the enchanting forest of Vrindavan on a whole moon night. Lord Krishna, who had returned to Vrindavan after a period of separation from the gopis (cowherd women), decides to perform the Rasa Lila, a divine dance.

The Rasa Lila: The Rasa Lila is a mystical and divine dance performed by Lord Krishna with the gopis. It is a profoundly spiritual and symbolic dance representing the highest level of divine love and union between the individual soul (the gopis) and the Supreme Soul (Lord Krishna). In this chapter, Lord Krishna expands Himself into multiple forms, allowing each Gopi to experience His presence individually. These multiple divine forms are to engage in the dance with each gopi simultaneously. This mystical aspect of the Rasa Lila highlights Krishna's omnipotence and His ability to reciprocate personally with each devotee.

The Gopis' Love and Devotion: The gopis are wholly absorbed in their love for Krishna, and their devotion is unparalleled. Their love is selfless, pure, and unconditional. As they dance with Krishna, they experience the highest spiritual ecstasy, transcending all worldly concerns.

Divine Intoxication: During the Rasa Lila, the gopis are described as becoming intoxicated with divine love. Their love for Krishna is so profound that they lose all sense of self and ego, merging their consciousness with the sacred.

Symbolism and Philosophy: The Rasa Lila is not merely a physical dance but a symbolic representation of the spiritual journey. It signifies the soul's longing for union with the Divine and the ultimate fulfilment of that desire. It also illustrates the concept of "bhakti," or holy love, as the highest path to God's realization.

Krishna's Benevolence: The chapter emphasizes Krishna's compassion and love for His devotees. He reciprocates with the gopis' devotion and fulfils their deepest spiritual desires.

10-34 Nanda Maharaja Saved and Shakatasura Slain

This chapter continues the narrative of Lord Krishna's childhood pastimes in the village of Vrindavan. It primarily focuses on two significant events: Nanda Maharaja's rescue and the demon Shakatasura's slaying.

Nanda Maharaja's Predicament: The chapter begins with Nanda Maharaja, Lord Krishna's foster father, being trapped in a gigantic tree by the demon Shakatasura. The monster had taken the form of a cart and fallen upon Nanda Maharaja, rendering him unconscious and immobile.

Krishna's Childhood Exploits: Lord Krishna, a young child at the time, was playing nearby with His friends when He heard about Nanda Maharaja's predicament. Krishna is portrayed as the all-powerful Supreme Lord who performs extraordinary feats even as a child.

Krishna's Rescue of Nanda Maharaja: Krishna comes to the rescue of Nanda Maharaja. With His divine strength, He effortlessly lifts the massive cart and frees Nanda Maharaja, saving him from danger. This incident highlights Krishna's divine nature and His role as the protector of His devotees.

Shakatasura's Demise: After saving Nanda Maharaja, Lord Krishna turns His attention to the demon Shakatasura, who had assumed the form of a cart. Krishna quickly realizes the demon's true identity and effortlessly kills him by overturning the cart. This event demonstrates Krishna's divine prowess and His role as the destroyer of evil forces.

Reunion with the Cowherd Boys: Krishna's friends, the Cowherd boys, who were initially frightened by the demon's appearance, are amazed and joyful to see Krishna's heroic actions. They celebrate Krishna's courage and are grateful for His protection.

The Astonishment of the Onlookers: The residents of Vrindavan, including Nanda Maharaja and the cowherd women, are astonished and filled with wonder at Krishna's divine deeds. They recognize that Krishna is not an ordinary child but the Supreme Lord Himself.

10-35 The Gopis Sing of Krishna

The Gopis' Love: The chapter begins with the gopis expressing their love for Lord Krishna. They are deeply attached to Krishna and long for His company. Their passion for Krishna is pure, selfless, and unconditional.

Krishna's Playful Nature: The gopis describe Krishna's playful and mischievous activities in the forest of Vrindavan. They recall how Krishna, as a young boy, would engage in various delightful pastimes with His friends, such as playing on swings, stealing butter, and herding cows. The gopis sing about Krishna's enchanting fluteplaying. They mention how Krishna's melodious flute captivates not only their hearts but the hearts of all living beings in the forest. The sound of Krishna's flute symbolises the call of the Divine, attracting souls towards Him.

The Gopis' Longing: The gopis express their intense desire to be with Krishna. They describe how separation from Him is unbearable and that every moment without Krishna feels like an eternity. The Gopis' love for Krishna goes beyond the mundane. They have attained a high level of spiritual realization. Their longing for Krishna is seen as symbolic of the soul's yearning for union with the Divine.

Krishna's Universal Form: The gopis describe how they perceive Krishna's universal form while meditating upon Him. They see Krishna as the Supreme Being who encompasses the cosmos, yet they love Him as their intimate friend and beloved.

The Gopis' Prayer: The chapter concludes with the gopis praying to Krishna, expressing their unwavering devotion, and requesting Him to remain with them always. They surrender completely to Krishna, acknowledging Him as their ultimate refuge.

Canto 10, Chapter 35 of the Srimad Bhagavatam is a beautiful portrayal of the deep love and devotion of the gopis for Lord Krishna. It highlights the spiritual significance of their love and their realization of Krishna's divinity. The chapter also emphasizes that the path to God's completion is through intense devotion and surrender to the Supreme Being, as exemplified by the Gopis' devotion to Krishna. This devotion is a central theme in the Bhakti tradition of Hinduism and serves as a source of inspiration for devotees.

10-36 The Slaying of the Demon Putana

This chapter narrates an essential episode from Lord Krishna's childhood in Vrindavan, where He defeats the demoness Putana. This episode is significant as it highlights Krishna's divine nature and His role as a protector of His devotees.

Here's a summary of the key points in Canto 10, Chapter 36:

Putana's Evil Intent: The chapter introduces Putana, a demoness who can change her form at will. Putana was sent by the wicked King Kamsa, who feared Lord Krishna and wanted to eliminate Him. Disguised as a beautiful woman, Putana approached the residents' homes of Vrindavan with evil intentions.

Putana's Deceptive Approach: Putana's disguise was so convincing that the residents of Vrindavan, including Lord Krishna's mother, Yashoda, were deceived by her appearance. They allowed her to approach baby Krishna.

Krishna's Divine Knowledge: even as an infant, Lord Krishna was aware of Putana's evil intent. He knew she intended to kill Him, but He did not show any fear. Krishna Sucks Putana's Life: As Putana picked up baby Krishna and offered Him her poisoned breast, Krishna sucked her milk and her life force. He exhibited His divine power by reducing Putana's enormous size and killing her. Putana, in her proper form, was revealed as a monstrous demoness.

The Demonic Revelation: The residents of Vrindavan, including Yashoda and the other gopis, were astonished to witness this divine feat. They realized their beloved Krishna was not an ordinary child but the Supreme Lord.

Cremation of Putana: After her death, Putana's body was so poisonous that it contaminated the entire area. The demoness's body grew so large that it had to be cremated on a massive scale, symbolizing the eradication of evil forces.

Krishna's Benevolence: This episode illustrates Krishna's compassion and his role as a protector of devotees. He saved the residents of Vrindavan from the threat of Putana and demonstrated His divine powers even as an infant.

10-37 The Gopis' Feelings of Separation

The chapter begins with the Gopis (cowherd girls of Vrindavan) expressing their intense love and longing for Lord Krishna. They are deeply attached to Krishna and feel great separation from Him when He is not present with them. Their passion for Krishna is pure and selfless, and they consider Him the centre of their existence.

As the night progresses, the Gopis sing and dance in the forest of Vrindavan, thinking of Krishna and hoping for His return. Their love for Krishna is so strong that it transcends ordinary human emotions. They share their feelings and describe how Krishna's enchanting flute music has captured their hearts.

Lord Krishna, fully aware of the Gopis' devotion and longing, eventually appears before them. His divine presence brings immense joy and relief to the Gopis. Krishna acknowledges their dedication and reassures them of His love and presence in their hearts.

The chapter beautifully describes the divine love and devotion between Lord Krishna and the Gopis. It highlights the concept of bhakti (devotion) and the idea that sincere and selfless devotion to God can lead to a deep and personal connection with the divine.

Overall, Canto 10, Chapter 37 of the Srimad Bhagavatam is a poetic and spiritually rich portrayal of the intense love and longing of the Gopis for Lord Krishna and His reciprocation of their devotion. Hindu literature considers it a profound expression of divine love and passion. It is often studied and recited by devotees to deepen their understanding of the path of devotion to God.

10-38 Akrura's Arrival in Vrindavan

The chapter begins with Akrura preparing to leave Mathura, King Kamsa's capital, for Vrindavan. Kamsa gives him specific instructions to bring Lord Krishna and Lord Balarama back to Mathura under the pretext of inviting them to a grand wrestling match, where Kamsa plans to kill them.

As Akrura embarks on his journey, he reflects on the wickedness of King Kamsa and the virtuous nature of Lord Krishna and Lord Balarama. He is filled with anticipation and devotion, hoping to have the Lord's darshan (divine sight) in Vrindavan.

Upon reaching Vrindavan, Akrura is welcomed by the residents of the village. He notices the extraordinary love and devotion of the cowherd boys and girls for Krishna and Balarama. He also witnesses the natural beauty of Vrindavan and the divine atmosphere permeating the land.

Akrura finally arrives at the home of Nanda Maharaja and Yasoda, the foster parents of Krishna. He is warmly received by them and invited to rest and refresh himself. Meanwhile, he eagerly awaits the opportunity to meet Lord Krishna.

As the chapter unfolds, Akrura is granted a divine vision by Lord Krishna. He sees the Lord's universal form (Vishvarupa), which encompasses the cosmos and all living beings. This vision profoundly impacts Akrura, who realizes the absolute divinity of Krishna.

The chapter ends with Akrura offering prayers to Lord Krishna, recognizing Him as the Supreme Personality of Godhead. Akrura expresses his unwavering devotion and surrenders himself entirely to Krishna's will, willing to carry out the mission Kamsa gave but with complete detachment from material desires.

Canto 10, Chapter 38 of the Srimad Bhagavatam is significant because it showcases the purity of Akrura's devotion and allows Lord Krishna to reveal His divine nature through the vision granted to Akrura. This chapter serves as a reminder of the transformative power of religious association and the importance of surrendering to the will of the Supreme Lord.

10-39 Akrura's Vision

This chapter is notable for the profound spiritual experience Akrura undergoes upon reaching Vrindavan. Here is a summary:

Akrura's Arrival in Vrindavan: The chapter begins with Akrura arriving in Vrindavan. He is filled with anticipation and eagerness to meet Lord Krishna and Lord Balarama. As he enters Vrindavan, he observes the enchanting beauty of the land and is struck by the pure devotion of the residents, who love Krishna with their hearts and souls.

Akrura's Inner Conflict: Akrura, while on his way to Nanda Maharaja's house to meet Krishna and Balarama, experiences an inner conflict. He understands that the wicked King Kamsa has sent him to bring the two brothers to Mathura for a sinister purpose, which troubles his conscience. However, he also yearns to see the divine forms of Krishna and Balarama.

Akrura's Purity of Heart: Akrura's internal struggle reflects his purity of heart and devotion. He contemplates the nature of Lord Krishna as the Supreme Personality of Godhead. He feels grateful for having the opportunity to be in His presence, even if it means carrying out Kamsa's orders.

Akrura's Vision of the Divine: As Akrura continues, he suddenly witnesses an extraordinary vision. He sees Lord Krishna and Lord Balarama as the ultimate Supreme Beings, manifesting a dazzling and universal form. This divine vision reveals the cosmic nature of Krishna and Balarama and their role in maintaining the universe.

Akrura's Prayers: Overwhelmed by this divine revelation, Akrura offers heartfelt prayers to Lord Krishna, acknowledging Him as the source of all creation and the ultimate shelter for all living beings. He recognizes Krishna as the Supreme Brahman and the ultimate goal of all spiritual seekers.

Krishna's Response: Lord Krishna is pleased with Akrura's devotion and humility. He acknowledges Akrura's pure intentions and tells him he will soon fulfil his mission by going to Mathura with him. Krishna assures Akrura that his devotion will bring him liberation.

10-40 Krishna Teases Brahma

Here is a summary of the chapter:

Krishna's Friends and Calves Disappear: In this chapter, the story begins with Lord Krishna, who, along with His cowherd friends and calves, goes to the forest of Vrindavan for a picnic. While enjoying their time, Krishna and all the cowherd boys and calves suddenly disappear.

Brahma's Confusion: Lord Brahma, the creator of the universe, notices the disappearance of Krishna's friends and the calves. He becomes bewildered and is unable to locate them anywhere in the forest. Unknown to Brahma, Lord Krishna has temporarily hidden the cowherd boys and calves within Himself through His divine mystic power. He does this to teach Brahma a lesson about His unlimited transcendental potency.

Brahma's Surprise: Brahma returns to the spot where he initially noticed the disappearance and is astonished to find that the identical cowherd boys and calves are present again. He realizes that this feat is beyond human or even demigod capabilities. Brahma's confusion and bewilderment lead him to realise that Krishna is the Supreme Lord, the ultimate source of everything, and the cause of all causes. He understands that Krishna's actions are part of His divine leela (pastimes).

Brahma's Prayers: Filled with awe and reverence, Lord Brahma offers eloquent prayers extolling the greatness and omnipotence of Lord Krishna. He acknowledges Krishna's supremacy over all living beings and the entire creation. Pleased with Brahma's prayers and understanding, Lord Krishna reveals His divine opulence to Brahma, displaying His universal form (Vishvarupa). Brahma witnesses countless universes, planets, and manifestations within Krishna's transcendental body.

Krishna's Benediction: After showing His universal form, Krishna reassures Brahma and forgives him for his momentary bewilderment. He promises to return the cowherd boys and calves to their original forms.

Reunion: Krishna fulfils His promise by returning the cowherd boys and calves to their original state, bringing immense joy and relief to Brahma.

10-41 Krishna Blesses Kubja

chapter narrates an endearing and spiritually significant episode from the life of Lord Krishna during His childhood in Vrindavan. It focuses on Krishna's interaction with Kubja, a hunchbacked woman, and the transformation she experiences through her devotion to the Lord.

Kubja's Introduction: Kubja, a hunchbacked and deformed woman, lived in Mathura when Lord Krishna resided there. Despite her physical deformity, Kubja possessed a pure and devoted heart. She was aware of Krishna's divine nature and longed to meet Him.

Krishna's Arrival: One day, Lord Krishna, along with His elder brother Balarama, visits Kubja's neighbourhood while playing in Mathura. Kubja seizes this opportunity to invite the Lord into her home.

Kubja's Devotion: Overwhelmed with love and devotion, Kubja offers sandalwood paste to Krishna and Balarama and various fragrant oils. She also brings them some fruits as a gesture of her deep reverence.

Krishna's Divine Playfulness: Lord Krishna, known for His playfulness and affection for His devotees, decides to bless Kubja. He asks her to apply the sandalwood paste to His body. As Kubja follows His instructions, Krishna reciprocates her devotion by using this opportunity to straighten her hunchback.

Kubja's Transformation: As soon as Krishna touches Kubja, her hunchback disappears, and she attains a stunningly beautiful and perfectly proportioned form. Her inner purity and devotion are reflected in her newfound external beauty.

Krishna's Mercy: Lord Krishna then lovingly accepts Kubja as His dear devotee and embraces her. This divine interaction leaves Kubja filled with bliss and gratitude.

Kubja's Devotional Offering: Kubja offers her heartfelt prayers to Lord Krishna, acknowledging His divine nature and expressing her gratitude for His grace.

Krishna's Blessings: Krishna, pleased with Kubja's devotion, blesses her with His mercy and assures her that she will always be remembered for her dedication to Him.

10-42 The Breaking of the Sacrificial Bow

chapter describes a significant event in the life of Lord Krishna, where He attends the royal assembly in Mathura and a grand bow-worship ceremony is organized by King Kamsa.

Preparations for the Ceremony: King Kamsa, aware of the prophecy that he will be killed by the eighth son of his sister Devaki (Lord Krishna), organizes a grand bow- worship ceremony in Mathura. A gigantic bow, known as the Shiva Dhanush, is placed in the assembly.

The arrival of Lord Krishna: Hearing about the ceremony, Lord Krishna, along with His elder brother Balarama, arrives at the royal assembly in Mathura. As Krishna enters the venue, He immediately captures the attention and admiration of everyone present due to His divine beauty and aura. King Kamsa challenges Krishna to string the massive Shiva Dhanush, which has been a formidable task for all those who attempted it in the past. Kamsa believes that if Krishna fails, he can harm Devaki's sons. Lord Krishna approaches the bow gracefully and quickly. He effortlessly lifts the heavy bow and, to the astonishment of all, expertly strings it. With one pull, Krishna breaks the bow into two pieces, producing a loud sound reverberating throughout the assembly.

Krishna's Divine Form Revealed: As the Shiva Dhanush shatters, Lord Krishna's proper divine form is revealed to everyone. His extraordinary beauty and radiance become even more apparent, and the assembly witnesses His transcendental nature as the Supreme Lord.

Kamsa's Panic: The breaking of the bow fills King Kamsa with terror and dread. He realizes that Krishna is not an ordinary boy but who has come to fulfil the prophecy of his demise. Lord Krishna delivers a message to Kamsa, declaring His purpose in coming to the world: to vanquish evildoers and protect the righteous. He warns Kamsa that his end is near. Filled with fear and anger, Kamsa orders Krishna and Balarama to be imprisoned, but Krishna calmly proceeds to release His parents, Vasudeva and Devaki, whom Kamsa has unjustly detained.

10-43 Krishna Kills the Elephant Kuvalayapida

This chapter narrates another significant event in the life of Lord Krishna during His time in Mathura. In this episode, Lord Krishna confronts and defeats a mighty elephant named Kuvalayapida, which King Kamsa sent as a deadly challenge to the Lord. Here's a summary of the chapter:

Kamsa's Malice: King Kamsa, witnessing Lord Krishna's divine prowess in breaking the Shiva Dhanush in the previous chapter, becomes even more convinced of Krishna's divine nature and the prophecy that Krishna will be the cause of his downfall. Kamsa hatches a new plan to eliminate Krishna out of fear and malice.

Sending Kuvalayapida: Kamsa sends his most potent and vicious elephant, Kuvalayapida, to trample and kill Lord Krishna. He believes this massive elephant is invincible and will defeat Krishna.

Krishna Confronts the Elephant: When the enormous and enraged elephant Kuvalayapida is released into the arena, it charges toward Krishna with violent intent. Krishna, a young boy now, stands calmly and fearlessly before the charging elephant.

Krishna Subdues the Elephant: As Kuvalayapida charges at Him, Krishna effortlessly grabs the elephant by its trunk. With His divine strength, Krishna whirls the elephant around and throws it to the ground with tremendous force, instantly killing it.

Awe and Fear in the Assembly: The assembly of onlookers, including Kamsa and other residents of Mathura, is left in a state of shock and awe at Krishna's divine display of power. They recognize that Krishna is not an ordinary human but the Supreme Personality of Godhead.

Krishna's Return to His Parents: After subduing the elephant, Krishna returns to His parents, Vasudeva and Devaki, who are overjoyed to see Him unharmed. They express their gratitude to the Lord for protecting them.

Kamsa's Fears Intensify: Kamsa's fear and paranoia about Krishna's divine nature and the prophecy continue to grow as each encounter with the Lord reveals His extraordinary abilities.

10-44 The Killing of Kamsa

This chapter narrates the dramatic and long-awaited confrontation between Lord Krishna and King Kamsa, which is a pivotal moment in the Krishna Leela (the divine pastime of Lord Krishna).

Kamsa's Fear and Preparations: after several failed attempts to harm or eliminate Lord Krishna, King Kamsa becomes increasingly fearful of Krishna's divine nature and the prophecy that Krishna will be his destroyer. Kamsa intensifies his preparations to face Krishna in a showdown. Kamsa arranges a wrestling match in the arena, inviting Krishna and Balarama to participate. The game is a grand spectacle attended by a vast crowd, including citizens of Mathura and other dignitaries. Krishna and Balarama enter the wrestling arena, and their divine beauty and presence captivate the assembled audience. They are dressed as wrestlers and are greeted with cheers and admiration.

The Encounter with Kamsa: During the match, Krishna and Balarama face various powerful wrestlers sent by Kamsa. Krishna effortlessly defeats each opponent, showcasing His supreme strength and skill. Kamsa, increasingly agitated and desperate, finally challenges Krishna to a one-on-one fight. Krishna accepts the challenge, and a tense silence falls over the arena. As Krishna confronts Kamsa, Kamsa attempts to attack Krishna with various weapons, including a massive iron mace. However, Krishna easily dodges Kamsa's attacks and finally disarms him.

Krishna's Defeat of Kamsa: Krishna then pounces on Kamsa, effortlessly defeating him in the wrestling match. In a pivotal moment, Krishna hurls Kamsa to the ground and kills him by pulling him down and crushing his body with His divine strength. Upon his death at the hands of Lord Krishna, Kamsa attains liberation (moksha) from the cycle of birth and death (samsara) as the Supreme Lord Himself kills him. Following Kamsa's death, the citizens of Mathura rejoice and celebrate Krishna and Balarama as their saviours. The parents of Lord Krishna, Vasudeva and Devaki are also freed from imprisonment.

10-45 Kamsa Begins His Persecutions

In this chapter, the narrative continues from the previous chapter, where Lord Krishna has killed Kamsa. After Kamsa's death, chaos and confusion prevail in Mathura, and the chapter describes the immediate aftermath of these events. Here's a summary of the chapter:

Panic in Mathura: Following King Kamsa's death at Lord Krishna's hands, there is widespread panic and confusion in Mathura. The citizens are shocked by the sudden events and fear for their lives.

Kamsa's Ministers: The ministers and advisors of King Kamsa are in a state of disarray and anxiety. They are worried about the consequences of Kamsa's death and the potential backlash from the powerful Yadava dynasty.

Krishna's Assurance: having fulfilled their mission of eliminating Kamsa, Lord Krishna and Balarama assure Mathura's citizens they no longer fear. Krishna reveals His divine form to them, reassuring them of His divine nature and protection.

Ugrasena Released: Krishna and Balarama release Ugrasena, Kamsa's father, from captivity. Kamsa had imprisoned Ugrasena due to his opposition to Kamsa's tyranny.

Kamsa's Brothers: Kamsa's younger brothers, who had also been imprisoned, are freed, and Krishna restores them to their royal positions. Krishna demonstrates His kindness and concern for the welfare of the Yadava dynasty.

The Coronation of Ugrasena: The citizens, along with Krishna and Balarama, decide to crown Ugrasena as the king of Mathura. Ugrasena is a righteous and wise ruler, unlike the tyrannical Kamsa.

Purification of Mathura: Krishna orders the city of Mathura to be cleansed and purified after the departure of Kamsa's oppressive rule. The citizens rejoice in the new era of peace and righteousness.

Krishna's Farewell: Krishna and Balarama, having established a just and righteous rule, bid farewell to Mathura and decide to return to Vrindavan, where their devotees, especially the Gopis and Gopas, are eagerly awaiting their return.

10-46 Uddhava Visits Vrindavan

Here's a the key points of the chapter:

Uddhava's Mission: Uddhava, a highly learned and devoted disciple and friend of Lord Krishna, is given a special mission by Krishna. Krishna recognizes the unparalleled love and devotion of the residents of Vrindavan, particularly the Gopis (cowherd girls), and wants Uddhava to deliver a message to them. Uddhava sets out on his journey to Vrindavan, carrying a message from Krishna to the Gopis. He is filled with anticipation and curiosity about the nature of their love and devotion. Upon reaching Vrindavan, Uddhava is struck by the village's natural beauty, which is deeply intertwined with the divine presence of Krishna. The residents of Vrindavan greet him with great warmth and affection.

The Message from Krishna: Uddhava meets the Gopis and other residents of Vrindavan and delivers Krishna's message. Krishna acknowledges their unparalleled love and devotion, which He considers the highest form of bhakti (request). He reassures them of His constant presence in their hearts and their love's unique place in His heart. The Gopis express their deep love and separation from Him upon hearing Krishna's message. They intensely long for Krishna and feel their lives are meaningless without Him. Their passion for Krishna is characterized by selflessness and surrender.

Uddhava's Realization: Uddhava, known for his intellectual and scholarly qualities, begins to realize the depth and purity of the Gopis' love. He realizes that their love is beyond the comprehension of ordinary scholars and even great devotees. Uddhava becomes deeply humble and recognizes the greatness of the Gopis' devotion. He wishes to be reborn as a blade of grass in Vrindavan to be trampled by the Gopis' feet, as that would be the highest perfection of life. After spending time in Vrindavan and experiencing the Gopis' love and devotion, Uddhava prepares to return to Krishna in Mathura. He is profoundly transformed by realising the Gopis' unique love and their supreme dedication to Lord Krishna.

10-47 The Song of the Bee

Here's a summary of the chapter:

Introduction: This chapter begins with the Gopis of Vrindavan expressing their intense love and longing for Lord Krishna. Their passion for Krishna is characterized by its depth, purity, and selflessness. They are constantly absorbed in the thoughts of Krishna.

The Metaphor of the Bee: In this chapter, the Gopis use the metaphor of a bee to describe their love for Krishna. They compare themselves to bees, who are attracted to the lotus of Krishna's feet, like a blooming lotus flower. The Gopis describes how the bee, eager to taste the honey of Krishna's lotus feet, hovers around Him. They use vivid and poetic language to depict the bee's restless and relentless search for the nectar of Krishna's presence. Through the metaphor of the bee, the Gopis express their yearning to attain the sweetness of Krishna's association. They long for Krishna with all their hearts and souls, and their love is unwavering and unending.

The Gopis' Description of Krishna: The Gopis describe Krishna's attributes, such as His enchanting beauty, charming smile, and the musical sound of His flute, which captivate their hearts and draw them to Him. The chapter highlights the depth of the Gopis' devotion and their willingness to endure any hardship or separation to be with Krishna. Their love is considered the highest form of faith, characterized by selflessness and surrender.

Conclusion: The chapter concludes with the Gopis' prayer to Lord Krishna, expressing their intense longing to be with Him and requesting His presence in their lives.

10-48 Krishna Pleases His Devotees

Here's a summary of the chapter:

Krishna's Return to Mathura: After completing His mission in Vrindavan, Lord Krishna returns to Mathura. However, He never forgets His devotees from Vrindavan, especially the Gopis, who are deeply pained by His absence. Krishna is aware of the longing and sorrow experienced by the Gopis due to His separation. He decides to console and please His devotees in Mathura.

The Akroora Message: Krishna asks His charioteer, Akroora, to convey a message to the Gopis on His behalf. The news is filled with affection and reassurance, assuring the Gopis that Krishna remembers them and treasures their love. Akroora reaches Vrindavan and delivers Krishna's message to the Gopis. He narrates Krishna's words, which express His love and concern for the Gopis. The Gopis express their deep love for Krishna and their eternal connection with Him upon hearing Krishna's message and are overwhelmed with joy and grief. Their emotions are a poignant blend of happiness and the pain of separation. In their love and devotion, the Gopis perform a dance known as the "Dance of Separation." In this dance, they express their feelings of longing and devotion for Krishna. Their love is so intense that it melts the hearts of those who witness it.

Krishna's Pleasure: Lord Krishna, who is in Mathura, is pleased by the devotion and love of the Gopis. He understands the unique nature of their love, which surpasses all other forms of prayer. Krishna treasures the Gopis' love and continues to be with them in their hearts.

This chapter emphasizes the profound and selfless devotion of the Gopis to Lord Krishna. It highlights the eternal connection between Krishna and His devotees and how Krishna reciprocates with the love of His devotees. Despite physical separation, the Gopis' intense love for Krishna sustains them, and Krishna's message and Akroora's visit bring them solace and joy. The "Dance of Separation" performed by the Gopis is a poignant expression of their love and longing for the Divine, a powerful symbol of devotion in the Bhagavatam.

10-49 Akrura's Vision

Here's a summary of the chapter:

Akrura's Arrival: Akrura, who previously visited Vrindavan to invite Lord Krishna and Lord Balarama to Mathura on King Kamsa's orders, has now returned to Vrindavan, but this time his intentions are different. He no longer serves Kamsa's malevolent interests but has developed a deep devotion to Lord Krishna. Akrura goes to the Yamuna River for a ritual bath and to purify himself. While in the river, he offers prayers and meditates on Lord Krishna, his beloved Lord.

Akrura's Spiritual Experience: As Akrura meditates on Krishna with a pure and devoted heart, he suddenly experiences a divine revelation. He sees a beautiful and glowing form of Lord Krishna within his heart. This form is none other than and it is described in great detail in the chapter.

Krishna's Universal Form: Akrura sees the entire universe within Krishna's transcendental body. He sees various cosmic manifestations, including countless planets, stars, galaxies, and demigods, all residing within the divine form of Krishna. This vision reveals the omnipotence and all-encompassing nature of the Supreme Lord.

Krishna's Four-Armed Form: Akrura also witnesses Krishna's fourarmed form, representing His identity as the ultimate controller and source of all creation. In this form, Krishna holds a conch shell, a discus, a lotus flower, and a mace, symbolizing His divine attributes.

Akrura's Prayers: Overwhelmed by the divine vision, Akrura offers prayers to Lord Krishna, acknowledging Him as the Supreme Lord and the ultimate goal of all spiritual seekers. He expresses his gratitude for having the opportunity to witness Krishna's divine form.

Krishna's Blessings: Lord Krishna is pleased with Akrura's devotion and blesses him. Krishna assures Akrura that his sincere devotion will lead to liberation (moksha) and that he will attain a spiritual abode in the presence of the Lord.

10-50 Krishna Establishes the City of Dwaraka

This chapter narrates the fascinating story of Lord Krishna's establishment of the city of Dwaraka, which became His princely kingdom and a symbol of divine luxury. After leaving Vrindavan and His beloved devotees there, Lord Krishna decides to establish a new city, Dwaraka, on the western coast of India. He consults with His divine father, Vasudeva, and seeks guidance. Lord Krishna selects a spot in the sea and asks Vishvakarma, the celestial architect, to build the city there. Vishvakarma is known for his exceptional skills in constructing divine and wealthy cities. Vishvakarma constructs the magnificent city of Dwaraka in moments. The city has grand palaces, beautiful gardens, wide streets, and impressive forts. The ocean surrounds it and is a sight to behold.

Krishna's Entry into Dwaraka: Krishna, along with His immediate family and close associates, enters the newly built city of Dwaraka. The citizens of Mathura, who have long awaited Krishna's return, follow Him to Dwaraka. In Dwaraka, Lord Krishna marries Rukmini, one of His principal queens and a devoted devotee. This divine wedding is celebrated with great pomp and grandeur, solidifying Krishna's royal status. In addition to Rukmini, Lord Krishna marries several other princesses and queens from various kingdoms. These marriages are celebrated grandly.

Lord Krishna takes on the role of a king in Dwaraka and becomes a beloved ruler. He governs with wisdom, justice, and compassion, and the citizens of Dwaraka adore Him. Krishna engages in various charitable activities, providing for the welfare of His subjects and distributing wealth to those in need. His rule exemplifies the qualities of a divine monarch. Although Krishna has established Dwaraka as His princely kingdom, He continues to engage in His divine pastimes (Leela) and maintains His transcendental nature as the Supreme Personality of Godhead.

10-51 Krishna's Deliverance of Mucukunda

This chapter is often called the "Krishna's Awakening of Mucukunda."

In this chapter, Lord Krishna considered an incarnation of the Supreme God in Hinduism, encounters Mucukunda, a great warrior and king from a previous age who had been in deep slumber for a long time due to a curse. Mucukunda had received a boon from Lord Indra, the king of the heavenly demigods, that anyone who disturbed his sleep would be burnt to ashes.

Krishna and His associates accidentally wake up Mucukunda while seeking shelter in the cave where he had been sleeping. However, Krishna, being aware of Mucukunda's past and the circumstances surrounding his curse, assures him that he has nothing to fear and that his nemesis has now been lifted. Krishna then converses with Mucukunda, where the king expresses his deep devotion and gratitude to the Lord.

This chapter is significant for several reasons:

Divine Encounter: It showcases a direct interaction between Lord Krishna and a devotee waiting for his divine encounter for a long time.

Devotion and Surrender: Mucukunda's devotion and surrender to Krishna exemplify the unwavering faith and dedication that devotees should cultivate.

Liberation: Mucukunda's story symbolizes sovereignty from the cycle of birth and death, emphasizing that surrendering to the Supreme Lord can lead to ultimate spiritual freedom.

Krishna's Compassion highlights Krishna's compassionate nature, as He mercifully frees Mucukunda from his curse and grants him a divine vision.

Overall, Canto 10, Chapter 51 of the Srimad Bhagavatam is a beautiful and spiritually significant episode that illustrates the relationship between God and His devotees, emphasizing the importance of devotion, faith, and surrender in the path of spirituality.

10-52 Rukmini's Message to Lord Krishna

Here is a summary of the key events and themes in this chapter:

Rukmini's Plight: At the beginning of this chapter, Rukmini, the princess of Vidarbha and an incarnation of Goddess Lakshmi, is in a state of distress. She has heard about Krishna's divine qualities, beauty, and compassion and has developed a deep love for Him. However, her brother, Rukmi, plans to marry her off to Shishupala, a prince who is hostile to Krishna. Fearing that she will be forcibly married to Shishupala against her will, Rukmini decides to take matters into her own hands. She writes a heartfelt letter to Krishna, expressing her love for Him and her desperate need for His rescue. In this letter, Rukmini conveys her plan to leave the palace and meet Krishna in person. Rukmini entrusts her letter to a Brahmana messenger and requests him to deliver it to Krishna in Dvaraka, explaining the situation's urgency. Meanwhile, Krishna, who is aware of Rukmini's devotion and her predicament, decides to go to Vidarbha to rescue her. He sets out on a chariot to fulfil her desire.

Krishna and Rukmini's Union: The chapter ends with Krishna's arrival in Vidarbha, where He meets Rukmini and rescues her from the impending marriage with Shishupala. Krishna and Rukmini get married, and their union is celebrated joyfully.

Canto 10, Chapter 52, is significant for several reasons:

It highlights the power of devotion and the role of a devotee's heartfelt prayers in attracting the grace of the Supreme Lord. It portrays Rukmini as a symbol of unwavering devotion, willing to risk everything for her love and devotion to Krishna. The chapter underscores the concept of divine intervention and how the Lord personally comes to the aid of His devotees in times of need. It marks a turning point in the story of Krishna's life, as He takes Rukmini as His chief queen and begins His divine pastimes in the city of Dvaraka.

10-53 Krishna Kidnaps Rukmini

chapter continues the narrative from the previous chapter and describes the events following Lord Krishna's rescue of Princess Rukmini from an unwanted marriage to Shishupala.

Rukmini's Arrival in Dvaraka: After her rescue by Lord Krishna, Princess Rukmini arrives in the city of Dvaraka, where Krishna resides. She is joyfully welcomed by Krishna's queens and other town residents. The citizens of Dvaraka celebrate Rukmini's arrival with great pomp and festivity. They are overjoyed that their beloved Lord Krishna has taken her as His chief queen.

Marriage Ceremony: A grand ceremony is arranged for Krishna and Rukmini in Dvaraka. This wedding is a significant event in the story of Lord Krishna and symbolizes His divine union with His devotees. It is important to note that Lord Krishna had several queens, each with her unique story and qualities. His marriages with them signify His divine Leela (pastimes) and the diverse aspects of His divine personality.

Krishna's Playfulness: The chapter also highlights Krishna's playful and mischievous nature. After the formal marriage ceremony, Krishna and Rukmini engage in an active conversation in which Krishna humorously teases Rukmini and brings laughter and joy to the scene.

Devotion of Rukmini: Rukmini's love and passion for Krishna are evident throughout this chapter. She is depicted as a devoted and virtuous queen deeply in love with the Lord.

It continues the story of Krishna's divine Leela and His relationship with His queens. It emphasizes the importance of devotion and the rewards of unwavering faith in the Lord, as seen in Rukmini's steadfast love for Krishna. The chapter portrays the grandeur and splendour of Lord Krishna's city, Dvaraka, and His divine pastimes in that sacred place. It showcases Krishna's ability to bring joy and happiness to the lives of His devotees through His playful interactions and divine presence.

10-54 Rukmini's Message to Lord Krishna

chapter continues the previous chapters that describe the events surrounding Lord Krishna's and Princess Rukmini's marriage. In this chapter, Rukmini sends a message to Krishna expressing her deep love and devotion for Him.

Rukmini's Devotion: Rukmini, who is now married to Lord Krishna and residing in Dvaraka, continues to be deeply devoted to the Lord. Her love for Krishna is unwavering, and she constantly thinks about Him.

Messenger's Arrival: Rukmini decides to send a message to Krishna through a trusted Brahmana messenger. In this message, she expresses her longing to see Him and her desire to serve Him passionately.

Message of Devotion: Rukmini's message is a beautiful expression of her devotion to Krishna. She describes how she chose Him as her husband in her heart even before their marriage, and she acknowledges His divine qualities and supremacy. She seeks His protection and prays for His presence in her life.

Brahmana's Journey: With Rukmini's message, the Brahmana messenger sets out on his journey to Dvaraka. He carries the message with utmost care and devotion, fully aware of the significance of the mission.

Krishna's Response: Upon receiving Rukmini's message, Krishna is deeply touched by her devotion and love. He immediately decides to go to Rukmini to fulfil her desire and enjoy her company.

Canto 10, Chapter 54, showcases Rukmini's unwavering devotion to Lord Krishna and her desire to have a personal connection with Him despite being His queen. The chapter emphasizes the importance of communication and the exchange of love and devotion between the devotee and the Lord. It highlights Krishna's compassionate nature, as He responds promptly to Rukmini's message and goes to meet her, thus reciprocating her love. This chapter underscores the concept of surrender and the idea that the Supreme Lord is always attentive to the prayers and calls of His devotees.

10-55 The History of Pradyumna

chapter narrates the fascinating story of Pradyumna, the son of Lord Krishna and Queen Rukmini. Pradyumna's life is full of extraordinary events, and this chapter provides insights into his birth, childhood, and various adventures.

Pradyumna's Birth: The chapter begins with the description of the birth of Pradyumna, who was born to Lord Krishna and Rukmini. His birth is a divine and miraculous event. Rukmini had desired to have a son with the qualities of Lord Krishna, and her wish was granted.

Abduction by the Demon Sambara: Soon after Pradyumna's birth, the demon Sambara abducts the infant from the palace. Sambara's actions are driven by a prophecy that predicts his death at the hands of Rukmini's son. Pradyumna proliferates in the demon's captivity. He exhibits extraordinary qualities and prowess even as a child, which astonishes those around him. Lord Krishna's family and associates become distraught over Pradyumna's disappearance. They are unaware of his whereabouts and believe him to be lost. However, Pradyumna eventually kills the demon Sambara and returns to Dvaraka.

Reunion with His Family: Upon his return, Pradyumna is reunited with his parents, Lord Krishna and Rukmini. This joyous reunion brings immense happiness to the entire city of Dvaraka.

Canto 10, Chapter 55, highlights the divine nature of Lord Krishna's family and the extraordinary qualities possessed by His children, such as Pradyumna. The chapter showcases the courage and bravery of Pradyumna as he defeats the demon Sambara, fulfilling the prophecy of his birth. It emphasizes the protective and loving nature of Lord Krishna, who ensures the safety and well-being of His family members. Pradyumna's story exemplifies how divine personalities and events are integral to the Bhagavatam's narrative, illustrating the intangible nature of Lord Krishna's pastimes.

10-56 The Syamantaka Jewel

chapter narrates an exciting story about the Syamantaka jewel, a valuable and magical gem in ancient times.

The Arrival of Satrajit: The story begins with the arrival of Satrajit in the city of Dvaraka. Satrajit was a respected and wealthy Yadava nobleman and the owner of the Syamantaka jewel, which was a divine gem capable of producing enormous quantities of gold each day.

Krishna's Request for the Jewel: Lord Krishna, aware of the jewel's significance and the benefit it could bring to the Yadava community, approaches Satrajit and requests him to place the treasure under His protection in Dvaraka. He assures Satrajit that He will safeguard the gem. Despite Krishna's assurance, the Syamantaka jewel disappears one day while in Satrajit's care. The jewel's disappearance leads to rumours and accusations, with some blaming Krishna for the theft. To clear His name and find the truth, Krishna conducts a thorough investigation. He discovers that a lion has taken the jewel and killed Satrajit's brother, Prasena, who had gone hunting with it. Krishna follows the lion's trail and finds the dead lion, the treasure, and Prasena's corpse.

With the discovery of the jewel and the lion, Krishna returns to Dvaraka with the evidence to vindicate His name. He reveals the true story to the community and reestablishes His innocence. The story leads to the reconciliation of Satrajit and Krishna, with Satrajit realizing that his false accusations had caused harm. He also recognizes Krishna's divine nature.

Canto 10, Chapter 56, showcases Lord Krishna's sense of justice and commitment to upholding righteousness. The chapter illustrates Krishna's ability to resolve conflicts and misunderstandings fairly and truthfully. It highlights the importance of trust and the consequences of false accusations within a community. The Syamantaka jewel is a valuable object, but the chapter also conveys that spiritual wealth and devotion to the Lord are far more precious.

10-57 The Killing of Satrajit and Satadhanva

Here's a summary of the key events and themes in this chapter:

Satadhanva's Crime: After the incident involving the Syamantaka jewel is resolved, a man named Satadhanva emerges as a central figure in the story. Satadhanva is a villainous character who was associated with Satrajit and the glory. Desire for Revenge: Satadhanva grieves against Krishna and decides to seek revenge for the deaths of Satrajit (his father) and the lion (which had killed Prasena). He plans to steal the Syamantaka jewel from Krishna's possession.

The Murder of Satrajit: Satadhanva successfully steals the jewel and escapes from Dvaraka. However, Krishna soon discovers the theft and pursues him. A fierce battle ensues, and Krishna eventually defeats Satadhanva and takes the jewel back. In the process, Krishna kills Satadhanva for his crimes. Krishna returns the Syamantaka jewel to the Yadava community and, specifically, to Akrura, a respected elder. This act demonstrates Krishna's commitment to justice and the well-being of His people.

Canto 10, Chapter 57, highlights several important themes:

Justice and Retribution: The chapter illustrates the principle of justice and the idea that wrongdoers face consequences for their actions. Krishna's actions are portrayed as maintaining dharma (righteousness). Protection of Dharma: Lord Krishna's role as a dharma protector is evident as He ensures that the stolen jewel is returned and that those who committed crimes are appropriately dealt with. Divine Leela: The chapter is part of Lord Krishna's divine pastimes and serves as a reminder of His multifaceted role as both a loving deity and a just ruler. Consequences of One's Choices: Satadhanva's story is a cautionary tale about the effects of harbouring ill intentions and seeking revenge.

10-58 Lord Krishna Kidnaps Rukmini

narrates an intriguing episode from the life of Lord Krishna, wherein He abducts Princess Rukmini, His chief queen, on the day of her planned wedding to Shishupala.

Rukmini's Plight: Princess Rukmini, deeply devoted to Lord Krishna, is in a dire situation. Her brother, Rukmi, has arranged her marriage to Shishupala, a prince hostile to Krishna. Rukmini is distressed and does not want to marry Shishupala.

Rukmini's Letter: Rukmini secretly sends a letter to Krishna, expressing her love and devotion to Him and her desperate plea for rescue. In her letter, she implores Krishna to save her from the impending marriage.

Krishna's Arrival: Krishna understands her predicament upon receiving Rukmini's message. He decides to go to the city of Vidarbha to rescue her. Along with His charioteer, Daruka, Krishna sets out on a chariot.

Krishna's Encounter with Rukmini: Krishna arrives in Vidarbha just as the marriage ceremony begins. He approaches Rukmini and abducts her from the temple where the wedding should occur. This dramatic event showcases Krishna's prowess and determination to protect His devotees.

Chase by Shishupala and Rukmi: Shishupala and Rukmi, furious over Rukmini's abduction, chase after Krishna. A brief confrontation occurs, but Krishna successfully defeats them and continues on His way with Rukmini.

Return to Dvaraka: Krishna and Rukmini return to Dvaraka, where the citizens and Krishna's queens are welcomed with great joy. Rukmini is officially married to Krishna in a grand ceremony.

Canto 10, Chapter 58, is significant for several reasons:

It illustrates Rukmini's unwavering devotion to Lord Krishna and her willingness to trust Him entirely for her rescue. The chapter portrays Krishna as the ultimate protector of His devotees, willing to go to great lengths to ensure their safety and happiness. It highlights the theme of divine love and the idea that the Supreme Lord reciprocates His devotees' pure love and devotion.

10-59 Rukmi's Story

provides insights into the character and actions of Rukmi, Princess Rukmini's brother. Rukmi played a significant role in the events leading up to Rukmini's abduction by Lord Krishna.

Rukmini's Disapproval: Rukmi, the elder brother of Rukmini, was vehemently opposed to her desire to marry Lord Krishna. He was against Krishna and wanted Rukmini to marry Shishupala, a prince who shared his hostility towards Krishna.

Rukmi's Plan: Rukmi was determined to prevent Rukmini from marrying Krishna. He hatched a plan to take her back from Krishna's custody and marry her off to Shishupala as initially planned. Rukmi assembled a significant army and marched towards Dvaraka, where Krishna and Rukmini were residing. He intended to take Rukmini away from Krishna forcefully.

Krishna's Intervention: When Krishna heard of Rukmi's intentions, he confronted Rukmi. Krishna mounted His chariot and set out to meet Rukmi and his army. A fierce and dramatic confrontation occurs between Krishna and Rukmi. They engaged in a heated verbal exchange, with Rukmi expressing his disdain for Krishna. Krishna, however, remained calm and composed. Krishna eventually defeated Rukmi in the duel. He disarmed Rukmi and shaved his head, marking him a defeated warrior. However, Krishna spared Rukmi's life, emphasizing that He did not want to kill His future brother-in-law. Rukmi was humiliated and left with his army after his defeat. Krishna returned to Dvaraka with Rukmini.

Canto 10, Chapter 59, highlights several important themes:

It portrays Rukmi's stubbornness and opposition to Rukmini's choice of Krishna as her husband. The chapter illustrates Krishna's courage and righteousness as He defends His beloved devotee, Rukmini, and ensures her freedom to choose her spouse. It emphasizes Krishna's mercy, as He spares Rukmi's life despite defeating him, underscoring His willingness to give a chance for reconciliation.

10-60 Lord Balarama Slays Rukmi

Here's a summary of the key events and themes in this chapter:

Rukmi's Vengeance: Rukmi, who had previously faced humiliation at the hands of Lord Krishna, nursed a deep grudge against Him. He was especially angered by Krishna's interference in his sister Rukmini's choice of husband.

Rukmi versus Jarasandha: Rukmi allie with Jarasandha. Jarasandha is the enemy of Krishna. Together, they plan to attack and defeat Krishna and the Yadava community.

Krishna and Balarama's Response: Upon learning of Rukmi and Jarasandha's hostile intentions, Lord Krishna and Lord Balarama decide to confront them. They and their associates set out to meet the evil forces.

Balarama's Duel with Rukmi: A fierce battle occurs between Lord Balarama and Rukmi. Balarama, who possesses extraordinary physical strength and prowess, easily defeats Rukmi in combat.

Mercy Shown to Rukmi: Although Balarama defeats Rukmi, He spares his life at the request of Rukmini, who pleads for her brother's life. Balarama, being compassionate, honours her request and forgives Rukmi.

Retreat of Jarasandha: After witnessing the defeat of Rukmi, Jarasandha realizes the futility of continuing the battle and decides to withdraw his forces.

Canto 10, Chapter 60, highlights several important themes:

It underscores the qualities of Lord Balarama, including His strength, courage, and sense of righteousness. The chapter illustrates the principle of forgiveness and mercy, as Balarama spares Rukmi's life at the request of Rukmini, showing His compassionate nature. The story emphasizes the ongoing enmity between Krishna and certain antagonistic kings like Jarasandha, setting the stage for future events in the epic. It serves as a reminder of the complex relationships and political intrigues in the Mahabharata, with alliances and conflicts playing a significant role in the narrative.

10-61 Lord Balarama Slays Dvivida Gorilla

This chapter narrates an intriguing and unique episode involving Lord Balarama and a mighty, mischievous gorilla named Dvivida. Here's a summary of the key events and themes in this chapter:

Introduction of Dvivida Gorilla: The story begins with the introduction of Dvivida, a gigantic and powerful gorilla wreaking havoc in the forests and disturbing the sages' peaceful activities. Dvivida possessed supernatural powers, causing fear and chaos among the local inhabitants.

Dvivida's Mischief: Dvivida's mischievous activities included uprooting trees, disturbing sacrifices, harassing sages, and even assaulting powerful beings like elephants and lions. His behaviour was a source of great concern for the residents and scholars of the region.

Balarama's Encounter with Dvivida: Lord Balarama, the elder brother of Lord Krishna, heard about Dvivida's destructive activities and decided to confront him. Balarama's purpose was to restore peace and order in the area.

Epic Battle: Balarama and Dvivida engaged in a fierce battle. Despite Dvivida's immense size and strength, Balarama, an avatar of Lord Vishnu, quickly overpowered him. Balarama eventually killed Dvivida by striking him on the head with His club.

Reactions of the Sages: The sages and inhabitants of the area were relieved and grateful for Lord Balarama's intervention. They praised Him for ending Dvivida's reign of terror and restoring peace to their region.

Canto 10, Chapter 61, highlights several important themes:

It illustrates Lord Balarama's divine strength and His role as a protector of dharma (righteousness) and peace.

The chapter emphasises the significance of divine intervention in dealing with disruptive and destructive forces that threaten the universe's balance.

It showcases the supernatural and sometimes whimsical nature of beings in Hindu mythology, including powerful entities like Dvivida.

The story serves as a reminder of the diverse and colourful narratives within the Mahabharata and other Indian epics.

10-62 The Meeting of Uddhava and Krishna

Uddhava, a close associate and cousin of Lord Krishna, arrives in Vrindavan, the idyllic village where Krishna spent His childhood. Uddhava has been sent by Krishna to deliver a message to the residents of Vrindavan and to understand their deep love and devotion to the Lord. Uddhava is deeply moved by the intense love and dedication that the residents of Vrindavan, especially the gopis (cowherd girls), have for Krishna. He observes their unwavering attachment to the Lord and their complete absorption in thoughts of Him. Uddhava, realising the unparalleled love of the residents of Vrindavan, becomes introspective and questions the nature of his devotion. He wonders why the Gopis' love for Krishna is so exceptional and how he can attain a similar level of faith.

Krishna's Response: In response to Uddhava's questions, Lord Krishna imparts profound spiritual knowledge. He explains the superiority of the gopis' devotion, emphasising the importance of selfless love and surrender to the Divine. Krishna reveals that the intense separation experienced by the gopis in His absence is the highest form of devotion, known as para bhakti. Krishna explains His transcendental form as the Supreme Personality of Godhead and His various incarnations to fulfil specific purposes. He clarifies that His pastimes in Vrindavan are meant to attract the hearts of devotees through loving relationships. Krishna delves into the nature of ultimate reality, explaining the oneness of the individual soul (atma) with the Supreme Soul (Paramatma). He elucidates the importance of meditation, self- realisation, and devotion to attain spiritual liberation.

It highlights the deep love and devotion that the residents of Vrindavan, especially the gopis, have for Lord Krishna, setting a profound example of pure passion. The chapter delves into the philosophical and spiritual teachings of Lord Krishna, including the nature of devotion, the relationship between the soul and the Supreme, and the importance of self-realisation. It emphasises the concept of parabhakti, the highest form of faith characterised by selfless love and complete surrender to the Lord.

10-63 Lord Krishna Fights with Banasura

chapter narrates an exciting and significant episode involving Lord Krishna and Banasura, a powerful demon and devotee of Lord Shiva. Banasura was a formidable demon king who ruled over the city of Sonitapura. Despite his demonic nature, he was a great devotee of Lord Shiva and had received blessings and boons from him, which made him exceptionally powerful.

Krishna's Arrival: Lord Krishna, along with His army and Lord Shiva's bull, Nandi, arrives near Sonitapura. Banasura receives news of Krishna's arrival and decides to confront Him. A fierce battle ensues between Lord Krishna and Banasura. Banasura, relying on his immense strength, engages in combat with Krishna. The action is intense and spectacular, with various celestial weapons being used.

Lord Shiva's Intervention: During the battle, Lord Shiva, aware of Banasura's devotion to him, arrives on the scene to mediate and protect his devotee. He requests Krishna to spare Banasura's life, as killing him would be against the principles of dharma (righteousness). Lord Krishna, respecting Lord Shiva's request and acknowledging Banasura's devotion to him, decides not to kill Banasura. Instead, He punishes him by severing his thousand arms, rendering him powerless in the battle. Realising his defeat and the divine nature of Lord Krishna, Banasura surrenders to Krishna and seeks His mercy. Krishna, in His kindness, forgives Banasura and assures him of protection. Canto 10, Chapter 63, highlights several important themes:

It showcases the power and courage of Lord Krishna in battle and His role as the Supreme Lord capable of defeating even the most formidable demons. The chapter emphasises the concept of devotion and the importance of a devotee's surrender to the Lord, as demonstrated by Banasura's ultimate surrender to Krishna. It portrays the relationship between Lord Krishna and Lord Shiva, highlighting their mutual respect and cooperation for the well-being of their devotees. The episode serves as a reminder of the principle of dharma, wherein even in battle, there is a code of conduct and respect for certain principles.

10-64 The Deliverance of King Nriga

chapter narrates the story of King Nriga and how he encountered Lord Krishna's divine mercy and justice. King Nriga was known for his immense wealth and generosity. He would often donate cows and other valuable possessions to Brahmins as acts of charity. He was so generous that he gave away thousands of cows daily.

The Mistake: Once, due to a mix-up by his servants, some cows that had been previously donated to Brahmins were mistakenly given to another Brahmin. When the error was discovered, King Nriga offered to compensate the Brahmin with an even more significant number of cows. The mistake was unintentional, but the Brahmin who initially received the cows was unwilling to accept more. Consequently, King Nriga faced a moral dilemma. He was later cursed to become a lizard due to the Brahmin's anger.

Krishna's Arrival: Many years later, Lord Krishna and His associates happened to pass by the area where King Nriga, now a lizard, was trapped in a dry well. The lizard was suffering greatly. Krishna recognised the lizard as King Nriga and understood the reason for his predicament. He ordered that water from His water jug be poured into the well. This divine water instantly transformed the lizard back into King Nriga. King Nriga's Gratitude: King Nriga, once restored to his human form, expressed his immense gratitude to Lord Krishna for His mercy and grace. He realised the significance of Krishna's presence in his life and the karmic consequences of his past actions.

Canto 10, Chapter 64, highlights several important themes:

It underscores the importance of dharma (righteousness) and the consequences of one's actions, even when unintentional. The chapter illustrates Lord Krishna's compassion and the principle that He is willing to deliver His devotees, even those who have made mistakes when they sincerely seek His help. It emphasises the power of divine intervention and the transformative effect of Lord Krishna's presence in the lives of devotees. The story is a moral lesson about integrity and fulfilling one's commitments.

10-65 The Meeting of Lord Krishna with Sudama Brahmana

This chapter narrates the heart-touching and spiritually enlightening story of the meeting between Lord Krishna and His dear friend, Sudama Brahmana. Here's a summary of the key events and themes in this chapter:

Introduction of Sudama Brahmana: Sudama was a poor and humble Brahmana living in abject poverty with his devoted wife. Despite their poverty, Sudama and his wife were ardent devotees of Lord Krishna.

Request by Sudama's Wife: Witnessing their difficult circumstances, Sudama's wife was concerned about their well-being and approached Sudama with a request. She asked him to visit Lord Krishna in Dvaraka, known for His generosity, and seek help.

Sudama's Reluctance: Sudama was initially reluctant to ask Krishna for material favours, believing that true devotion should be selfless and not driven by desires. However, he agreed to go to Dvaraka at his wife's insistence.

Sudama's Gift: Sudama, with a pure heart, decided to take a humble gift for Krishna. He carried a small bag of chipped rice (poha) as an offering, as it was the only thing they had to offer.

Sudama's Arrival in Dvaraka: Upon reaching Dvaraka, Sudama was mesmerised by the opulence and grandeur of the city. He met Lord Krishna in His palace, but instead of presenting his gift immediately, he was so overwhelmed by Krishna's divine presence that he forgot about the facility.

Krishna's Loving Reception: Lord Krishna, who is omniscient and knows Sudama's intentions, welcomed Sudama with great love and respect. He embraced Sudama and honoured him as a dear friend.

Sudama's Return: Sudama spent some time in Krishna's company, experiencing divine bliss and forgetting his material concerns. He returned home to find his humble hut transformed into a magnificent palace filled with opulence and wealth.

10-66 The Deliverance of Akurara

This chapter is significant because it narrates a pivotal event in the life of Lord Krishna.

Here is a summary of Srimad Bhagavatam Canto 10, Chapter 66:

In this chapter, the story revolves around Akurara, a noble and devoted devotee of Lord Krishna. Akurara was sent by Lord Krishna's maternal uncle, Kamsa, to bring Krishna and Balarama from Vrindavan to Mathura under the pretext of participating in a wrestling match. However, Kamsa's real intention was to harm Krishna because he knew the prophecy that Krishna would eventually kill him.

When Akurara arrives in Vrindavan, he is warmly welcomed by Krishna's parents and the residents. He is filled with awe and admiration upon meeting Lord Krishna, who is revered as the Supreme Personality of Godhead by the people of Vrindavan.

As Akurara prepares to take Krishna and Balarama back to Mathura, he becomes overwhelmed with devotion and longing for the Lord. While journeying to Mathura, Akurara reflects upon Krishna's divine qualities, His childhood pastimes, and the deep love the residents of Vrindavan have for Him.

Upon reaching Mathura, Akurara takes Krishna and Balarama to the wrestling arena, where they eventually confront Kamsa. The chapter describes the events that unfold in Mathura, including Krishna's defeat of various demons and His ultimate confrontation with Kamsa, leading to the liberation of the people of Mathura from Kamsa's oppressive rule.

Canto 10, Chapter 66, is not only a narrative of historical events but also serves as a profound spiritual teaching. It highlights the importance of devotion and surrendering to Lord Krishna. It illustrates how a sincere devotee like Akurara can experience a deep connection with the divine and be transformed by it.

Overall, this chapter is a beautiful and significant episode in the Bhagavatam, emphasising the divine nature of Lord Krishna and the power of devotion to connecting with the Supreme Being.

10-67 Lord Krishna's Daily Activities

provides insights into the daily life and activities of Lord Krishna during His stay in Dwarka, a city He established after leaving Mathura.

Krishna's Morning Activities: The chapter describes Lord Krishna's morning routine. He would wake up early, offer prayers, meditate, and do yoga. Krishna's daily life exemplified the importance of spiritual practices and disciplined living.

Krishna's Audience with His Ministers: As the king of Dwarka, Krishna would hold meetings with His ministers and advisors to discuss various administrative matters. His rule was characterised by justice and wisdom, and He always acted in the best interests of His subjects.

Krishna's Love for His Queens: The chapter portrays Krishna's deep love and affection for His queens, including Queen Rukmini and others. He would spend time with each of His queens individually, making them feel unique and cherished.

Krishna's Playful Pastimes: Lord Krishna's playful nature is highlighted as He engages in active activities with His family members, friends, and subjects. These activities include joking, singing, dancing, and enjoying the company of His loved ones.

Krishna's Responsibility as Protector: Even as He enjoys these joyful moments, Lord Krishna never neglects His role as the protector of Dwaraka. He would often patrol the city and its environs to ensure the safety and security of its residents.

Krishna's Approachability: Despite being the Supreme Lord and the king of Dwarka, Krishna was incredibly approachable. The chapter emphasises how people from all walks of life, including the common folk, could quickly meet and interact with Him.

Krishna's Divine Glories: The chapter concludes by acknowledging the infinite divine qualities and metaphysical nature of Lord Krishna. It reminds readers that Krishna, though engaged in worldly activities, remained untouched by material limitations.

10-68 The Marriage of Samba

The chapter begins with Samba, the son of Lord Krishna and Jambavati, playing a playful prank on some sages. Samba dresses like a woman in his youthful exuberance and imitates the sages' behaviour. This action leads to an unintended consequence as the sages, angered by his antics, curse him with leprosy. Samba, now afflicted with leprosy, feels great remorse for his actions and suffering. He seeks forgiveness from the sages but is told that his curse can only be lifted if he worships Lord Surya (the sun god) and follows a particular ritual.

Krishna's Arrival: When Samba cannot cure himself through the prescribed ritual, Lord Krishna intervenes. He suggests that Samba undertake severe penance and austerities at the place of a saintly sage named Dvadasaditya (literally, "twelve suns"). Krishna and Rukmini Visit Dvadasaditya: Lord Krishna, accompanied by His principal queen Rukmini, visits the hermitage of Dvadasaditya. They are warmly received by the sage and his wife, who recognise Krishna's divine nature.

Samba's Penance: Samba diligently follows the instructions given by the sage Dvadasaditya, engaging in rigorous penance, worship of Lord Surya, and self- purification. Lord Surya, pleased with Samba's devotion and penance, appears before him and offers him a boon. Samba requests the cure for his leprosy and restore his original form. Lord Surya grants his request, and Samba is healed.

Marriage Proposal: While at the hermitage, Rukmini becomes impressed with the sage's daughter, and she suggests her as a suitable bride for Samba. The sage and his wife agree to the proposal, and the marriage between Samba and the sage's daughter is arranged.

Canto 10, Chapter 68, demonstrates several critical themes in the Srimad Bhagavatam, including humility, repentance, and devotion. It also highlights Lord Krishna's compassion and ability to alleviate His devotees' suffering. Additionally, this chapter illustrates the divine nature of Krishna and His ability to perform miracles and grant boons to His devotees.

10-69 The Lord's Daily Activities

The chapter begins by describing the early morning activities of Lord Krishna. He would wake up, perform His daily rituals, and then visit the temple to offer prayers and worship to the deities.

Krishna's Conversations: Krishna would have delightful conversations with His queens, ministers, and friends. His discussions were filled with wisdom, humour, and love, and they charmed everyone around Him.

Krishna's Meals: Lord Krishna would take His meals with His queens, and each queen felt that Krishna was exclusively dining with her, showcasing His divine omnipresence and love for His devotees.

Krishna's Sporting Activities: Krishna often indulged in sporting activities with His friends, such as wrestling, archery, and other outdoor games. His presence brought immense joy to those privileged to participate in these activities with Him.

Krishna's Visits to His Subjects: Lord Krishna would regularly visit the homes of His devotees and subjects, allowing them to have personal interactions with Him. This action strengthened their bond of devotion and love for the Lord.

Krishna's Dispensation of Justice: As the ruler of Dwarka, Krishna was responsible for upholding justice. He would listen to the grievances of His subjects and ensure that justice was served impartially.

Krishna's Benevolence: The chapter highlights how Krishna generously provided for His devotees' needs and desires, ensuring they lacked nothing. He blessed them with material and spiritual well-being.

Krishna's Enchanting Presence: The residents of Dwarka were captivated by Krishna's enchanting personality, divine beauty, and loving interactions. They considered themselves fortunate to be in His presence.

Krishna's Ultimate Purpose: While engaging in these worldly activities, Lord Krishna's ultimate purpose remained to guide His devotees toward the path of spiritual realisation and to inspire love and devotion toward the Supreme.

10-70 Lord Krishna's Daily Activities

Similar to previous chapters in this canto, this chapter continues to provide insights into the daily life and activities of Lord Krishna during His time in Dwarka.

Krishna's Morning Routine: The chapter describes Lord Krishna's morning activities. He would rise early and engage in personal cleanliness, such as bathing and dressing in delicate garments. Krishna's care reflects His divine charm and attractiveness.

Krishna's Worship of the Sun God: as the Supreme Lord, Lord Krishna would worship the Sun god by offering water and prayers. His worship of the sun god demonstrates His respect for the universal principles and the interconnectedness of all divine aspects.

Krishna's Visit to the Royal Courtyard: Krishna would then proceed to the royal courtyard of Dwarka, where He was received with great reverence by His subjects, ministers, and queens. His arrival brought immense joy to everyone.

Krishna's Playful Pastimes: The chapter highlights Lord Krishna's playful interactions with His queens, who were deeply enamoured by His divine beauty and personality. These pastimes included joking, gentle teasing, and loving exchanges.

Krishna's Meals: Lord Krishna would take His meals with His queens and other family members. Each queen felt that Krishna was exclusively dining with her, illustrating His omnipresence and the bond He shared with each devotee.

Krishna's Conversations and Entertainment: Krishna would engage in delightful conversations filled with wisdom and humour. He would also enjoy the performances of musicians and dancers, adding to the joyous atmosphere of Dwarka.

Krishna's Evening Activities: In the evening, Krishna would again visit His queens and engage in affectionate pastimes. He continued to provide His devotees with love, attention, and spiritual guidance.

Krishna's Departure: After a day filled with divine interactions and activities, Krishna would eventually retire for the night, ending another day in His transcendental life.

10-71 The Lord Travels to Indraprastha

This chapter describes an important journey undertaken by Lord Krishna from Dwarka to the city of Indraprastha (also known as Hastinapura), which was ruled by His dear friend and devotee, Maharaja Yudhishthira, of the Pandava dynasty.

The Request of Maharaja Yudhishthira: Maharaja Yudhishthira becomes eager to meet Him after hearing about Lord Krishna's pastimes in Dwarka and knowing that Krishna was about to leave for Dwarka after completing His mission. He sends a message expressing his desire to have Krishna's association with Indraprastha. Lord Krishna, who deeply cherishes His friendship with the Pandavas, gladly accepts Yudhishthira's invitation and prepares to travel to Indraprastha with His queens and other associates. The chapter describes the grand departure of Lord Krishna from Dwarka. The citizens of Dwarka, including His family members, queens, and friends, are saddened at His departure but understand that it is His divine plan.

Krishna's Journey to Indraprastha: Lord Krishna, accompanied by His entourage, embarks on the journey there. The description of this journey includes the passing of various towns and villages along the way, where people come out to offer their respects and seek the Lord's blessings. Krishna eventually reaches Indraprastha, where He is warmly welcomed by Maharaja Yudhishthira, his brothers, Queen Draupadi, and all the residents of the city. The joyous reunion of Krishna and the Pandavas is a central theme of this chapter.

Krishna's Stay in Indraprastha: Lord Krishna stays in Indraprastha for several months, during which time He enjoys the company of His dear friends and devotees. He participates in various activities and pastimes with the Pandavas, further strengthening their bond of love and friendship. Eventually, Lord Krishna takes leave from Indraprastha to return to Dwarka, as He had commitments and responsibilities there. Emotional farewells and a deep longing among the Pandavas and the citizens of Indraprastha mark his departure.

10-72 The Pastimes of Lord Krishna

The chapter begins with Sukadeva Goswami, the narrator of the Bhagavatam, summarising the glorious pastimes of Lord Krishna that were described in detail in the previous chapters of the Tenth Canto. He expresses the significance and metaphysical nature of Krishna's activities, which include His childhood leelas (pastimes), His interactions with the cowherd boys and girls, His playing of the flute, and His love-filled relationships with the residents of Vrindavan. Sukadeva Goswami recalls the miraculous circumstances of Krishna's birth in Mathura, His escape from the clutches of the evil King Kamsa, and His upbringing in the loving care of His foster parents, Nanda and Yasoda, in the village of Vrindavan. He highlights Krishna's divine nature and His role as the Supreme Lord.

The chapter recounts various endearing pastimes of Krishna in Vrindavan, such as His playful interactions with the cowherd boys and girls, His lifting of the Govardhan Hill, His vanquishing of demons, and His charming pastimes with the gopis (cowherd maidens), especially the renowned Raslila dance. Krishna's departure from Vrindavan to Mathura is to fulfil His mission of protecting and liberating His devotees. Sukadeva Goswami describes the sorrow and longing experienced by the residents of Vrindavan upon Krishna's departure.

The chapter briefly mentions some of Krishna's activities in Mathura and Dwarka, including His battles with various demons, His marriage to queens, and His establishment of Dwarka as a prosperous and wellprotected city. Sukadeva Goswami explains that after completing His pastimes on Earth, Lord Krishna returned to His eternal abode, Vaikuntha, along with His associates and devotees.

The chapter concludes with Sukadeva Goswami highlighting the extraordinary significance of hearing and studying the Srimad Bhagavatam, which is a sacred scripture that reveals the Supreme Truth and the divine pastimes of Lord Krishna. He emphasises that those who regularly hear and contemplate the Bhagavatam attain spiritual enlightenment and liberation.

10-73 Brahma's Prayers and Lord Krishna's Glories

This chapter presents a beautiful and philosophical conversation between Lord Brahma, the creator of the universe, and Lord Krishna.

Brahma's Realisation: At the beginning of the chapter, Lord Brahma, the universal creator, becomes bewildered when he sees that all the cowherd boys and calves in Vrindavan have disappeared. In his ignorance, Brahma thought that he had bewildered Lord Krishna and wanted to test His divinity.

Krishna's Divine Play: Lord Krishna, who is omniscient and fully aware of Brahma's intentions, decided to reveal His divine luxury and power. He expanded Himself into multiple forms, each identical to the missing cowherd boys and calves. Brahma's Realisation of Krishna's Divinity: Brahma's attempts to test Krishna's power are in vain, as he cannot find any discrepancies in Krishna's actions or forms.

Gradually, Brahma begins to understand the profound truth about Krishna's divine nature as the Supreme Personality of the Godhead.

Brahma's Prayers: Overwhelmed by awe and realisation, Lord Brahma offers a series of heartfelt prayers extolling the glories and omnipotence of Lord Krishna. He recognises that Krishna is the universe's source of all creation, maintenance, and destruction. Brahma humbly acknowledges his limitations and ignorance.

Krishna's Benediction: Pleased with Brahma's humility and prayers, Lord Krishna reveals His universal form (Vishvarupa) to Brahma, displaying His cosmic, all- encompassing nature. Brahma witnesses the entire universe within the body of Krishna.

Conclusion: Lord Krishna assures Brahma that everything in Vrindavan is an expansion of His divine energy, and he orchestrated Brahma's test to increase the devotion and love of the residents of Vrindavan. Brahma, having realised his mistake and the true identity of Krishna, returns to his abode with a transformed understanding and deep reverence for the Lord.

10-74 The Deliverance of Shishupala

This chapter narrates an incident during the Rajasuya Yajna (sacrifice) performed by Maharaja Yudhishthira, where Lord Krishna exhibits His divine qualities and protects His devotees by dealing with Shishupala, a resentful and hostile king.

The chapter begins with Maharaja Yudhishthira performing the Rajasuya Yajna, a grand Vedic sacrifice meant to establish his imperial authority and demonstrate his prowess as a righteous ruler. Lord Krishna is the honoured guest at this event. Shishupala, a king from the Chedi kingdom and a cousin of Krishna holds a deep-seated grudge against Lord Krishna. He resents Krishna because Krishna had married Rukmini, whom Shishupala had intended to match. The attendees must offer their respects to Lord Krishna as part of the yajna. However, when it is Shishupala's turn, he unleashes a torrent of insults and blasphemy against Krishna. He criticises Krishna's birth, character, actions, and divine qualities, displaying his intense jealousy and hostility.

Lord Krishna remains calm and composed, patiently listening to Shishupala's vitriolic tirade. He understands that Shishupala's animosity results from past karmic factors and that Shishupala's end will be in Krishna's hands. Lord Krishna acts when Shishupala's blasphemy reaches its zenith and exceeds the limit. He invokes His Sudarshana Chakra, a divine disc weapon, and releases it towards Shishupala. The Sudarshana Chakra swiftly decapitates Shishupala, ending his life. Shishupala's soul attains liberation (moksha) and merges into Krishna's transcendental body upon being killed by Krishna, signifying the ultimate goal of independence through devotion to the Lord.

Reaction of the Assembly: Initially, the assembly is stunned by Krishna's act, but they eventually recognise its divine justice. They praise Krishna's actions, understanding that Shishupala's blasphemy had reached its limit and his death was a means of spiritual liberation for him. Lord Krishna explains to the assembly that Shishupala's fate resulted from his actions and that Krishna, as the Supreme Lord, had acted according to dharma (righteousness) and the laws of destiny.

10-75 The Deliverance of Shishupala

This chapter narrates an incident during the Rajasuya Yajna (sacrifice) performed by Maharaja Yudhishthira, one of the Pandava brothers, with Lord Krishna as the honoured guest.

Maharaja Yudhishthira decided to perform the Rajasuya Yajna, a grand Vedic ritual, to assert his imperial authority and establish himself as the rightful emperor. Lord Krishna is invited to grace the occasion as the chief guest. Shishupala, a cousin of Krishna and a powerful king, harbours deep enmity and jealousy toward Lord Krishna. He holds a grudge against Krishna because Krishna had married Rukmini, whom Shishupala wanted to marry. Many noble and powerful kings from various kingdoms gathered for the Rajasuya Yajna. As part of the ceremony, the guests must honour the chief guest, Lord Krishna, by offering their respects. When it's Shishupala's turn to show his respects to Krishna, he becomes incensed and launches into a tirade of insults and accusations against Krishna. He criticises Krishna's ancestry, character, and actions and accuses Krishna of stealing Rukmini and other offences.

Lord Krishna listens patiently to Shishupala's insults without reacting. He understands that Shishupala's enmity results from past karma and that destiny has ordained his death. However, Krishna intervenes when Shishupala's blasphemy exceeds a specific limit. As Shishupala continues to insult Krishna, Krishna invokes His Sudarshana Chakra, a divine disc weapon. The Sudarshana Chakra swiftly decapitates Shishupala, ending his life. At that moment, Shishupala's soul is liberated and merges into Lord Krishna's transcendental body.

The assembly of kings and sages at the yajna is initially stunned by Krishna's act. However, they understand the justice of the situation, as Shishupala's blasphemy had reached its limit, and his death was a means of liberation for him. Maharaja Yudhishthira expresses his concern about the propriety of Krishna's actions. He worries that Krishna's involvement in killing a relative could have negative consequences. Lord Krishna assures Yudhishthira that His actions were by dharma (righteousness) and were meant to uphold virtue and protect the sanctity of the yajna.

10-76 Dantavakra, Viduratha, and Romaharshana

Dantavakra and Shalva: Dantavakra, the king of Karusha, and Shalva, a mighty warrior, were adversaries of Lord Krishna. They conspired to attack Dwarka, the city ruled by Lord Krishna, to avenge previous conflicts.

The Battle: A great battle ensues between Lord Krishna, who wields his divine weapon, the Sudarshana Chakra, and these adversaries. Lord Balarama also participates in the action.

Death of Dantavakra: Dantavakra, a cousin of Lord Krishna, engages in combat with Him. Lord Krishna kills Dantavakra by striking him with the Sudarshana Chakra during the battle.

Death of Shalva: Lord Balarama confronts Shalva and defeats him in battle. Shalva is killed, bringing an end to his menace.

The Story of Romaharshana: The chapter also briefly mentions the story of Romaharshana, a sage who disrespected Lord Balarama. As a consequence, Lord Balarama kills him.

Overall, Canto 10, Chapter 76 of the Srimad Bhagavatam illustrates the divine nature of Lord Krishna and Lord Balarama and their ability to conquer powerful adversaries threatening the religious order. It's an essential chapter in the Bhagavata Purana that showcases the culmination of Lord Krishna's earthly pastimes before He departs from the mortal world.

10-77 Lord Krishna Slays the Demon Salva

This chapter continues the narrative of Lord Krishna's heroic deeds and divine encounters. Here's a summary of the key events in this chapter:

The Demon Salva: Salva was a powerful and evil demon with a flying city known as Saubha. He was a staunch enemy of Lord Krishna and had previously conspired with Dantavakra and Shalva (mentioned in the previous chapters) to attack Dwarka.

Salva's Attack: Salva, riding his flying city Saubha, launched a devastating attack on Dwarka. Dwarka and its residents were in great distress due to Salva's assault.

Lord Krishna's Response: Lord Krishna, along with His divine weapon, the Sudarshana Chakra, decided to confront Salva and his flying city.

Destruction of Saubha: A fierce battle between Lord Krishna and Salva took place in the sky. Eventually, Lord Krishna skillfully hurled His Sudarshana Chakra at Saubha, which led to the destruction of Salva's flying city and the death of Salva himself.

Rescue of Princesses: During the battle, Lord Krishna rescued 16,100 princesses whom Salva had imprisoned. He later married them, expanding His divine household.

Return to Dwarka: After defeating Salva and saving Dwarka from the threat, Lord Krishna returned to His city, where He was celebrated for His courage and heroism.

Canto 10, Chapter 77 of the Srimad Bhagavatam, showcases the extraordinary divine powers of Lord Krishna and His unwavering commitment to protecting His devotees and upholding righteousness. It emphasises the belief in the sacred as the ultimate saviour and protector in adversity.

10-78 The Killing of the Demon Śālva

This chapter continues the narrative from the previous chapters, explicitly focusing on the events following the defeat of the demon Śālva. Here's a summary of the key events in this chapter:

After defeating Śālva and destroying his flying city, Saubha (as described in the previous chapters), Lord Krishna returns to Dwarka with great honour and celebration from the citizens.

The episode then shifts to the Yadava dynasty, of which Lord Krishna is a part. There is growing pride and arrogance among the Yadavas due to their association with Lord Krishna's divinity, which leads to conflicts and discord among them.

A Quarrel Among Yadavas: In the absence of Lord Krishna, a heated argument erupts among the Yadavas, which soon escalates into violence. They begin fighting with each other.

Curse of Sages: During this chaos, a group of sages arrive in Dwarka and witness the Yadavas' unruly behaviour. In response, the sages curse the Yadavas, predicting their eventual destruction.

Omens and Divine Signs: Unusual and frightening omens and celestial signs start appearing, indicating impending calamity and the Yadavas' doom.

The Yadavas' Self-Destruction: As the divine curse takes effect, the Yadavas lose control of their senses. They start fighting each other with even greater intensity, and in a tragic turn of events, many of them are killed in the violence.

Lord Krishna's Departure: Lord Krishna, witnessing the destruction and recognising that His mission on Earth has been fulfilled, decides to leave His mortal body. He sits down in meditation and departs from the world in a transcendent form, marking the end of His earthly pastimes.

Canto 10, Chapter 78 of the Srimad Bhagavatam is significant in Lord Krishna's life narrative. It highlights the concept of divine leelas (pastimes) and the ultimate divinity of Lord Krishna. The chapter also teaches the consequences of arrogance and discord, even among those closely associated with the divine.

10-79 Lord Balarama Goes on Pilgrimage

This chapter focuses on the divine adventures of Lord Balarama, the elder brother of Lord Krishna. Here's a summary of the key events in this chapter:

Lord Balarama's Desire: After the departure of Lord Krishna, Lord Balarama, who is an incarnation of Lord Vishnu and a significant deity in Hinduism, expresses his desire to go on a pilgrimage to holy places to purify his heart and soul.

The Pilgrimage Begins: Lord Balarama sets out on his Pilgrimage, accompanied by an entourage of Yadava followers. He visits several sacred places of Pilgrimage across India.

The Pilgrimage Sites: Some of the sacred places visited by Lord Balarama include Prabhasa, where Lord Krishna had departed; Kurukshetra, the site of the great Mahabharata war; and the holy rivers like the Ganges.

Meeting Sages and Saints: Along the way, Lord Balarama meets and receives blessings from various sages and saints who reside in these sacred places. He engages in spiritual discussions and performs acts of charity.

Subduing Rogues: Lord Balarama encounters a few groups of arrogant and unruly individuals who challenge him during his Pilgrimage. In response, Lord Balarama uses His immense strength and subdues them, teaching them humility.

Return to Dwarka: After completing his Pilgrimage and purifying himself, Lord Balarama returns to Dwarka, where the residents and devotees welcome him with great reverence.

Canto 10, Chapter 79 of the Srimad Bhagavatam emphasises the importance of Pilgrimage and spiritual purification. It showcases Lord Balarama's divine qualities, his commitment to dharma (righteousness), and his role as a spiritual guide and protector of devotees. The chapter also highlights the significance of visiting sacred places and seeking the blessings of holy sages and saints in Hindu tradition.

10–80 The Liberation of Aghasura

In this chapter, the young Lord Krishna and His friends and cows encounter a gigantic demon named Aghasura. Aghasura assumes the form of a massive snake-like creature with a gaping mouth in his attempt to devour Krishna and His companions.

Krishna enters Aghasura's mouth with His friends and cows, showing His divine prowess. Inside Aghasura's body, they witness a frightening but wondrous scene as the demon's fiery interior resembles a hellish landscape. Despite the danger, Krishna remains calm, and His friends and cows remain unharmed.

Ultimately, Krishna expands Himself within Aghasura's body, causing the demon's enormous form to burst open, releasing Krishna and His companions unharmed. This chapter highlights Krishna's divine nature and ability to protect His devotees from even the most formidable threats.

In summary, the 80th chapter of the 10th canto of the Srimad Bhagavatam narrates the miraculous incident of Krishna and His friends' encounter with the demon Aghasura, showcasing Krishna's divine powers and His unwavering protection of His devotees.

10-81 The Lord Blesses Sudama Brahmana

Sudama Brahmana's Visit: Sudama Brahmana, a dear friend and devotee of Lord Krishna, decides to visit Lord Krishna in Dwarka. Sudama and his wife are experiencing extreme poverty and hunger.

Sudama's Gift: Sudama's wife urges him to seek Lord Krishna's help in their time of need. Sudama hesitates to ask for material assistance but agrees to take some chipped rice (poha or aval) as a humble gift for Lord Krishna.

Sudama's Arrival in Dwarka: Sudama reaches Dwarka and is welcomed by Lord Krishna with great love and affection. Despite his shabby appearance and the humble gift, Lord Krishna treats Sudama as an honoured guest.

The Gift of Devotion: Lord Krishna accepts the chipped rice from Sudama with immense joy. He recognises Sudama's pure devotion and the sincerity of his heart.

Sudama's Return: After spending time with Lord Krishna, Sudama returns home. On reaching there, he finds his humble cottage transformed into a magnificent palace, and his family is prosperous.

Sudama's Realization: Sudama realises that Lord Krishna, in His divine form, blessed him with immense wealth and prosperity as a reward for his unwavering devotion.

This chapter beautifully illustrates the importance of devotion, and the Lord values the sincerity and love of His devotees above all else. Lord Krishna's interaction with Sudama highlights the principle that faith and pure love for God are more precious than material wealth.

10-82 Lord Kṛṣṇa Meets the Inhabitants of Vṛndāvana

This chapter is a deeply emotional and touching part of the Bhagavatam that describes the reunion of Lord Krishna with the inhabitants of Vrindavan, His childhood home. Here's a summary of the key events in this chapter:

A Message from Uddhava: Uddhava, a dear devotee and friend of Lord Krishna, is sent to Vrindavan by Lord Krishna to deliver a message to the residents there. The message conveys Lord Krishna's love and concern for the people of Vrindavan, who have been pining for His presence.

Vrindavan's Response: Upon hearing Uddhava's message and learning about Lord Krishna's well-being, the residents of Vrindavan become overwhelmed with joy. They remember their beloved Krishna and His childhood pastimes with deep affection.

Vrindavan's Love for Krishna: The people of Vrindavan express their love for Lord Krishna through various prayers, songs, and stories of His childhood. Their devotion and longing for Him are portrayed as pure and unalloyed.

The Gopis' Love: The Gopis mainly express their love for Krishna through heartfelt songs and memories of their divine love for Him. Their devotion is considered the pinnacle of passion and dedication in the Bhagavatam.

Krishna's Arrival: Lord Krishna arrives in Vrindavan with Uddhava. His presence brings immense joy and ecstasy to the residents. They feel that their hearts are fulfilled by seeing Him again.

Divine Embrace: Lord Krishna embraces the residents of Vrindavan, and their ecstatic love for Him intensifies. The reunion is filled with tears of joy, love, and deep spiritual connection.

This chapter is a moving depiction of the intense love and devotion that the residents of Vrindavan have for Lord Krishna. It underscores the central theme of loving surrender to the divine and highlights the eternal bond between God and His devotees.

10-83 Draupadī Meets the Queens of Kṛṣṇa

This chapter describes an emotional and significant meeting between Draupadi, the Pandavas's wife, and Lord Krishna's queens. Here's a summary of the key events in this chapter:

Draupadi's Pilgrimage: After the Kurukshetra war and the eventual departure of Lord Krishna from this world, Draupadi embarks on a pilgrimage along with the Pandava brothers and other associates. She is filled with grief due to the loss of her husband and the departure of Lord Krishna.

Arrival in Dwarka: Draupadi and her group arrive in Dwarka, where the queens of Lord Krishna warmly welcome them. These queens include Rukmini, Satyabhama, and others.

Draupadi's Lament: Draupadi expresses her deep sorrow and lamentations to the queens, describing her family's hardships and tragedies during and after the Kurukshetra war. She particularly laments the loss of her sons and the difficulties faced by the Pandavas.

The Queens' Compassion: The queens of Lord Krishna, who are known for their devotion and wisdom, listen empathetically to Draupadi's sorrows. They console her and share their experiences of Lord Krishna's divine presence and support.

Reminiscing About Krishna: The queens share stories and memories of their interactions with Lord Krishna. They describe His divine qualities, compassion, and role as Godhead's Supreme Personality.

Draupadi's Renewed Faith: Draupadi is deeply moved by the queens' words and the stories of Lord Krishna's divine pastimes. Her faith and devotion to Lord Krishna are renewed, and she finds solace in their company.

This chapter highlights the emotional and spiritual aspects of Draupadi's journey, her encounter with Lord Krishna's queens, and the shared devotion and reminiscences of the divine pastimes of Lord Krishna. It emphasises the importance of seeking solace and strength by associating devoted and spiritually wise individuals, even in times of great sorrow.

10-84 The Sages' Teachings at Kurukṣetra

This chapter contains teachings and discussions between Lord Krishna and a group of sages at Kurukshetra, the site of the great Mahabharata war. Here's a summary of the key events and teachings in this chapter:

Gathering of Sages: Many sages and learned scholars assemble at Kurukshetra, eager to hear the wisdom and teachings of Lord Krishna.

Request for Teachings: The sages approach Lord Krishna and express their desire to learn from Him. They seek spiritual knowledge and guidance to attain liberation (moksha) and transcend the cycle of birth and death.

Lord Krishna's Instructions: Lord Krishna imparts spiritual wisdom to the assembled sages. He speaks about the material world's impermanence, the soul's eternal nature (atman), and the importance of devotion and surrender to the Supreme Divine.

Detachment and Renunciation: Lord Krishna emphasises the significance of separation from material possessions and the performance of one's duties with a sense of devotion and surrender to God. He explains that one can attain spiritual liberation by practising selflessness and dedicating all actions to the Divine.

Worship of the Formless and Personal God: Lord Krishna explains that while some devotees worship the formless, impersonal aspect of the Divine (Brahman), others, like Himself, choose to honour the personal form of God (Bhagavan). He asserts that both paths ultimately lead to the same goal of liberation, but the direction of devotion to the personal God is considered the most direct and accessible.

The Importance of Bhakti: Lord Krishna stresses the importance of bhakti (devotion) as the most effective means to attain God-realization and liberation. He explains that pure, unwavering dedication and sincere surrender lead to a deep connection with the Divine.

This chapter profoundly teaches spirituality, emphasising devotion, renunciation, and selfless action to attain spiritual realisation. It highlights the central message of the Bhagavad Gita and the essence of Lord Krishna's teachings on dharma (righteousness) and moksha (liberation).

10-85 The Lord Instructs Vasudeva

chapter contains a conversation between Lord Krishna and Vasudeva, His father, where Lord Krishna imparts spiritual wisdom and instructions. Here's a summary of the key events and teachings in this chapter:

Vasudeva's Arrival: Vasudeva, the father of Lord Krishna, arrives at Dwarka to meet his divine son. He expresses his desire to receive spiritual knowledge and guidance from Lord Krishna.

Vasudeva's Humility: Vasudeva approaches Lord Krishna with great humility and reverence despite being the father of the Supreme Lord. He acknowledges Lord Krishna as the Supreme Personality of Godhead and seeks wisdom to uplift his consciousness. Lord Krishna's Teachings: Lord Krishna imparts profound spiritual teachings to Vasudeva. He explains the nature of the soul (atman) and the concept of the eternal self that transcends the physical body.

The Importance of Devotion: Lord Krishna emphasises the significance of devotion (bhakti) as the highest path to attain the Divine. He explains that pure faith, characterised by love and surrender to God, leads to liberation (moksha).

Surrender to God: Lord Krishna encourages Vasudeva to surrender entirely to the divine will and offer God all actions and thoughts. He advises Vasudeva to perform his duties as an offering to the Supreme.

The Illusory Nature of Material World: Lord Krishna elaborates on the temporary and illusionary nature of the material world. He teaches Vasudeva to see beyond the fleeting material pleasures and to focus on the eternal spiritual realm.

Freedom from Rebirth: Lord Krishna explains that those who cultivate a loving relationship with the Divine and live a life of devotion and selflessness can attain liberation from the cycle of birth and death (samsara).

This chapter underscores Lord Krishna's profound spiritual wisdom to Vasudeva, emphasising the importance of devotion, surrender, and selfless action to attain spiritual realisation and liberation. It highlights the central teachings of the Bhagavad Gita and the essence of Lord Krishna's guidance to lead a meaningful and spiritually fulfilling life.

321

10-86 Arjuna Kidnaps Subhadrā

This chapter contains two distinct narratives. Here's a summary of the key events in each description:

Arjuna, one of the Pandava brothers and a close friend of Lord Krishna, visits Dwarka. He falls in love with Subhadrā, Lord Krishna's sister, during his stay.

Given the familial and social complexities, Arjuna wishes to marry Subhadrā but hesitates to express his feelings openly.

With the help of Lord Krishna, Arjuna devises a plan. During Lord Jagannath's Ratha Yatra (chariot festival), Arjuna kidnaps Subhadrā and takes her away to marry her.

Lord Krishna approves of this union, as it aligns with His divine plan.

Krishna Instructs the Gopīs in Mathurā:

In Mathura, Lord Krishna's childhood home, He comes across some of the Gopis from Vrindavan who are searching for Him.

These Gopis have deep love and devotion for Lord Krishna and express their desire to always be with Him.

Lord Krishna imparts spiritual wisdom to the Gopis, emphasising the importance of pure devotion and single-minded love for the Divine.

He explains that the Gopis' unwavering love and longing for Him have made them the most fortunate souls, as they are always in His thoughts.

Overall, this chapter highlights the themes of love and devotion in two distinct contexts: Arjuna's love for Subhadrā and the Gopis' love for Lord Krishna. It underscores the idea that genuine love and dedication to the Divine are highly cherished in the Bhagavatam and can lead to a deep spiritual connection with the Supreme.

10-87 The Prayers of the Personified Vedas

In this chapter, the personified Vedas offer prayers to Lord Krishna, acknowledging His supreme divinity and expressing their devotion and gratitude. Here's a summary of the key events and teachings in this chapter:

Personified Vedas Approach Lord Krishna: The personified Vedas, representing the sacred knowledge and wisdom of the universe, approach Lord Krishna in a mood of humility and reverence.

Acknowledgement of Krishna's Supremacy: The personified Vedas acknowledge Lord Krishna as the ultimate source of all knowledge, wisdom, and the essence of all scriptures. They recognise Him as the Supreme Personality of Godhead.

Prayer for Mercy: The personified Vedas express their desire to attain the mercy of Lord Krishna. They seek His blessings to understand His transcendental nature and qualities.

Description of Krishna's Divine Qualities: The Vedas describe various divine qualities and attributes of Lord Krishna, including His compassion, beauty, wisdom, and the power to grant liberation (moksha) to devotees.

Role of the Vedas: The personified Vedas explain their purpose is to guide human beings toward righteousness, devotion, and spiritual realisation. They emphasise that all knowledge ultimately leads to the understanding of Lord Krishna.

Prayers for Devotional Service: The Vedas pray to Lord Krishna for the ability to engage in devotional service (bhakti) with unwavering faith and love. They recognise that pure devotion is the highest form of spiritual practice.

Krishna's Response: Lord Krishna acknowledges the prayers of the personified Vedas and expresses His pleasure at their devotion and humility. He assures them of His blessings and mercy.

This chapter emphasises the significance of devotion and humility in pursuing spiritual knowledge and realisation. It underscores the idea that the ultimate purpose of all knowledge and wisdom is to lead one toward a loving and holy relationship with the Supreme Lord, Lord Krishna.

10-88 Lord Kṛṣṇa Beholds the Forests of Vṛndāvana

This chapter contains a deeply emotional and poetic description of Lord Krishna's reunion with the forests of Vrindavan, where He spent His childhood. Here's a summary of the key events and emotions expressed in this chapter:

Lord Krishna's Visit: Lord Krishna, along with His elder brother Balarama, visits the forests of Vrindavan, filled with the memories of His divine childhood pastimes.

Overwhelming Emotions: As Lord Krishna enters Vrindavan, He is overcome with intense emotions. He recalls his loving interactions with the cowherd boys, cows, and Gopis (cowherd girls) during His time there.

Poetic Description: The chapter is filled with lyrical descriptions of the natural beauty of Vrindavan, including the lush forests, blooming flowers, and flowing rivers. Lord Krishna's senses are inundated with the place's sights, sounds, and fragrances.

Reunion with the Residents: Lord Krishna encounters the residents of Vrindavan, who are overjoyed to see Him again. They express their deep love and longing for Him, and Lord Krishna reciprocates affectionately.

Playing His Flute: Lord Krishna plays His divine flute, which enchants the hearts of all living beings in Vrindavan. The cows, birds, and Gopis are drawn to Him by the melodic tunes.

Spiritual Significance: The chapter conveys the spiritual significance of Vrindavan as a place of pure devotion and love for Lord Krishna. It illustrates the eternal bond between God and His devotees.

Departure with Promises: Lord Krishna departs from Vrindavan, promising the residents that He will return and continue to bless them with His divine presence.

Chapter 88 of Canto 10 is a beautiful and poignant depiction of the deep love and affection between Lord Krishna and the residents of Vrindavan. It portrays the divine charm of Lord Krishna and the enduring spiritual connection between God and His devotees.

10-89 Krishna and Balarama Enter Mathura

This chapter describes the momentous occasion when Lord Krishna and Lord Balarama enter the city of Mathura, which holds great significance in their life's journey. Here's a summary of the key events in this chapter:

Arrival in Mathura: Lord Krishna and Lord Balarama, along with their companions, arrive in Mathura, ruled by Kamsa, their maternal uncle and a tyrant who has been the source of much turmoil and suffering.

Kamsa's Fear: The news of Krishna and Balarama's arrival in Mathura spreads quickly. Kamsa, who is aware of the prophecy that Krishna will be the cause of his downfall, becomes fearful.

Krishna's Encounter with a Washerwoman: On their way into the city, Lord Krishna and Lord Balarama meet a simple washerwoman. Krishna requests water from her, but the woman, not recognising Him, jests that she will give them water only if they pay for it. The exchange showcases Krishna's playful nature and willingness to engage with everyone, regardless of social status.

Krishna and Balarama at the Wrestling Arena: Krishna and Balarama proceed to the wrestling arena in Mathura, where they plan to confront Kamsa's wrestlers and, eventually, Kamsa himself.

Defeating the Wrestlers: Krishna and Balarama engage in combat with Kamsa's strongest wrestlers in the wrestling arena. They easily beat them, displaying their divine strength and prowess.

The Challenge to Kamsa: Having defeated the wrestlers, Lord Krishna challenges Kamsa to face Him in a duel, fulfilling the prophecy that predicts Kamsa's defeat by Krishna's hands.

Chapter 89 sets the stage for the story's climax of Lord Krishna's divine mission to remove evil forces and establish dharma (righteousness). It portrays Krishna's fearlessness and determination to confront the oppressor, Kamsa, and highlights His divine qualities, such as playfulness and compassion, even in challenging circumstances.

10-90 Summary Description of Lord Krishna's Pastimes

This chapter concisely summarises some of Lord Krishna's critical pastimes and events, showcasing His divine activities and their significance.

The Creation of the Material World: The chapter describes how Lord Krishna is the ultimate cause of the material universe's creation, maintenance, and destruction. He is the source of all existence.

Lord Krishna's Divine Birth: The chapter recounts the miraculous birth of Lord Krishna in Mathura and His transfer to Gokul, where He was raised by His foster parents, Yasoda and Nanda Maharaja.

Childhood Pastimes: It highlights some of Lord Krishna's charming childhood pastimes, including His stealing of butter, playing with the cowherd boys, and dancing on the hoods of the serpent Kaliya.

The Killing of Demons: Lord Krishna's heroic deeds are summarised, such as slaying demons like Putana, Trinavarta, and Bakasura. Each of these events demonstrates His divine power and protection of His devotees.

The Lifting of Govardhan Hill: The chapter briefly mentions the extraordinary event where Lord Krishna lifts Govardhan Hill on His little finger to protect the residents of Vrindavan from the wrath of Lord Indra.

Rasalila: Lord Krishna's enchanting dance with the Gopis during the Rasalila on the moonlit night is described as a pinnacle of divine love and devotion.

The Killing of Kamsa: The chapter narrates Lord Krishna's eventual confrontation with and defeat of His tyrannical maternal uncle, Kamsa, fulfilling the prophecy of His arrival.

Lord Krishna's Return to Dwarka: After killing Kamsa, Lord Krishna and Lord Balarama return to Dwarka, where the residents joyously welcome them.

Chapter 90 serves as a brief overview of the remarkable and divine pastimes of Lord Krishna, highlighting His multifaceted personality as a naughty child, a fearless warrior, and the Supreme Lord who brings joy, love, and liberation to His devotees.

Canto 11

11-01 The Curse upon the Yadu Dynasty

In this chapter, Lord Krishna is preparing to leave the Earthly plane. Uddhava, His devoted disciple, is distressed by His impending departure. Krishna imparts profound wisdom and spiritual teachings to Uddhava, addressing various aspects of life, devotion, and the nature of reality. The chapter also narrates the curse that led to the eventual destruction of the Yadu dynasty. It is a pivotal point in the text, emphasising the impermanence of worldly power and the importance of seeking spiritual enlightenment.

11-02 Mahārāja Nimi Meets the Nine Yogendras

In Chapter 2 of Canto 11 in Srimad Bhagavatam, titled "," the great King Nimi seeks spiritual guidance from the Nine Yogendras, who are enlightened sages and masters of yoga. He inquires about the nature of the self, the path to liberation, and how to transcend the material world. The Yogendras respond by teaching him about various aspects of yoga, meditation, and the significance of devotion to Lord Vishnu. This chapter emphasises the importance of seeking spiritual wisdom from enlightened beings and highlights the path to transcendental knowledge and liberation.

11-03 Liberation from the Illusory Energy

In this chapter, Lord Krishna continues to impart spiritual wisdom to Uddhava. He explains the nature of the material world, the illusory energy that binds living beings, and the concept of liberation (moksha). Krishna emphasises the need to transcend material desires and attachments, attain a state of stability, and surrender to the Supreme Lord in devotion. He also elaborates on the characteristics of a true devotee and the significance of self-realisation to attain liberation from the cycle of birth and death. This chapter serves as a profound discourse on the path to spiritual liberation and the importance of devotion to the divine.

11-04 Drumila Explains the Incarnations of Godhead

In this chapter, the sage Drumila imparts spiritual knowledge to King Nimi. He explains the various incarnations of the Supreme Lord and their divine purposes. Drumila discusses how the Lord incarnates in different forms to protect and guide humanity, emphasising that all these incarnations are transcendental and beyond the limitations of material existence. This chapter highlights the significance of understanding and acknowledging the divine manifestations of the Supreme Being and their role in maintaining cosmic order and spiritual evolution.

11-05 Lord Kṛṣṇa's Explanation of the Vedic Path

335

In this chapter, Lord Krishna imparts profound spiritual knowledge to Uddhava. He explains the essence of the Vedic scriptures and the importance of understanding the ultimate purpose of life, which is to attain pure devotion and love for the Supreme Lord. Krishna discusses the various paths of yoga, including karma yoga (the yoga of selfless action), bhakti yoga (the yoga of devotion), and jnana yoga (the yoga of knowledge). He emphasises that faith is the most direct and effective way to realise the divine and attain liberation. This chapter is a comprehensive discourse on the spiritual journey and the significance of unwavering devotion to the Supreme.

11-06 The Yadu Dynasty Retires to Prabhāsa

In this chapter, Lord Krishna instructs the Yadu dynasty to retire to Prabhāsa, a sacred pilgrimage site, to prepare for their ultimate departure from the world. In their pride and intoxication, the Yadus unwittingly provoke a conflict that destroys them. In the end, Lord Krishna departs from the world by entering meditation, and a great flood submerges the city of Dvārakā. This chapter marks the culmination of Lord Krishna's earthly pastimes. It serves as a powerful reminder of the impermanence of worldly glory and the importance of surrendering to the divine will.

11-07 Lord Kṛṣṇa Instructs Uddhava

In this chapter, Lord Krishna imparts his final teachings to Uddhava before he departs from the earthly realm. Krishna emphasises the importance of renunciation, devotion, and spiritual wisdom. He explains that the material world is temporary and full of suffering, and true liberation can only be attained through unwavering faith in the Supreme. Krishna also describes the characteristics of a genuine devotee and advises Uddhava to meditate upon his form to achieve spiritual realisation. This chapter is a culmination of the profound wisdom shared by Lord Krishna throughout the Srimad Bhagavatam and serves as a guide for seekers on their spiritual journey.

11-08 The Lord's Opulence

Lord Krishna continues instructing Uddhava in this chapter, revealing His divine opulence and universal form. He describes how He is the source of all creation and the ultimate goal of all spiritual paths. Krishna explains that His luxury and power are beyond human comprehension and that devotion to Him is the surest way to attain liberation.

The chapter also describes Lord Krishna's transcendental pastimes, His relationship with His devotees, and the importance of cultivating a loving relationship with the Lord. It emphasises the all-encompassing nature of the Supreme Lord and the boundless love and devotion that can lead to spiritual realisation.

11-09 Detachment from All that Is Material

In this chapter, Lord Krishna continues His discourse with Uddhava, emphasising the importance of detachment from material possessions and relationships. He explains that true renunciation is not merely external but involves a profound internal separation from the material world.

Krishna describes the impermanent nature of material wealth and pleasures, urging Uddhava to focus on devotion and spiritual realisation. He provides insights into the heart of the soul, the illusory energy (Maya), and how one can transcend material bondage. The chapter underscores the significance of cultivating detachment and unwavering devotion to the Supreme Lord to attain spiritual liberation and eternal bliss.

11-10 The Nature of Fruitive Activity

In this chapter, Lord Krishna imparts profound wisdom to Uddhava about the nature of karmic actions (fruitive activity) and the importance of performing one's duties without attachment to the results.

Krishna explains that everyone is bound by their past karma, which influences their present life. However, by dedicating all actions to Him and performing them selflessly, one can gradually transcend the cycle of karma and attain liberation. He emphasises that true renunciation is not the abandonment of duties but the renunciation of attachment to the fruits of one's actions.

The chapter serves as a teaching on karma yoga, emphasising the need to act in a spirit of devotion and selflessness, ultimately leading to spiritual liberation and freedom from the cycle of birth and death.

11-11 The Vision of the Cosmic Form

Lord Krishna reveals His divine universal form (Vishvarupa) to Uddhava in this remarkable chapter. This cosmic form is a magnificent display of His omnipotence, showing that He is the source of all existence.

Krishna's universal form encompasses all living beings, deities, and the cosmos. Uddhava witnesses this form's awe-inspiring and terrifying aspects, which signify the destructive power of time and the cycle of birth and death. Krishna explains that those who can see beyond this external cosmic manifestation to His personal, loving form are the proper recipients of His grace.

This chapter highlights the boundless majesty and metaphysical nature of the Supreme Lord. It reinforces the significance of devotion and surrender to understand and connect with the divine.

11-12 Beyond Renunciation and Knowledge

342

In this concluding chapter, Lord Krishna imparts his ultimate teachings to Uddhava. He explains that the highest form of spiritual realisation goes beyond mere renunciation and knowledge.

Krishna emphasises the significance of pure devotion (bhakti) as the most direct and effective path to attain His divine presence and grace. He describes the different types of devotees, including those in pure love and surrender, and highlights their elevated spiritual status.

The chapter underscores that loving devotion to the Supreme Lord surpasses all other spiritual practices and leads to the ultimate liberation and eternal union with the divine. It serves as a profound conclusion to the teachings of Srimad Bhagavatam, emphasising the supremacy of devotion and love for the Supreme Being.

11-13 The Hymn of the Lord's Illusory Energy

In this chapter, Lord Krishna instructs Uddhava about the illusory energy of the Supreme, known as Maya. He explains how Maya deludes living beings into thinking they are the doers of their actions and separate from the divine.

Krishna describes how Maya creates a false sense of ego and attachment to material desires, trapping individuals in the cycle of birth and death. He emphasises that only through sincere devotion and surrender to Him can one transcend the influence of Maya and attain liberation.

The chapter includes a hymn known as the "Yogamaya Hymn," where Lord Krishna praises the power of His illusory energy and how it facilitates the divine pastimes of the Lord. It reflects profoundly on the nature of illusion and the need for spiritual awakening to break free from its grip.

11-14 The System of Universal Management

In this chapter, Lord Krishna imparts knowledge to Uddhava about how universal creation and management function. Krishna explains the intricate system of the material world, including the hierarchy of deities responsible for various cosmic parts.

He describes the importance of maintaining dharma (righteousness) in society and how each person has a role in upholding it. Krishna also discusses the four types of varnas (social orders) and ashramas (stages of life) that help guide individuals in their spiritual and societal responsibilities.

This chapter serves as a comprehensive guide to the principles of cosmic management and the importance of leading a life by dharma for the welfare of all beings. It provides insights into the organised structure of the universe and the need for individuals to perform their duties selflessly while remaining devoted to the Supreme Lord.

11–15 Instructions for Civilised Human Beings

345

In this chapter, Lord Krishna imparts valuable guidance to Uddhava on how civilised human beings should conduct themselves in society. He emphasises principles of virtuous living and ethical conduct.

Krishna discusses various aspects of human behaviour, including humility, compassion, truthfulness, and detachment. He advises Uddhava on how to treat others with respect and kindness, irrespective of their social status, and encourages the pursuit of knowledge and spiritual wisdom.

This chapter is a moral and ethical guide, highlighting the importance of leading a life of righteousness, compassion, and selflessness. It underscores the need for individuals to cultivate virtuous qualities and align their actions with dharma (right) to progress spiritually and contribute positively to society.

11-16 The Lord's Opulence

346

In this chapter, Lord Krishna imparts profound spiritual knowledge to Uddhava. He discusses the different forms of God, the importance of devotion, and the nature of reality. Krishna emphasises the significance of surrendering to the divine and explains that pure devotion is the most direct path to God's realisation. The chapter highlights the intangible qualities and opulence of the Supreme Lord.

11-17 Lord Krishna's Description of the Varnasrama System

In this chapter, Lord Krishna instructs Uddhava about the varnashrama system, a social and occupational structure that promotes righteousness and spiritual growth. Krishna explains the four varnas (castes) and four ashramas (stages of life) and how they contribute to an individual's spiritual development. He emphasises that spiritual progress comes from performing one's prescribed duties with devotion and without attachment. Krishna also discusses the importance of maintaining harmony and unity in society. This chapter guides leading a virtuous and balanced life by dharma (righteousness).

11–18 Description of Varnasrama–Dharma

In this chapter, Lord Krishna continues instructing Uddhava, providing a detailed description of the varnashrama-dharma. This social and occupational system guides individuals in leading righteous and spiritually meaningful lives.

Krishna explains the duties and responsibilities of the four varnas (castes) and four ashramas (stages of life). He emphasises that one should perform their prescribed duties with devotion and without attachment to attain spiritual growth and liberation from the cycle of birth and death.

Throughout the chapter, Krishna underscores the importance of self-realisation, practising non-violence, and cultivating detachment. He also discusses the significance of one's conduct, character, and intention in adhering to dharma (righteousness). This chapter provides valuable insights into living a life aligned with spiritual principles and societal responsibilities.

11–19 Description of the Varnasrama System

In this chapter, Lord Krishna continues his discourse with Uddhava, elaborating on the principles of the varnashrama-dharma, the social and occupational system.

Krishna emphasises that everyone should follow their prescribed duties according to their varna (caste) and ashrama (stage of life) without attachment. He explains that such actions performed selflessly and in devotion to the Supreme lead to spiritual growth and liberation.

The chapter also delves into topics like the importance of cleanliness, the significance of pilgrimages, and the role of devotion in transcending the material world. Overall, it reinforces the idea that living by dharma (righteousness) and pursuing a spiritual path is the key to attaining eternal bliss and liberation.

350

In this chapter, Lord Krishna imparts profound wisdom to Uddhava about the supremacy of pure devotional service over knowledge and detachment.

Krishna explains that while knowledge and detachment are valuable, they should ultimately lead to unalloyed devotion to the Supreme. He emphasises that loving surrender to God is the highest path to spiritual realisation, transcending material knowledge and renunciation.

The chapter emphasises that genuine devotion is characterised by unwavering love and a desire for a personal relationship with the Divine. Krishna describes the qualities of a true devotee and the power of bhakti (devotion) in attaining liberation.

This chapter highlights the preeminence of devotion and the profound spiritual fulfilment it brings, surpassing even the pursuit of knowledge and detachment.

11-21 Lord Krishna's Explanation of the Vedic Path

In this chapter, Lord Krishna imparts profound spiritual wisdom to Uddhava regarding the various paths to realisation mentioned in the Vedas.

Krishna explains that the Vedas prescribe different paths for individuals based on their inclinations and abilities. These paths include karma yoga (the yoga of selfless action), jnana yoga (the yoga of knowledge), and bhakti yoga (the yoga of devotion). Krishna emphasises that the ultimate goal of all these paths is to attain a loving, holy relationship with the Supreme.

The chapter underscores the importance of sincere spiritual practice, surrender to the Divine, and cultivating inner purity. Krishna explains that all these paths ultimately converge into pure devotion as the most direct and effective way to realise God.

In summary, Chapter 21 of Canto 11 elucidates the unity and diversity of the Vedic paths, all leading to realising the Divine through devotion and self-realisation.

11–22 Elements of Material Creation

352

In this chapter, Lord Krishna imparts spiritual knowledge to Uddhava by explaining the creation and dissolution of the material universe.

Krishna describes the primary elements of material creation, such as Earth, water, fire, air, and ether, along with the subtle aspects of mind, intelligence, and ego. He explains how these elements interact and combine to form the material world.

The chapter also delves into the concept of time and the cycle of creation, maintenance, and destruction that governs the universe. Krishna emphasises that understanding these cosmic principles helps one transcend the material world and attain spiritual realisation.

Overall, Chapter 22 provides insights into the intricate workings of the material universe and underscores the importance of seeking spiritual truth beyond the material realm.

11–23 The Song of the Avanti Brahmana

353

In this chapter, Uddhava encounters a self-realised brahmana from the city of Avanti, who imparts spiritual wisdom through a song.

The Avanti Brahmana's song praises the path of devotion to Lord Krishna as the most direct and effective means of attaining liberation. He narrates the stories of various devotees who achieved profound spiritual realisations through their unwavering love and devotion to the Lord.

The song underscores the importance of surrendering to the Divine with full faith and devotion, highlighting that such surrender transcends all other spiritual practices and ultimately leads to liberation.

In essence, Chapter 23 emphasises the power of bhakti (devotion) and the stories of devotees who found divine grace and liberation through their dedication to Lord Krishna.

11-24 The Philosophy of Sankhya

354

Lord Krishna imparts deep spiritual knowledge to Uddhava in this chapter, focusing on the Sankhya philosophy.

Krishna explains the Sankhya philosophy, which systematically analyses the material and spiritual realms. He discusses the principles of creation, the categories of material elements, the nature of the soul, and the concept of liberation.

Krishna emphasises that the soul is eternal and distinct from the material body. He describes how detachment from material desires and attachments leads to spiritual realisation and liberation. He also underscores that one must cultivate discrimination and self-realisation to attain the ultimate goal of life.

In essence, Chapter 24 delves into the profound Sankhya philosophy, emphasising the eternal nature of the soul and the path to spiritual enlightenment through detachment and self-realisation.

11–25 The Three Modes of Material Nature and Beyond

355

In this chapter, Lord Krishna imparts spiritual wisdom to Uddhava, focusing on the three modes of material nature—sattva (goodness), rajas (passion), and tamas (ignorance).

Krishna explains how these modes influence human behaviour, desires, and actions, keeping individuals in the material world. He emphasises the importance of transcending these modes through spiritual knowledge and devotion to attain liberation.

The chapter also discusses the superiority of devotion to the Supreme Lord over all other paths, as it enables one to rise above the influence of material nature and attain the highest spiritual realisation.

In essence, Chapter 25 highlights the significance of understanding the modes of material nature and how devotion to the Divine is the ultimate means to transcend them and achieve spiritual liberation.

11–26 The Aila-gītā

The chapter begins with Uddhava expressing his deep sorrow over the impending departure of Lord Krishna from the earthly realm. Uddhava is eager to receive Krishna's final instructions and guidance.

The impermanence of the Material World: Krishna explains the transient and temporary nature of the material world, emphasising the importance of focusing on spiritual pursuits and realising the eternal nature of the soul.

Detachment and Renunciation: Krishna advises Uddhava on the importance of objectivity and renunciation to attain spiritual realisation. He explains that attachment to material possessions and relationships binds the soul to the cycle of birth and death.

Bhakti Yoga: Krishna praises the path of bhakti yoga, the loving devotional service to the Supreme, as the most direct and effective means to attain Him. He emphasises the significance of surrendering to the divine will and cultivating a loving relationship with God.

Self-realisation: Krishna describes the stages of self-realisation, culminating in pure love and devotion for the Supreme Being. He also elucidates the qualities of a true devotee.

The Nature of God: Krishna reveals His divine and universal form to Uddhava, demonstrating that He is the source of all creation and the ultimate reality. He explains that all living beings are His manifestations.

Importance of Guru: Krishna emphasises the necessity of a qualified spiritual guide or guru in one's journey towards spiritual enlightenment.

The 26th chapter of the 11th canto, the Aila-gītā, is a profound conversation between Lord Krishna and Uddhava, where Krishna imparts spiritual wisdom, stressing the importance of devotion, detachment, and self-realisation as the means to attain the ultimate truth and liberation from the cycle of birth and death. It is a valuable text for those seeking spiritual enlightenment and guidance in the Bhakti tradition.

11-27 Process of Deity Worship

357

In this chapter, Lord Krishna guides Uddhava on the proper method of deity worship and the significance of worshipping the form of the Divine.

Krishna explains the importance of devotion and sincere intent in deity worship. He emphasises that worshipping the deity with love and faith can establish a personal relationship with the Supreme and receive spiritual blessings.

The chapter outlines the procedures for deity worship, including rituals and offerings, and underscores that the essence of prayer lies in one's devotion and devotion's purity. Krishna highlights the transformative power of deity worship in purifying the heart and elevating one's consciousness.

In summary, Chapter 27 provides instructions on deity worship and underscores the importance of devotion and sincerity in connecting with the Divine through this sacred practice.

11–28 Jnana-yoga

In this chapter, Lord Krishna imparts spiritual wisdom to Uddhava, focusing on the path of Jnana-yoga, the yoga of knowledge and insight.

Krishna explains the importance of discerning the difference between the material and spiritual realms. He emphasises that proper knowledge leads to understanding the soul's eternal nature and relationship with the Supreme. Krishna also discusses the material world's heart, the ego's illusory nature, and the significance of self-realisation.

The chapter highlights that the pursuit of knowledge should ultimately lead to the realisation of the oneness of the self with the Supreme Self. Krishna emphasises that such realisation is the highest form of spiritual attainment, surpassing all other forms of knowledge and yoga.

In essence, Chapter 28 provides insights into the path of Jnana-yoga, stressing the importance of spiritual wisdom and self-realisation in attaining union with the Divine.

11-29 Bhakti-yoga

In this chapter, Lord Krishna imparts profound wisdom to Uddhava, focusing on the path of Bhakti-yoga, the yoga of devotion and love for the Divine.

Krishna explains that Bhakti-yoga is the most direct and accessible path to attain God's realisation. He discusses the qualities of a true devotee and the significance of pure, unalloyed devotion to the Supreme.

The chapter emphasises that devotion is not bound by material considerations and is characterised by selfless love and surrender to the Divine. Krishna describes how true prayer purifies the heart, removes all material desires, and leads to a deep and loving relationship with the Lord.

In summary, Chapter 29 underscores the paramount importance of Bhakti-yoga, highlighting that genuine devotion and love for the Divine are the most effective means to attain spiritual realisation and union with the Supreme.

11-30 The Disappearance of the Yadu Dynasty

In this chapter, the Bhagavatam narrates the events leading to the decline and disappearance of Lord Krishna's Yadu dynasty.

The chapter describes how a curse from a group of sages led to a series of events, including a drunken brawl among the Yadava clan members, culminating in their destruction. Lord Krishna, foreseeing the destiny of His dynasty, decided to conclude their earthly presence.

Krishna and His family and close associates retreated to the Prabhasa Tirtha, where they performed a sacred ritual and entered the ocean waters. A great cataclysm then occurred, leading to the destruction of the Yadava dynasty.

The chapter ends with the narration of Lord Krishna's departure from this world, His universal form, and the transformation of His divine body into a deity form for future worship.

In summary, Chapter 30 recounts the tragic events that led to the end of the Yadu dynasty, culminating in Lord Krishna's departure from the mortal world and the transformation of His physical form into a deity for eternal devotion.

11-31 The Disappearance of Lord Sri Krishna

In this poignant chapter, the Bhagavatam narrates the departure of Lord Krishna from the earthly realm.

After witnessing the Yadu dynasty's destruction, Lord Krishna sat beneath a banyan tree. A hunter, mistaking Krishna for a deer, shot an arrow that struck Him in the foot. Realising the Lord's transcendental nature, the hunter and his dog approached Krishna, who bestowed His blessings upon them.

Krishna then decided it was time for Him to leave His mortal form. He entered a meditative state and, amidst the presence of His devoted associates, allowed His divine form to merge into the Supreme Brahman, concluding His earthly pastimes.

This chapter marks the culmination of Lord Krishna's presence in His avatar as He returns to His eternal abode. It reflects the cyclical nature of divine incarnations and underscores the importance of devotion to the Supreme to attain spiritual realisation and liberation.

Canto 12

12-01 The Birth of Emperor Parikshit

This chapter describes how Emperor Parikshit, Arjuna's grandson and Abhimanyu's son, was born. The chapter narrates the circumstances surrounding his birth, including his father's untimely death in the Kurukshetra War, which led to his mother's grief and how Lord Krishna intervened to save Parikshit's life in the womb. Ultimately, Parikshit was born and would become a great king and a prominent figure in the Mahabharata and Srimad Bhagavatam. This chapter sets the stage for the events that follow in the final canto of the Srimad Bhagavatam.

12-02 Maharaja Parikshit Cursed by a Brahmana Boy

In this chapter, Maharaja Parikshit, the ruler of the Kuru dynasty, encounters a young Brahmana boy who is deeply immersed in meditation and utterly unaware of his surroundings. Out of curiosity, Parikshit places a dead snake around the boy's neck to test whether the boy's reflection is genuine.

When this act disrupts the boy's meditation, he becomes angry and curses Parikshit, declaring that the king will die in seven days due to a snake bite from the serpent, Takshaka. Maharaja Parikshit accepts the curse as the will of destiny and decides to spend the remaining days of his life in spiritual contemplation and preparation for his impending death.

This chapter highlights the theme of karma, the consequences of one's actions, and the importance of being mindful and respectful of spiritual seekers and ascetics.

12-03 The Deliverance of Maharaja Parikshit

In this chapter, Maharaja Parikshit prepares for the impending arrival of Lord Takshaka, the serpent destined to bite and kill him as per the curse of the Brahmana boy from the previous chapter.

As Takshaka approaches, Parikshit seeks refuge in the shelter of the Supreme Lord, Sri Krishna. He renounces his kingdom and all material possessions, dons simple clothing, and embarks on a pilgrimage. Throughout the seven days leading up to his death, Parikshit remains absorbed in the thoughts of Lord Krishna. He listens to the narrations of Srimad Bhagavatam, which the sage Sukadeva Goswami recites.

On the seventh day, Takshaka arrives as a deadly snake; he bites Parikshit. However, Parikshit remains utterly detached from his physical body and continues to meditate on Krishna. The king achieves liberation and attains the spiritual world due to his pure devotion and surrender to the Supreme Lord.

This chapter illustrates the power of devotion, the significance of spiritual knowledge, and the concept of achieving liberation at the time of death through unwavering faith and meditation on the divine.

12-04 The Process of Bhagavata Dharma

In this chapter, Suta Goswami continues narrating Sukadeva Goswami's teachings to Maharaja Parikshit.

Sukadeva Goswami explains the significance of the Srimad Bhagavatam and its profound impact on spiritual realisation. He emphasises that the Bhagavatam is the essence of all Vedic scriptures and that hearing and discussing its verses can attain the highest state of devotion and love for the Supreme Lord, Krishna.

The chapter also touches upon the principles of Bhagavata Dharma, which involves surrendering to the will of the Lord, engaging in devotional service, and cultivating a loving relationship with God. Sukadeva Goswami underscores the importance of pure devotion. He emphasises that through such faith, one can transcend the cycle of birth and death and attain eternal bliss in the association of the Supreme.

In essence, Chapter 4 of Canto 12 emphasises the significance of Srimad Bhagavatam as a spiritual guide and elaborates on the path of devotion and surrender to the Supreme Lord to attain spiritual realisation and liberation.

12-05 Sacrifice of Maharaja Parikshit

In this chapter, Maharaja Parikshit, having been bitten by the serpent Takshaka, is lying down and awaiting the inevitable approach of death.

Parikshit remains calm and undisturbed despite his impending death, fully absorbed in meditation on Lord Krishna. Many sages and ascetics gather around him to witness the great soul's departure from his body. They understand the significance of his impending death and the elevated state of consciousness he has achieved.

Meanwhile, Takshaka, the serpent, arrives with his poison to deliver the fatal bite. However, Parikshit's devotion and righteousness have invoked the protection of Lord Krishna. As Takshaka attempts to bite the king, a brilliant and luminous personality known as the Sudarshana Chakra, Lord Krishna's divine discus, appears and counteracts Takshaka's venom.

The chapter underscores the power of devotion, the protection of the Supreme Lord, and the significance of a saintly life. It is an inspiring example of how a devotee, even in the face of death, remains steadfast in their faith and ultimately attains liberation through their unwavering devotion to God.

12-06 The Perfect Society: Four Social Classes

In this chapter, Maharaja Parikshit, after being saved from the snake bite by the Sudarshana Chakra, expresses his gratitude to Lord Krishna and Sukadeva Goswami for the spiritual wisdom he has received. He inquires about how society can be organised for the welfare of all.

Sukadeva Goswami explains the ideal social structure known as Varnashrama dharma. This system comprises four social classes or varnas: Brahmanas (priests and scholars), Kshatriyas (warriors and rulers), Vaishyas (merchants and farmers), and Shudras (labourers and service providers). Additionally, there are four spiritual orders or ashramas: Brahmacharya (student life), Grihastha (married life), Vanaprastha (retired life), and Sannyasa (renounced life).

The chapter emphasises that these divisions should be based on one's qualities and qualifications, not birth and that all members of society should collaborate harmoniously to pursue spiritual realisation. Sukadeva Goswami elaborates on the responsibilities and duties of each varna and ashrama. He emphasises the importance of self-realisation and devotion to the Supreme Lord for everyone, regardless of their social position.

In summary, Chapter 6 of Canto 12 guides the ideal social structure. It highlights the importance of spiritual development and devotion as the ultimate goal of life, accessible to people from all social backgrounds.

12-07 The Purification of the Yadu Dynasty

In this chapter, Sukadeva Goswami continues his narration of Maharaja Parikshit.

The chapter describes how, after Lord Krishna departs from this world, a time of great disturbance and discord arises among the Yadu dynasty, Krishna's family. Due to a curse from the sages, the Yadavas become intoxicated and engage in a drunken brawl, which leads to the destruction of the entire Yadu dynasty.

As the conflict escalates, Lord Krishna decides to end the dynasty himself. He enters a forest and sits under a tree. A hunter, mistaking Krishna's foot for the face of a deer, shoots an arrow, which fatally wounds the Lord. Lord Krishna then leaves His earthly form and returns to His divine abode.

This chapter underscores the idea that even the Lord's own family is not exempt from the laws of karma, and it illustrates the principle of divine detachment, showing that Lord Krishna is not affected by the events of the material world. It also marks the conclusion of Lord Krishna's pastimes on Earth.

12-08 The Disappearance of Lord Sri Krishna

In this chapter, Sukadeva Goswami continues to narrate to Maharaja Parikshit.

After Lord Krishna departs from the earthly realm in the previous chapter, this chapter describes the reactions of His devotees, especially the residents of Dwaraka. They are overwhelmed with grief upon hearing of Krishna's departure, and many of them decide to leave their mortal bodies behind through yoga, meditation, or self-immolation in the sacred fire, desiring to be with Krishna in the spiritual world.

The chapter also highlights the devotees' intense separation and love for Krishna. As the residents of Dwaraka witness His departure, they experience a deep sense of loss, which only intensifies their devotion.

In the end, it is described how Lord Balarama and Lord Krishna's queens and Arjuna continue to perform religious rites and rituals to honour the departed Lord. The chapter emphasises the metaphysical nature of Lord Krishna and the profound impact He had on His devotees.

Chapter 8 of Canto 12 serves as a poignant conclusion to Lord Krishna's earthly pastimes, emphasising the themes of devotion, love, and the eternal nature of the spiritual realm.

12–09 The Dynasty of Amsuman

In this chapter, Sukadeva Goswami continues his narration of Maharaja Parikshit.

After the departure of Lord Krishna and Lord Balarama, the Yadu dynasty faced challenges and difficulties due to the curse that led to their downfall. Maharaja Parikshit's son, Janamejaya, performs a great Sarpa Yagna (snake sacrifice) to cleanse the dynasty and restore its glory. During this sacrifice, the snakes in the lineage of Takshaka, who had bitten Parikshit, are intended to be destroyed.

However, as the sacrifice progresses, the great sage Astika intervenes and saves the snakes from extermination, ensuring their survival. Astika's intervention is booming, and he earns the respect and admiration of Janamejaya and the other assembled sages.

This chapter highlights the importance of dharma (righteousness) and the significance of compassion and respect for all living beings, even amid rituals and sacrifices. It also introduces the character of Astika, an essential figure in the Mahabharata and the Bhagavatam, known for his wisdom and compassion.

12-10 The Story of King Puranjana

374

In this chapter, Sukadeva Goswami tells Maharaja Parikshit an allegorical story to illustrate spiritual truths.

The story revolves around a king named Puranjana, who represents the soul, and a city called "Pura," which symbolises the physical body. King Puranjana is obsessed with his queen and spends his life pursuing material pleasures, represented by various household attachments and desires. He becomes entangled in the cycle of birth and death, symbolised by his repeated marriages and deaths in different bodies.

In this story, Puranjana's life is a metaphor for the soul's entanglement in the material world and its attachment to the physical body. Ultimately, King Puranjana realises the futility of his pursuits and the transient nature of worldly pleasures. He renounces his attachments and turns toward spiritual wisdom and devotion.

This chapter is symbolic teaching, emphasising the importance of detaching from material desires and seeking spiritual realisation to break free from the cycle of birth and death and attain liberation.

12-11 Summary Description of Lord Krishna's Pastimes

In this chapter, Sukadeva Goswami concisely summarises Lord Krishna's various pastimes and activities, which are the subject of the entire Bhagavatam.

Sukadeva Goswami highlights Krishna's birth in Mathura, His childhood pastimes in Vrindavan, His role as a charioteer in the Kurukshetra War, His teachings to Arjuna in the form of the Bhagavad Gita, His glorious transcendental activities, and His interactions with devotees, including the Pandavas and residents of Vrindavan.

The chapter emphasises that Lord Krishna is the Supreme Personality of Godhead and that His pastimes are not ordinary but are filled with divine significance. One can attain spiritual realisation and liberation by hearing and meditating on these pastimes.

Chapter 11 serves as a summary and reminder of the extraordinary life and teachings of Lord Krishna, inspiring devotees to reflect on His divine nature and the path of devotion.

12–12 The Age of Kali

In this concluding chapter, Sukadeva Goswami shares profound insights about the nature of the Kali Yuga, the current age characterised by an increase in irreligion, a decline in spiritual values, and moral degradation.

Sukadeva Goswami describes the symptoms and challenges of the Kali Yuga, such as deceit, hypocrisy, greed, and a lack of spirituality. He explains that devotion to the Supreme Lord through chanting His holy names, especially the Hare Krishna mantra, is the most effective means to attain spiritual salvation during this age.

The chapter also portrays the departure of Sukadeva Goswami, who, after imparting the Srimad Bhagavatam's wisdom to Maharaja Parikshit, ascends to the spiritual realm in a self-ignited fire. This action signifies the completion of his divine mission.

Ultimately, the chapter highlights the power of the Srimad Bhagavatam as a spiritual guide and the importance of devotion and divine consciousness, particularly in the challenging times of the Kali Yuga. It serves as a concluding message, inspiring seekers to pursue love and spiritual enlightenment in our age.